Supporting health at work:

international perspectives on occupational health services

Edited by Peter Westerholm
and David Walters

This book is printed on chlorine-free, acid-free stock produced from woodpulp originating from managed, sustainable plantations. The paper and board are recyclable and biodegradable.

© IOSH Services Limited 2007
Printed in England by Greenshires Group Limited

ISBN-13: 978 0 901357 39 7

Published by IOSH Services Limited
The Grange
Highfield Drive
Wigston
Leicestershire
LE18 1NN
UK
t +44 (0)116 257 3100
f +44 (0)116 257 3101
www.iosh.co.uk

Contents

About the editors

Peter Westerholm is Professor Emeritus in the Department of Medical Sciences at Uppsala University. Until his retirement in 2000, he was Professor of Occupational Epidemiology at the Swedish National Institute for Working Life. He has published research on cancer epidemiology, work-related cardiovascular disease and occupational health services, and is a former chairman and founding member of the International Commission on Occupational Health's committee for health services research and evaluation in occupational health.

David Walters is currently Professor of Work Environment and Director of the Centre for Work Environment Research (CWERC) at Cardiff University. He was formerly Professor of Occupational and Environmental Safety and Health at South Bank University, London. He has researched and written extensively in the fields of labour relations and regulation in occupational safety and health, focusing especially on comparative aspects of these issues in the UK and other countries of the European Union. His recent publications include *Health and safety in small enterprises* (2001), *Regulating health and safety management in the EU* (2002) and *Working safely in small enterprises in Europe* (2002).

Acknowledgments

This volume represents the work of a number of contributors and it would be remiss not to offer sincere thanks to all of them for their time and effort to present chapters on the provision and role of occupational health services in supporting health at work in their countries. It is also pleasing to be able to thank a particularly distinguished panel of reviewers, including Professor Frank van Dijk (Netherlands), Professor John Harrison (UK), Dr Tim Carter (UK) and Professor Mansel Aylward (UK), who provided extensive and constructive reviews of all of the material in the pages that follow. Dr Jon Kimber undertook the first stages of language editing and Alex Cameron at IOSH provided final language and technical editing. Both made essential contributions to the final version of the material published here, for which the editors are especially grateful. Last, but by no means least, it is a pleasure to acknowledge the special debt owed to Peter Westerholm, who has co-edited this volume, whose idea it was originally, and who has worked unstintingly to bring about its publication.

David Walters

Introduction: occupational health services in a changing world

David Walters, Cardiff University, UK

Providing relevant and effective occupational health (OH) services in the changing world of work is widely recognised as a major challenge in most advanced market economies. Economic changes that are occurring on a world scale and the efforts of states to achieve or maintain competitiveness in global markets create new environments in which traditional approaches to requiring or supporting service provision for OH are no longer seen as appropriate. In many countries, the shift away from the regulatory state to one in which the state is a facilitator of free market initiatives has produced many contradictions, some of which are directly relevant to the provision and role of OH services. Change in the structure of work and the labour market offers further significant challenges to the coverage and operation of traditional provision. In addition, the nature of the relationship between work and health is increasingly regarded as considerably more complex than in the past. Negative health outcomes have changed as employment has shifted away from heavy industry towards services; this has led, for example, to a reduction in cases of traditional occupational diseases but parallel increases in stress-related conditions. At the same time, greater attention is being paid to providing support for keeping people in work and returning to productive employment those who have left work for health reasons. In these latter scenarios, traditional views of the negative effects of work on health are to some extent being reoriented to accommodate notions of positive effects that productive economic activities have on the health and wellbeing of individuals in modern societies.

Clearly all these changes have significant implications for the nature of support for maintaining the health and wellbeing of people at work. They affect the aims of such support, its targets and priorities, the way in which it is delivered and its coverage. They also concern the roles and expected contributions of health professionals and the meaning of OH prevention, as distinct from OH curative or reparative programmes or activities. It is to examine these implications for OH service provision in a range of countries that this volume has been compiled. But we hope to offer something more than a description of service provision. There are critical matters of evaluation, quality and scale of service provision that need to be addressed in order to understand the issues involved in providing professional health services to companies and organisations in production and services in the modern world of work. These matters further include the challenges involved in interacting with management and executives of client organisations, the staff they employ and the trade unions to which the staff may belong.

A shift has occurred in some countries away from state-subsidised services to market-based provision. It is important to know what the impact of this change has been on the nature of the services now offered and their quality. In this context, there are important issues of evaluation to address, as well as strategic approaches to ensuring quality in changed circumstances of delivery in which, for example, it cannot be assumed that client satisfaction will necessarily always be the best measure of how OH services support the health needs of workers.

Equally important is the question of support for health professionals engaged in service provision. Beginning with the nature of education and training of professionals and the adequacy with which it reflects current issues, concerns are also evident in relation to continuing training and professional development as well as to changes in the qualities and competences that are relevant and required to provide support for OH in the modern economy. How or to what extent these issues are addressed in different countries is therefore of considerable interest.

More generally, there are questions that can be asked about the nature of evaluation of provisions and practices in different countries and the evidence base for policy development in OH. Changes that have taken place in the organisation of provision are partly dictated by markets, but the state obviously has not been a passive player in this process. There are therefore important questions for macro-level analysis of state policies on health services and the role of support for health at work within these policies. Rhetorical links between workplace health support, work retention, return to work and rehabilitation have been made in recent governmental policies in some countries. But what is the reality of practice at the workplace level? Here too, major questions should be addressed to micro-level evidence and evaluation in each country as well as to questions of regulation and market liberalisation in OH. While there is little dispute that productive and paid work is overall a more healthy situation than unemployment, the quality of such work and the support that makes it safe and without risks to health for all workers are important aspects in which there is a central role to be played by preventive services. Significant issues about practice also concern, for example, relationships between the preventive work environment functions of OH services and those needed to support rehabilitation and return to work, and the extent to which these functions are integrated or separated at the level of the workplace and service provider.

A further related but relatively unexplored area concerns the role of workplace health promotion (WPHP) in ensuring improving health at work. The evaluations in this book allow a degree of comparative analysis of a number of important questions, such as the extent to which approaches to WPHP exist in different countries, how they are linked to other means of support for health improvement at work, and what the roles and responsibilities of employers are in such essentially public health issues.

Linked to all these questions, of course, is the challenge of coverage of OH services in the modern economy. It is widely recognised that the trend away from work in large stable organisations in which the employment relationship is legally defined creates major challenges to traditional approaches to the management of health and safety in general. In terms of OH service provision, it is important to review what is known about support of this kind for workers who are employed in small enterprises, or in other contingent and peripheral forms of employment, since it is clear that in many respects the health of these workers is particularly vulnerable.

This book is devoted to consideration of these issues in OH service provision across a range of countries, representing a variety of different responses to challenges presented by modern economic change in advanced market economies. In each case, the authors have provided a rich source of description and analysis of the national situations with which they are familiar in their respective countries. Not all changes or their consequences are evident to the same extent in all countries. At a descriptive level, one clear feature that emerges from the accounts is that of variation in national approaches. At the same time, however, there are strong signs of convergence. Generally, research on all the issues outlined above is relatively underdeveloped. Therefore contributions often raise more questions than answers. This is inevitable and, indeed, to be welcomed, if such questions help to give a clear pointer to future needs.

As a result, we have a unique contribution to the literature on OH service provision, in which the role of the state and the market, professional standards and competences, the position of OH services in public health support more generally, and issues of quality and effectiveness are addressed. For British readers, such a contribution is particularly timely since policy development and the changing focus of support for work and health has been especially prominent in recent times. The international nature of the content of the present volume therefore provides an important source of comparison and contrast that is relevant to current debates in the UK. However, such relevance is by no means restricted to British experiences. Indeed, the issues covered in the following pages have widespread international application and provide a firm bedrock for future analysis of the quality and development of OH service provision in all modern economies.

This book consists of a series of contributions describing and analysing developments in OH service provision in Austria, the Czech Republic, Denmark, Finland, France, Germany, the Netherlands, Norway, Sweden and the UK (where separate accounts are given for experiences in England and Scotland). We have also included a contribution from Japan, which offers some interesting comparisons from outside Europe. There are two comparative and analytical chapters. In the first of these, Laurent Vogel presents some thoughts on the state of OH service provision in Europe and on the wider implications of the national contributions. The volume concludes with an overview from Peter Westerholm, who played a major role in selecting and editing the national contributions, which offers further reflections on the range of issues addressed.

Occupational health services in Austria

Reinhard Jäger, Austrian Society for Occupational Medicine, Vienna

The historical development of occupational health in Austria

Until the late 1970s, only a few large enterprises in Austria, mainly in nationalised industry, had occupational physicians. Usually they were fully employed by these enterprises. In many cases, their function was more curative than preventive, and where prevention was part of their function, it focused on medical examinations, with little attention, if any, paid to the workplace environment or to primary prevention.

During the 1970s and early 1980s, new legislation[1-3] obliged all companies with more than 250 employees to employ staff to prevent ill health in the workplace, namely occupational physicians and safety engineers. The number of hours per week they worked in the company depended on the number of employees. The safety engineer was usually directly employed by the company itself. The occupational physician, on the other hand, was usually a general practitioner with some additional training in occupational medicine, who was engaged by contract. In the early 1980s, postgraduate training for occupational physicians was extended (from four to 12 weeks full time), but for most of them their work as an occupational physician was just a sideline. This reflected the policy of the Österreichische Ärztekammer (Austrian Medical Association) at the time: working as a part-time company doctor provided a good opportunity for a general practitioner to obtain some extra income.

At the same time, the first initiatives were taken to establish more permanent occupational health (OH) services. The earliest were in Hall/Tirol (1980) and Linz (1985). During the first years of this development, the previously part-time occupational physicians were the only experts in the service, but in most cases they now worked full time in that specialism. This was an important step towards specialisation and professionalisation among the physicians involved. Another incentive for the development of OH services in Austria was the country's membership of the European Union (EU) from 01 January 1995. Council Directive 89/391/EEC of 1989[4] – the Framework Directive – had to be applied to Austrian national health and safety legislation. The Directive obliges employers to have 'one or more workers to carry out activities related to the protection and prevention of occupational risks', irrespective of the number of employees in the company. This obligation has been transposed into Austrian law, which requires companies to employ or contract an occupational physician and a safety engineer if they have more than 50 employees. EU legislation also requires Austrian employers to 'be in possession of an assessment of the risks to safety and health at work'. Such workplace risk assessment is carried out in most companies by external experts, mainly safety engineers, in co-operation with in-house occupational physicians.

As demand for OH services increased, more organisations providing them were founded. Today there are 41 such organisations in Austria. Occupational medicine has been recognised by the Austrian Ministry of Health as a separate professional medical specialism (as it is in other European countries), and the Austrian Medical Association has taken the new specialism on board. The number of physicians who aim to specialise in occupational medicine and to work as full-time occupational physicians is steadily increasing.

Structure, distribution and coverage of OH services in Austria

The structure of OH activities in Austrian companies is largely determined by legislation, which covers both services for occupational medicine and services for safety at work. This does not encourage the idea of multiprofessional services, but the latest legislative amendment[5] allows companies to bring in experts other than occupational physicians or safety engineers – such as occupational psychologists – for 25 per cent of the so-called 'prevention time'. However, employers are entitled to decide whether they want to engage 'other experts' and, if so, which. An increasing number of OH units are already accumulating experience in occupational psychology, and many have occupational psychologists on their staff. Furthermore, many organisations have a service for occupational medicine and for work safety as well, and also have occupational nurses. So, the first steps towards a multiprofessional approach to occupational health in Austria have been taken.

The organisational structure of the services can vary considerably. A few are part of a large company, some are companies of their own, and others are associations founded with the support of social partners, mainly workers' organisations. The general manager in many cases is an occupational physician, who is sometimes also a business manager. Officially, the head of an occupational medicine service must be an occupational physician, and the head of an occupational safety service a safety engineer.

The services are spread all over the country, so that, except in the sparsely populated Alpine region, they are generally 100km or less apart. As would be expected, there is a higher concentration in industrial districts.

It is difficult to gauge what proportion of the Austrian workforce is covered by OH services. Around 70 per cent of the Austrian workforce is employed in small or medium-sized enterprises (SMEs) of 50 employees or fewer. In SMEs there is no requirement to provide continuous monitoring of workers' health and conditions. They receive one visit a year from an occupational physician and a safety engineer as part of the government's social security provisions, at no cost to the company. For very small organisations (under 10 employees), these visits happen every two years.

Companies with more than 50 employees are obliged to engage preventive staff of their own, at their own expense. There are three ways of complying with this obligation:

- by employing preventive staff of their own (in practice, mainly safety engineers)
- by agreeing a contract with an individual specialist (mainly occupational physicians)
- by agreeing a contract with an organisation providing OH services.

There are no published statistics on the proportion of Austrian employees who receive continuous in-house OH services at work. Around 30 per cent of the Austrian workforce is employed by companies with more than 50 employees, and the present author estimates that between a third and a half of these have access to full-time OH services. This means that between 10 and 15 per cent of the Austrian workforce obtains its preventive healthcare from an in-house OH service provider. The most common solution is to have a safety engineer in the company and to have a contract with an occupational physician.

Legislative basis for OH services

As mentioned above, all companies with 50 or more employees have to employ an occupational physician and a safety engineer, and if necessary other experts as well. Their main tasks are also stipulated by legislation.[5] The most important is to advise the employer and employees on all aspects of health and safety at work. The minimum time to be spent on these tasks is specified in the legislation: 1.5 hours per worker per year for blue-collar workers, 1.2 hours for white-collar workers. Of this minimum 'prevention time', 35 per cent is reserved for the occupational physician, 40 per cent for the safety engineer, and the remaining 25 per cent for either of them or for another expert that the individual employer can choose. 'Prevention time', as the name implies, is limited to preventive strategies. The occupational physician is not allowed to use this time to treat existing conditions, except in cases of first aid. Moreover, the time to be spent on medical examinations is restricted – it should take up no more than 20 per cent of the 'prevention time'.

The most important tasks of an occupational physician are to:

- advise the employer, work council and employees on all aspects of health and safety in the workplace, healthy work conditions and ergonomic workplace design
- inspect the workplace
- establish possible causes of work-related diseases and health risks
- perform medical examination of the workers (up to a maximum of 20 per cent of 'prevention time')
- carry out vaccinations, if there is a risk of work-related infections
- attend conferences and meetings as part of continuous professional development (up to a maximum of 15 per cent of 'prevention time')
- attend company meetings with other experts, representatives of the employer and work council, and other workers responsible for health and safety
- document all these activities.

The medical examinations mentioned above are legally compulsory where there are workplace hazards that can cause occupational diseases (eg toxic chemicals, asbestos, noise). The employer must arrange them during working hours, and the workers are obliged to take part. Other examinations – such as eye tests for workers who use display screen equipment or health examinations for shift workers – are voluntary for employees. The point of these examinations is to allow the effects of over-exposure to this kind of hazard to be detected early. The outcome has to be reported to the Labour Inspectorate. In the case of health hazards, follow-up inspections are required not only of the worker but also of the workplace. Sometimes it is necessary to move an employee to another task in a less hazardous environment. There is not normally any evaluation of the results of these examinations at group level, unless they form part of a research project.

These regulations apply to all branches of industry in the private sector, and there are similar regulations for the public sector. The legal authority that controls whether and how the regulations are implemented in companies is the Labour Inspectorate, which is now part of the Ministry for Economy and Work.

The relationship between OH and public health services
Even in cases of occupational or work-related disease, medical treatment is provided by the public health services – in other words, by a general practitioner or medical specialist, or in hospital. Occupational physicians do not normally offer treatment within the company for existing conditions, as their tasks are mainly to do with prevention and rehabilitation. This implies that they must analyse the workplace environment, workload and work organisation to find factors causing or promoting ill health, and to advise the employer and employees on

what to do in terms of prevention and rehabilitation. Regardless of the causation of their ill health, patients have a free choice in who treats them and how.

Because treatment and prevention are separated in this way, it is important that occupational physicians and general practitioners co-operate effectively. This is a key area in which OH services in Austria need to improve.

Staffing and competence

Most OH organisations consist mainly of occupational physicians, assisted by OH nurses and administrative staff. The law stipulates how many assisting and administrative personnel an OH unit has to employ per occupational physician. The larger OH units may have around 20 occupational physicians, with some working part time. One full-time occupational physician can take care of around 2,000–3,000 employees, depending on the size, structure and geographical location of the company. Some OH service providers have specialists, such as trainers in physiotherapeutic exercises, or analytical chemists for biomonitoring.

Occupational physicians are obliged to have 12 weeks' postgraduate training in occupational medicine, safety engineers eight weeks' postgraduate training, and occupational nurses four weeks' additional training. Occupational physicians and safety engineers must have a specialist OH diploma – without this, they cannot work legally in a company. Occupational physicians' formal training ends with an examination, which is then followed by a *Diplomfortbildungs-programm*, or continuing professional development (CPD).[6] CPD remains voluntary, but many occupational physicians take part in the courses and conferences.

Postgraduate training for occupational physicians is provided by two institutions:

- Österreichische Akademie für Arbeitsmedizin (Austrian Academy for Occupational Medicine), situated in Klosterneuburg near Vienna, founded in the early 1980s
- Linzer Akademie für Arbeitsmedizin und Sicherheitstechnik (Linz Academy for Occupational Health and Safety), founded in 1988.

These are both non-academic private associations, with members from national and local authorities, the social security system, trade unions and employers' organisations. On the board of the Austrian Academy there is also a representative of the Austrian Medical Association. Both institutions are financed mainly by student fees. The basic curriculum is defined by the Ministry of Health, which must also approve the training institutions.

The curriculum covers not only traditional physical and chemical hazards, but also risks arising from heavy workload and psychosocial or organisational factors. The main emphasis of the training programme is on all work-related diseases, not only legally recognised ones.

The academies also provide CPD, as do the Österreichische Gesellschaft für Arbeitsmedizin (Austrian Society for Occupational Medicine) and the department for occupational medicine at the Medical University of Vienna (which is the only such department in Austria so far).

There are no statistics on the number of active occupational physicians and other OH professionals. It is estimated that there are around 2,000 occupational physicians, of whom a third work full time.

Main focus of preventive programmes

During the 1980s and early 1990s, preventive programmes were mainly geared towards health surveillance, workers' protection and risk assessment in the workplace. But, in line with the European trend, over the last decade health promotion has become more and more important. Now, not only physicians but also occupational psychologists and various 'health advisers' offer health promotion projects to companies. This is a free market, without any specific legal restrictions. Not all of these projects follow the Ottawa Charter for Health Promotion and the Luxembourg Declaration on Workplace Health Promotion, which give the definitions accepted in the social security system and by the Labour Inspectorate. Some are merely screening programmes for individual risk factors, others aim to reduce tobacco and alcohol dependency and abuse, and still others address occupational risk factors and require the involvement of employees in group work. These projects are mainly financed by companies. The more demanding programmes are often supported by health insurance companies.

The new trend has led to a discussion about whether health promotion should be part of occupational physicians' work during their prescribed 'prevention time'. In cases of individual screening programmes the answer must be no. In discussing health promotion, it is important not to forget the protection of workers from 'old' hazards in the workplace which are still present, as well as from the 'new' risks of recently developed technologies and new chemical substances and – last but not least – from stress at work and organisational risk factors.

Developing quality

Quality management and control of OH services in Austria needs further development. Austrian legislation contains some regulations designed to achieve good quality in preventive activities within companies (eg by defining the tasks occupational physicians have to fulfil, and requirements for documenting their activities), but there is no overall quality management system. Some OH service providers have achieved ISO certification, but in the author's opinion, the sector would benefit from a system that is more specific to OH. Furthermore, the Labour Inspectorate's monitoring of how well regulations are implemented is not very effective.

So, it is an important objective of the Austrian Society for Occupational Medicine to promote quality assessment. The society has a checklist on its website,[7] which occupational physicians can use to monitor whether they meet the society's quality criteria. A working group of the society is discussing further development of quality activities, for example by setting up an auditing system similar to that of the Gesellschaft zur Qualitätssicherung in der betriebsärztlichen Betreuung (Society for Quality Assurance in Occupational Medicine, GQB) in Germany,[8] and determining whether or not it should be obligatory.

Financing structures

There are two main sources of funds for OH services. Individual companies pay for the services of OH professionals – whether directly employed or brought in as consultants or contractors – depending on the amount of 'prevention time' needed, as determined by the size of the company. On the other hand, obligatory medical examinations are funded by the social security system.

On top of these funding streams, some OH service providers gain additional funds from running special projects concerned with health promotion, participating in research projects, or running laboratory services for biomonitoring.

The services for SMEs (with 50 employees or fewer) are provided and financed by the Allgemeine Unfallversicherungsanstalt (AUVA) health insurance organisation; all employers have to be insured against occupational diseases and accidents.

Public awareness and surveillance

Most duties deriving from legislation are aimed at the employer. The Labour Inspectorate has to check whether the occupational physician and the safety engineer are doing their job, whether risk assessment in all workplaces is being performed properly, whether maximum allowable concentrations of chemical substances in the workplace are being considered, whether employees are using their personal protective equipment, and so on. The intention is that labour inspectors (who are mainly technicians, with only a few physicians) should visit every company at least once a year. But the Inspectorate has a shortage of personnel, which is why the controls cannot be as detailed and strict as they should be.

A second point is that public awareness of the importance of OH is not very high in Austria, in contrast to the many discussions among the public and in the media about environmental hazards. Also, among other medical specialists occupational medicine is still not really recognised as a component of the public health system. This perception persists because of some distinguishing features of OH services: they work 'only' preventively, not curatively; they are financed by companies, not by the social security system; they give advice to employers and employees, but not in the well-known setting of the doctor–patient relationship; and they offer their services in a free market.

The combination of weak control and poor public consciousness means that some companies pay little attention to occupational safety and health.

Problems

The main problem faced by OH services is increasing competition and the decreasing prices for services that result. It is the author's opinion that this is partly the fault of OH providers themselves. For years, many occupational physicians felt themselves to be in a secure position. Companies had to use them, and the providers failed to highlight the additional benefits of their activities to companies. Many employers regard OH services as a more or less useless financial burden, and they have no idea what the benefit of high standards might be. Therefore, their main (or even only) criterion for contracting a service is the price per hour of 'prevention time'. This forces OH providers to offer services at very low, sometimes sub-market prices, which then tends to put quality under strain.

Moreover, there are no results from evaluations or research programmes on the effectiveness of prevention. When talking about preventive medicine, most people in Austria will think of screening programmes for individual risk factors, rather than avoiding or reducing risks in the workplace.

Strategies for developing OH services

To cope with these problems and to encourage OH services in Austria to develop further, action at several different levels is necessary.

- Within companies, occupational physicians must sharpen the arguments they use to convince employers and employees of the benefits of good quality in-workplace health protection and promotion. Accompanying evaluation programmes at company level would also be helpful.

- The Austrian Society of Occupational Medicine is playing an important role in pushing its discussion of quality control forward, towards its aim of establishing an obligatory quality system with periodical audits.
- How the service is financed has a major influence on its provision. Therefore, a fixed-price system should be considered – this would help employers focus more on the quality of different providers' services rather than just on the cost. Discussion is also needed on whether the quality or quantity of service should depend on the size of the organisation being served (for example by treating SMEs with up to 50 employees differently from larger companies), and on how services for SMEs are to be financed. The current situation is the result of a political compromise; it is not satisfactory and does not lead to equal treatment of companies.
- A more intensive public relations campaign is needed to attract attention to OH and its benefits. OH services must become an important and generally accepted part of the Austrian public health system, rather than an imposition on companies that is seen to increase payroll costs without yielding obvious benefits.

In summary, it is fair to say that Austria has made some important first steps towards developing OH services, but it is equally fair to point out that there is still a long way to go and there are many problems to overcome. The most influential factor will be the future development of political attitudes towards OH services. The previous Austrian government, in power until December 2006, followed a neo-liberal economic agenda and aimed to reduce employers' costs and legal obligations as much as possible, in the process disregarding the evidence that OH benefits employers and company productivity as well as employees. The new government has issued a policy statement that calls for a more preventive approach to healthcare – this may be a positive signal that OH services will be developed further in the coming years.

References

1.   Bundesgesetz vom 30. Mai 1972 über den Schutz des Lebens, der Gesundheit und der Sittlichkeit der Arbeitnehmer (Arbeitnehmerschutzgesetz), BGBl. 234/1972. Available online at ris1.bka.gv.at/bgbl-pdf/RequestDoc.aspx?path=bgblpdf/1972/19720071.pdf& docid=19720071.pdf (viewed 26 March 2007).
2.   Bundesgesetz vom 20. Oktober 1982, mit dem das Arbeitnehmerschutzgesetz und das Allgemeine Sozialversicherungsgesetz geändert werden, BGBl. 544/1982. Available online at ris1.bka.gv.at/bgbl-pdf/RequestDoc.aspx?path=bgblpdf/1982/19820218.pdf& docid=19820218.pdf (viewed 26 March 2007).
3.   Bundesgesetz vom 3. Juli 1986, mit dem das Arbeitnehmerschutzgesetz geändert wird, BGBl. 393/1986. Available online at ris1.bka.gv.at/bgbl-pdf/RequestDoc.aspx?path= bgblpdf/1986/19860164.pdf&docid=19860164.pdf (viewed 26 March 2007).
4.   Council Directive 89/391/EEC of 12 June 1989 on the introduction of measures to encourage improvements in the safety and health of workers at work (the Framework Directive). *Official Journal* L183; 29 June 1989: 1–8.
5.   Bundesgesetz vom 28. Dezember 2001, mit dem das Arbeitsinspektionsgesetz 1993, das ArbeitnehmerInnenschutzgesetz und das Bauarbeitenkoordinationsgesetz geändert werden (Arbeitnehmerschutz-Reformgesetz), BGBl. 259/2001. Available online at ris1.bka.gv.at/bgbl-pdf/RequestDoc.aspx?path=bgblpdf/2001/2001a159.pdf&docid= 2001a159.pdf (viewed 26 March 2007).
6.   Diplomfortbildungsprogramm (DFP) der Akademie der Ärzte. See www.arztakademie.at/ diplom-fortbildungs-programm (viewed 26 March 2007).
7.   Österreichische Gesellschaft für Arbeitsmedizin. Checkliste zur Qualitätssicherung.

Available online at www.gamed.at/uploads/media/checkliste.pdf (viewed 26 March 2007).

8. Gesellschaft zur Qualitätssicherung in der betriebsärztlichen Betreuung. See www.gqb-online.de (viewed 26 March 2007).

Policy and practice in occupational health services in the Czech Republic

Miroslav Cikrt, Centre for Occupational Health, National Institute of Public Health, Prague, Milan Tuček, Society of Occupational Medicine, Czech Medical Society of J E Purkyně, Prague, Daniela Pelclová, First Medical Faculty, Univerzita Karlova, Prague, and Pavel Urban, Centre for Occupational Health, National Institute of Public Health, Prague

Structure of Czech occupational health services and their distribution and coverage

In the Czech Republic (and in its predecessor, the former Czechoslovakia), there is a long history of governmental commitment to occupational health (OH) issues. The first Department for Occupational Medicine in Czechoslovakia was established at the Charles University in Prague in 1932. The system of Czech OH services before 1989 arguably served as a model worth following in several respects, including in its approaches to resources and staffing. Research in OH was at a very high level, and work environment standards were relatively strict in comparison with many European countries. In practice, however, the system did not always work as expected.[1] For example, during the Communist era (1948–1989), there were frequent bans on the disclosure of information about workplace hazards and risk management. The gap between political proclamations and reality was widening. Nevertheless, there were some progressive practices in place during that time which, unfortunately, have been abandoned and almost completely lost since the Velvet Revolution in 1989.

During the 1990s, dramatic changes in the economic system had a deep impact on working life. Although differences between the structure of the labour market in the Czech Republic and that of the labour market in the pre-2004 European Union (EU) are relatively small, the way the workforce is structured is still influenced by the former economic arrangement, and is likely to remain so for the next few years.

The introduction of new technologies and changes in demographic structure and socio-cultural life have influenced the work environment. Unfortunately, the social dimension of these processes has often been underestimated.[2] The restructuring of OH services after the revolution in 1989 resulted in a reduction in the number of physicians and nurses engaged in the services, thus largely failing to meet the OH needs of workers and companies alike.

Coverage

It is very difficult to estimate the coverage of OH services in the Czech Republic because no precise statistics are available. The only useful information comes from the annual surveys organised by the Chief Public Health Officer. In 2005 (2004 figures are in parentheses), a total of 11,743 (7,159) checks on enterprises were performed. These checks were to verify that there was a signed contract between the employer and an OH service provider, and that the full range of OH services prescribed by law were being provided. According to the surveys, some 9 per cent (15 per cent) of employers did not provide OH services at all, while 37 per cent (45 per cent) of employers did not provide adequate services. Workers in small and medium-sized enterprises (SMEs) are especially likely not to be covered by OH services because of the costs to employers, a lack of service providers or the remote geographic location of the companies.

Equality
Equality in the provision of OH services has not yet been achieved. There are still differences in coverage between workers in SMEs and those in larger companies; between low-risk and high-risk occupations; and between different employment sectors, such as agriculture, services and industry. There is also still a large shortfall between the services needed and what is currently available.

Models
The way OH services are provided in the Czech Republic is very similar to that in other EU member states.

At the primary level, services are provided by the general healthcare system. This level encompasses several models of OH service provision, which can largely be characterised by the size of the organisation receiving the service: a big industry model, a group service model, and a private healthcare centre model. Services are mostly provided by general practitioners, who usually have no formal training in occupational medicine, on the basis of a contract with an employer.

The need for improvements in OH service provision is more urgent in SMEs and among the self-employed than in big enterprises. In SMEs, provision is especially dependent on the individual initiative of employees and employers, and the high rate of staff turnover in SMEs tends to result in patchy coverage.

The secondary level includes specialised services (methodological, consultative and other) for providers at primary level. Secondary level providers also offer primary services to clients who cannot find another provider (especially SMEs). This type of service is based on a network of regional or municipal centres incorporated into hospitals, polyclinics and institutes of public health which provide specialised services. Both systems are financed in the same way.

The quality assurance system needs further development. Currently the most important area for improvement is in the field of guidelines and standards in occupational medicine, by which providers can be measured. There are already standards which define the range and frequency of preventive medical examinations performed by authorised occupational physicians and the ways in which workers must be consulted in particular types of workplace. These instructions and guidelines are published by the Ministry of Health or by Společnost Pracovního Lékařství (the Society of Occupational Medicine).

However, there is currently no unified system for quality assurance in either health services in general or for OH services in particular. Nevertheless, pilot projects are in progress that should provide a basis for building a Czech national system of quality assurance and for its subsequent incorporation into legislation. The Society of Occupational Medicine has begun a project that aims to create such a system for assessing OH services, following World Health Organization recommendations and guidelines.[3]

The Czech legislative framework
During the process of accession to the EU, the Czech Republic transposed into national legislation all EU directives in the field of occupational safety and health, particularly the

Framework Directive 89/391/EEC[4] on the introduction of measures to encourage improvements in the safety and health of people at work.

Framework legislation at national level
The main legislation on occupational safety and health in the Czech Republic is Act No. 20/1966 Dig. on national health, along with subsequent amendments. The most important paragraphs relating to OH services are:

- section 9, paragraphs 1 and 2: citizens' rights to healthcare. In general healthcare, patients have the right to free choice of a physician who provides curative care. However, preventive OH services are exempt from this right. Workers must accept the OH service provider contracted by their employer
- section 18a: OH services are available so that employers can comply with their legal obligation to protect the health of their employees at work, and to prevent occupational diseases and accidents
- section 35a: OH service providers perform special consultations on issues of health protection, health promotion and the social wellbeing of employees, regularly inspect workplaces, evaluate the influences of work and work conditions on employees, perform preventive examinations, give first aid, co-operate with the public health service, and participate in education and training in health protection and promotion
- section 40: every individual who is economically active as an employer, and every organisation that is legally defined as an employer, is obliged to establish OH services for their employees according to Decree No. 145/88 Dig. This is a transposition into Czech law of the International Labour Organization convention on OH services, No. 161.[5]

Other important regulations at national level
There are two other pieces of legislation that affect the provision of OH services in the Czech Republic:

- Act No. 48/1997 Dig. on general health insurance. Section 13 requires OH care to be paid for by general health insurance; this includes preventive examinations, first aid, some regular examinations, specially ordered extraordinary examinations, and dispensary examinations for occupational diseases whose purpose is not solely for assessing financial compensation
- Decree of the Ministry of Health No. 49/67 on the assessment of fitness to work. Sections 3, 8, 9 and 11 cover epidemiologically important activities; section 12 deals with examinations in workplaces at risk; section 13 covers activities that jeopardise the health of employees; section 14 addresses specific health capabilities, and section 15 looks at routine examinations and change or termination of work.

Relationships between OH services, public health services and the general health service
Under Czech legislation (the Public Health Act), occupational healthcare is a component of public healthcare. Regional institutes of public health that have OH departments are therefore involved in the system of ensuring health at work. The regional public health institutes (hygiene inspectorates) and recently also the Labour Inspectorate may also penalise employers for failing to meet their legal OH obligations.[6,7]

Each worker is in the care of a general practitioner (GP), whom he or she has the right to choose. The GP provides diagnosis and treatment in case of a disease. Co-operation between

GPs and OH service providers is very important, especially after long periods (more than four weeks) of sickness absence or whenever there are concerns regarding long-term or permanent changes in capacity to work. Accordingly, the principles of co-operation, in particular mutual exchange of relevant information between physicians, are to be defined in new legislation, which is under preparation. If a GP or a specialised physician suspects that a patient is suffering from ill health caused by work, he or she can send the patient to a regional occupational medical centre for examination or hospitalisation. At these centres, the patient's condition is evaluated by public health officers. If they agree that the condition was caused by the patient's work, a level of compensation is decided on. If it is decided that the illness is not work related, the patient is informed in writing.

Relationships between OH services and inspection bodies

There are two independent state inspection bodies in the field of occupational safety and health: the Public Health Inspectorate and the Labour Inspectorate (established in July 2005). The Public Health Inspectorate provides an arbitration service in cases of disagreement between OH service providers and employers, but it is not authorised to control the quality of OH services. The newly established Labour Inspectorate also has no formal direct link to OH activities.

Staffing and competencies

The working population in the Czech Republic totals about 5 million employees. Of these, about 10 per cent are deemed to be at high risk because of hazards they face at work.

There are two types of OH providers in the Czech Republic, differentiated by their level of medical training:

- occupational physicians, who have specialised in occupational medicine
- non-specialists, usually general practitioners.

The involvement of GPs is usually limited to health examinations of workers. They do not generally undertake any other significant activities to do with OH provision, such as workplace visits, risk assessment, or consultations for employers and employees. Only exceptionally will these physicians address multidisciplinary problems with other specialists. This simplified approach may have serious consequences, particularly in terms of incorrect assessment of someone's ability to work. General practitioners, despite being untrained in occupational medicine, have been permitted to take on the role of occupational physician in order to make it possible for employers to fulfil their legal obligation to provide OH services for their employees. A principal reason for this is a lack of specialists in occupational medicine.[8]

OH services in the Czech Republic are provided by both the national health service and private healthcare facilities. The latter have to be registered by a regional authority and licensed by the Czech Medical Chamber. Among the providers are:

- private general practitioners (about a third of the country's total of 7,000 general practitioners). Almost 300 of them have passed a one-year basic course in occupational medicine
- physicians who specialise in industrial hygiene and occupational diseases or occupational medicine (of which there are about 200)
- public healthcare centres (polyclinics)

- healthcare centres established by large companies
- specialist occupational medicine departments in hospitals and teaching hospitals (approximately 25 certified physicians)
- institutes of public health (418 employees, of whom 64 are physicians and 36 certified occupational physicians).

Employers can use their own employees to provide in-company preventive care, provided that the provision of healthcare is within the scope of the chosen employees' activities. Companies that do not possess specialised facilities for providing OH services can make use of a network of contracted OH providers. Such companies can also take advantage of medical facilities that specialise in counselling and interpreting results of preventive medical examinations performed by others. In all cases, the independence of healthcare providers has to be guaranteed.

It is estimated that the Czech Republic needs around 1,000–2,500 primary level specialists in OH. General practitioners represent the largest proportion of physicians working in OH (about 70 per cent). About 300 of them have attended a one-year weekend course (a total of 150 hours) organised by the department of occupational medicine at the Institut Postgraduálního Vzdělávání ve Zdravotnictví (Institute for Postgraduate Medical Education) in Prague and Brno.

Currently, only about 200 physicians working in OH are certified in occupational medicine. They have completed a three-year course in occupational medicine, also organised by the Institute for Postgraduate Medical Education. At the end of their course, they take a specialisation examination, consisting of a practical section, a written thesis, and an oral examination. These specialists work mostly at the secondary level of OH service provision (see above under the heading 'Models').

Any provider of OH services is obliged to carry out the following tasks:

- helping an employer to identify and assess health hazards in the workplace
- surveillance of workers' health, based on legal requirements, the severity of occupational risks to workers' health or voluntary requests from workers
- surveillance of the factors in the work environment and working practices that may affect workers' health
- advising on occupational safety and health, hygiene and ergonomics, and on personal and collective protective equipment
- organising first aid and emergency treatment
- advising on the planning and organisation of work, including the design of workplaces and the choice, maintenance and condition of machinery and other equipment, as well as on substances used at work
- promoting the adaptation of work to the worker, assessing disability and fitness for work, and promoting working ability
- advising on fitness for work and adaptation of work to the worker in specific cases to meet the needs of vulnerable groups and of particular legislation
- helping to provide information, training and education in the field of occupational safety and health and ergonomics to the management and the workforce
- advising on, supporting and monitoring the implementation of occupational safety and health legislation
- participating in workplace health promotion programmes.

A keystone of high performance by an occupational physician lies in familiarity with specific work conditions and the demands of the job, as well as knowledge of individual workers' state of health.[6,7]

Main orientation of programmes

Reliable information and valid data are essential for setting priorities and allocating resources in the field of OH. To make such information available, three major information systems have been established in the Czech Republic. On one hand, these systems collect data on exposure to various occupational risk factors; on the other, they monitor the impact of such exposures, as reflected in the prevalence of occupational diseases. This approach makes it possible to estimate the national burden of occupational diseases and ill health.

Categorisation of work operations

The system is based on the Public Health Protection Act (No. 258/2000 Dig.), and the Labour Code (No. 155/2000 Dig.). These enactments oblige employers to perform risk assessment – in other words, to identify all health hazards in the workplace and to estimate the level of risk for each. All work activities are put into four categories according to their risk level. Depending on how work operations in a particular enterprise are categorised, different measures for risk management have to be adopted. These include requirements for frequency and content of health examinations where appropriate. Data from the categorisation system make it possible to estimate the magnitude of a problem and to analyse the risk associated with exposure to any specific noxious factor.[9,10]

National Registry of Occupational Diseases

According to Czech legislation, specialised centres for occupational disease and occupational medicine must recognise the occupational diseases that are enumerated in the official list of occupational diseases and meet the prescribed medical and exposure criteria for dealing with them.[11] Subsequently, the cases are reported to the National Registry of Occupational Diseases, which is a component of the National Health Information System. The Registry was founded in 1991 and is run by the Centre for Occupational Health at the National Institute of Public Health in Prague. Its operations are based on Act No. 156/2004 Dig., which established 13 national health registries, and on the Decree of the Ministry of Health No. 552/2004 Dig., which regulates the collection of data for the National Health Information System. About 20 items are stored in the registry on each case of an occupational disease. Currently, the registry contains data on approximately 40,000 cases of occupational disease. In 2004, the registry joined EUROSTAT/EODS. The Czech registry was invited to join the multinational study DELPHI, which is researching the quality of national registration systems for occupational diseases, organised by the Coronel Institute in Amsterdam. The link between the information system, the categorisation of work operations, and the National Registry of Occupational Diseases provides an opportunity to estimate the national burden of work-related health problems.[12]

The registry of persons occupationally exposed to carcinogens (REGEX)

REGEX has been developed as a tool for the surveillance of occupational cancer. It has been designed to cover three functions:

- maintaining a nationwide collection of data on occupational exposures to chemical, physical and biological carcinogens (which functions as a 'passive' exposure registry)
- keeping track of periodic check-ups of exposed subjects
- generating data suitable for analytic epidemiological research.

The functions of the project determine its output. REGEX enables:

- assessment of the level of exposure in specific industries, plants, occupations or workplaces
- co-ordination of inspection activities
- initiation of measures for risk reduction
- estimation of expected health impacts
- analysis of long-term trends in exposures
- evaluation of the effects of implemented preventive measures.

The database is updated yearly. The number of registered subjects was 3,786 (with a total of 5,253 entries) in 2004.[10,13]

Health promotion in the workplace

The Czech Republic's concept of health promotion is based on the Luxembourg Declaration, which defines health promotion as 'the combined efforts of employers, employees and society to improve the health and well-being of people at work'.[14] The Czech Republic is involved in the activities of the European Network for Workplace Health Promotion.

Although health promotion is not a standard component of OH services in the Czech Republic, it has been incorporated into a government programme called 'Health for all 21'. Item 13.6 of this programme includes a commitment to ensure that at least 10 per cent of SMEs comply with principles of health promotion. Within the framework of this task, the National Institute of Public Health put together a manual called *Criteria for workplace health promotion*, to which it appended its own commentary. There is also an annual competition, 'Enterprises promoting health at work', funded by the Ministry of Health and the National Institute of Public Health. In 2005, around 20 firms entered the contest, and 10 of them received awards.

Financing structures

At present, OH services are funded partly by health insurance, and partly by employers, employees and government institutions. Funding by health insurance is based on Act No. 48/1997 Dig. and other associated acts, such as No. 242/1997 Dig.; it covers activities such as first aid, periodical preventive examinations of workers at risk, extraordinary examinations performed for medical reasons (see sections 11–14 of the Directive of the Ministry of Health, No. 49/1967 Dig.), follow-up examinations of workers with notified occupational diseases, and check-ups of workers exposed to hazardous factors with long-term or delayed effects. In general, it is possible to arrange pre-employment examinations for a fee (paid either by the employee or the employer). Employers pay for periodical examinations of firefighters and, in part, of drivers, and for extraordinary examinations performed for non-medical reasons. State institutions pay for vaccination programmes and grant-supported programmes, such as the 'Enterprises promoting health at work' competition.

This system of multisource financing cannot be considered acceptable in the long term. All OH services should be provided solely by employers. This is also the intention of new legislation currently being prepared.

Public surveillance

The government established a council for occupational safety and health in 2004 to serve as an advisory body. The council is composed of representatives of several ministries, employers, employees (via trade unions) and independent experts in the field. The inspecting authority for

OH services is represented on the council by the Ministry of Health. A committee of the council focuses on tasks related to risk assessment in the workplace, OH services and work rehabilitation.

One non-governmental organisation is active in the field of occupational health and safety, namely the Akademie práce a zdraví České republice (Academy of Work and Health of the Czech Republic). It arranges meetings and conferences, and also participates in research. Although its main interest is in OH policy, it also actively supports the role of OH service providers.

Problems in OH in the Czech Republic

Education is needed to change workers' views on what are acceptable health risks. To help such a change, it is necessary to break the link between pay and exposure to hazards by abandoning the common practice of paying higher wages or bonuses to employees working in high-hazard workplaces. Although this practice may be attractive to both workers and employers in the short term (especially given the present low level of wages), a long-term strategy needs to be developed that gives the introduction of better industrial hygiene methods into the workplace the same priority as the improvement of production technology.

Less than 4 per cent of the working population is employed in agriculture, but this sector of the economy is one of the most risky. Therefore, the need for a comprehensive hazard assessment and intervention strategy for farm workers is crucial to any public health plan for the rural population. There is an urgent need to develop an OH service model for farm workers, and also to carry out research on the OH issues facing rural populations. This would allow risk factors to be determined and intervention strategies for the prevention of occupational diseases and accidents at work to be designed.[9]

It is useful to summarise the main OH problems in the Czech Republic today. They can be divided into two groups: strategic issues which need to be addressed at the national level, and operational issues facing individual enterprises. The national issues are:

- incomplete legislation (the part of the Framework Directive that relates to preventive and protective services has not yet been implemented)
- delays in passing several important laws, especially those relating to accident insurance and OH services
- an absence of effective co-operation between stakeholders in OH
- limited collaboration and exchange of information between OH providers and general practitioners or other healthcare specialists
- a lack of co-operation between the two state bodies responsible for occupational safety and health inspection, the Public Health Inspectorate (which is part of the Ministry of Health) and the Labour Inspectorate (which is part of the Ministry of Labour and Social Affairs)
- ineffective control of employers
- a lack of professionals with the required level of expertise in OH, industrial hygiene, safety engineering, OH nursing and other fields
- gaps in the coverage of OH services, fragmentation of the OH support system, and the danger that OH provision could become a purely commercial business
- a lack of unified concepts for and practical usage of risk assessment methodology.

At the level of individual organisations, the main problems are:

- employers' limited knowledge of their duties in the field of occupational safety and health
- a reduction of investment in the field of occupational safety and health to the lowest possible level (and its replacement by financial compensation for hazardous work)
- the tendency to use outdated machinery and to buy the cheapest types of personal protective equipment
- organisational cultures that tend to lead to large amounts of quasi-compulsory overtime, which often increases ill health and absence among workers
- stress on staff resulting from fear of job loss
- a failure to incorporate health and safety management into the overall business management system
- a failure of the consultative function of OH services to meet employers' needs (they generally concentrate only on periodical medical examinations)
- a similar failure to address employees' needs – there is limited scope for employees to give feedback on OH services and to ask for solutions to their specific needs and problems
- insufficient involvement of trade union (or other employee) representatives in health and safety matters. Although unions play an important role in the government's council on occupational safety and health, they need to be more active at the level of individual enterprises.

Anticipated developments and strategies in OH services

On the basis of evaluation of current trends and the present situation, the following developments in OH services in the Czech Republic can be expected:

- modification of the system of social insurance, health insurance and healthcare, focusing on prevention and including healthcare for the working population
- more restructuring, reorientation and renovation of the national OH system, including allocation of sufficient resources to make these aims fully achievable
- increasing awareness of policy makers, employers and workers of the importance of OH as a part of socio-economic development
- improvements in training of all groups of OH personnel.

In order to facilitate these developments, the following strategic approaches need to be considered:

- use of an incremental strategy for the development of OH services, starting with 'basic OH services', as described by Rantanen[15]
- implementation of the Czech national system for evaluation and surveillance of quality of OH services
- further development of the information system for OH service providers, employers, employees and other stakeholders, currently available on the internet homepage of the Czech Society of Occupational Health[16] and the Centre for Occupational Health at the National Institute of Public Health[17]
- implementation and evaluation of the programmes for screening for and intervening against work stress, and methods for identifying people who are most suitable for highly stressful jobs
- improvement of co-operation between the experts in a multidisciplinary team to ensure the greatest collective benefit from their individual skills
- provision of OH services by multidisciplinary teams with special training, with an increasing role for some new professions, such as ergonomists, psychologists and specialists in health promotion

- inclusion of OH services as a fundamental part of the commercial strategy of each workplace
- updating of pre- and post-graduate training programmes for OH professionals to reflect changes in working life and new OH risks.

References

1. Cikrt M, Pelclová D, Markvart K, Lukáš E & Kříž J. Occupational and environmental medicine in the Czech Republic. *International Archives of Occupational and Environmental Health* 1997; 69 (2): 79–82.
2. World Health Organization Europe. *Organizational models and functions of OHSs in countries in socioeconomic transition: present state and perspectives. Summary report on a WHO meeting.* Łódź, Poland: WHO, December 1994.
3. Westerholm P & Baranski B (eds). *Guidelines on quality management in multidisciplinary occupational health services.* Bilthoven: WHO European Centre for Environment and Health, 1999.
4. Council Directive 89/391/EEC of 12 June 1989 on the introduction of measures to encourage improvements in the safety and health of workers at work (the Framework Directive). *Official Journal* L183; 29 June 1989: 1–8.
5. International Labour Organization. Occupational Health Services Convention. C161. Geneva: ILO, 1985. Available online at www.ilo.org/ilolex/cgi-lex/convde.pl?C161 (viewed 23 April 2007).
6. Tuček M, Pelclová D & Cikrt M. *Pracovní lékařství pro praxi. Příručka s doporučenými standardy* (Occupational medicine for practice. A handbook with recommended standards; in Czech). Prague: Grada, 2005.
7. Tuček M. Analýza pracovně lékařské péče v České republice (Analysis of occupational medical care in the Czech Republic; in Czech with abstract in English). *České pracovní lékařství* 2005; 6 (1): 28–36.
8. Leino T, Räsänen K, Kauppinen T, Liira J, Jakkola J, Carnevale F, Baldasseroni A, Van Damme K, Casteleyn L, Veidebaum T, Kahn H, Vilkis A, Eglite M, Jekabsone I, Vanadzins I, Jankauskas R, Černá M, Tuček M, Málek B, Cikrt M, Pelclová D & Šmerhovský Z. *Comparative analysis of occupational health systems and practices as part of preventive healthcare systems in seven European countries. Part 1: Document-based analysis.* EU-INCO Copernicus Project No. PL 973108. Helsinki: Työterveyslaitos (Finnish Institute of Occupational Health), 1999.
9. Cikrt M. Occupational health services in candidate countries. *Proceedings of the European conference 'Joint OSH strategy for the enlarged Europe', 30–31 January 2004.* Brussels: ETUC-TUTB, 2004: 43–54.
10. Cikrt M & Urban P. Centre of Occupational Health at the National Institute of Public Health. WHO Collaborating Centre for Occupational Health. *Central European Journal of Public Health* 2005; 13 (3): 107–111.
11. Pelclová D, Weinstein C & Vejlupková J. Occupational health in the Czech Republic. *New Solutions* 1994; 4 (3): 70–75.
12. Urban P, Cikrt M, Hejlek A, Lukáš E & Pelclová D. The Czech National Registry of Occupational Diseases. Ten years of existence. *Central European Journal of Public Health* 2000; 8 (4): 210–212.
13. Šmerhovský Z, Landa K & Kauppinen T. CAREX – mezinárodní informační systém profesionálních exposic karcinogenům a jeho použití v České republice (CAREX – international information system of occupational exposure to carcinogens and its application in the Czech Republic; in Czech with abstract in English). *České pracovní lékařství* 2003; 49 (3): 108–113.

14. European Commission. The Luxembourg Declaration on Workplace Health Promotion in the European Union. 27–28 November 1997. Available at www.enwhp.org/fileadmin/downloads/Luxembourg_Declaration_June2005_final.pdf (viewed 02 April 2007).

15. Rantanen J. *Basic occupational health services. Strategy, structures, activities, resources* (2nd edition). Helsinki: Työterveyslaitos (Finnish Institute of Occupational Health), 2005. Available at www.who.int/occupational_health/publications/bohsbooklet.pdf (viewed 02 April 2007).

16. Společnost Pracovního Lékařství České Lékařské Společnosti Jana Evangelisty Purkyně (Society of Occupational Medicine, J E Purkyně Czech Medical Society): website at www.pracovni-lekarstvi.cz.

17. Centrum Pracovního Lékařství, Státní Zdravotní Ústav (Centre for Occupational Health at the National Institute of Public Health): website at www.szu.cz/chpnp/index_en.php.

Occupational health services in Denmark – the rise and fall of a multidisciplinary and preventive approach

Anders Kabel, Association of Health and Preventive Service Units, Copenhagen, Peter Hasle, Institute of Occupational Health, Copenhagen, and Hans Jørgen Limborg, TeamArbejdsliv, Valby, Denmark

Introduction

The story of Danish OH services is one of the development of a unique system – quite different from the ones found in many other countries. The almost exclusive emphasis has been on preventive activities in the workplace, while more traditional medical services have been excluded. The system took off in the late 1970s, with nearly unanimous support from both the major blocs in the Danish parliament, and from employers and unions. For 25 years, the system's actors fought to develop services, quality and professionalism. However, at the same time, the system became entangled in a damaging political process, which started with conflicts between the social partners about compulsory affiliation and payment for administrative staff in industrial companies 12 years ago.

The final result came in 2004 as part of a major reform of work environment legislation carried out by the Liberal–Conservative government and supported by the right-wing parties in the parliament. The OH service system is now being dismantled and replaced by a system of private certified advisers, who have no regular relationship to the companies they advise and no real influence over employees.

This chapter describes the evolution of Danish OH services, and their structure, staffing, activities and quality assurance. It also presents and discusses the new system which will replace the present OH service in the coming years.

Legal development

The establishment of the Danish OH and preventive service followed the Work Environment Act, which was passed by parliament in 1975 and came into force in 1977. The new reflexive law was, to a large extent, based on self-regulation[1] in accordance with similar developments in the other Scandinavian countries[2] and the UK.[3] The Act stipulates that the employer has sole responsibility for the avoidance of risks at work and for the application of the control measures necessary to secure a healthy and safe work environment. Some clauses in the Act offered the authorities the possibility of issuing more detailed rules in co-operation with social partners in the labour market.

In order to support reflexivity, one of the frame clauses included provisions for an OH system that was supposed to support self-regulation by companies. The Act, and a departmental order with details of the system, required all companies in certain specified sectors to affiliate to an OH service unit. Furthermore, it was established that the companies affiliated to a unit should be the owners of that unit. They should have a bipartite board of directors, equally divided between representatives of employers and employees. An employer's representative chaired each board. The staffing level for the service was specified at 1.3 hours of advisory service per employee in each member company per year. The government provided a small subsidy for the establishment of new units.

The number of industries with compulsory affiliation to OH service units was gradually expanded by amendments to the OH services order in 1980, 1987, 1993 and 2001. In a total of 10 steps, coverage was gradually expanded to include approximately 40 per cent of the labour force by 2002. The first sectors covered were a number of well-known hazardous industries, such as shipyards, foundries, slaughterhouses and chemicals. Later, other manufacturing industries followed, as did the construction industry, hotels and restaurants, printing, and finally parts of the public health sector such as care for the elderly and hospitals.

An important part of enforcement was not formal legislation but a guidance note published jointly by Arbejdstilsynet (the Work Environment Authority) and its social partners.[4] This has been referred to as an early kind of 'soft law regulation'[5] and is an indication of the close co-operation between the partners during the establishment of the system.

An extensive evaluation took place between 1982 and 1986, resulting in a number of reports.[6,7] The general conclusion was that OH services had a positive effect in workplaces, but that there was still need for improvement. The evaluation generated several recommendations:

- assurance of the qualification of OH staff
- improved service to small and medium-sized enterprises (SMEs)
- clarification of the ratio of OH staff to general staff required
- improved OH support during the development of in-house health and safety departments.

A committee consisting of representatives of the social partners and the OH service authorities was formed in 1990. Its aim was to produce a plan for the further development of the OH system that would both expand it and improve its quality. After lengthy negotiations, the committee agreed on a joint white paper for the development of OH services up to 2000.[8] The white paper included a number of recommendations supported by employers and unions. The recommendations were intended to enhance multidisciplinary, cross-unit collaboration, postgraduate education, and closer co-operation with the work environment regulatory system. Among the specific proposals were requirements for both health and technical professionals, and a minimum of four staff members. Additionally, and importantly, the two parties agreed to expand the OH service further in order to cover approximately 60 per cent of the labour market.

However, because of a conflict over the prescribed ratio of OH service staff to administrative personnel in industries already covered by compulsory OH services, the private employers' federation withdrew its support for the recommendations made in the white paper of 1994. The employers failed to achieve a reduction of the compulsory 1.3 hours' advisory service per employee per year, and the conflict saw the collapse of consensus-oriented collaboration between the social partners on OH.

This left a political problem for the Social Democratic government, which wanted to keep the support of both employers and employees for work environment policy. In an attempt to reopen the dialogue, the government initiated several actions, which involved:

- an authorisation system, which required quality assurance, a certain composition of professional staff, and compulsory postgraduate education
- a number of pilot projects aimed at testing alternative OH systems, especially for the affiliation of new groups of workers
- a new evaluation of the OH system.

The results of the new evaluation indicated[9] that the OH system had a positive effect on the ability of companies to control their own work environment. The findings were based partly on telephone interviews with management and employees, and partly on a number of case studies of companies that had received assistance from OH services. In addition, most of the interviewees from management and employees expressed satisfaction with the OH service they received.

The government took the opportunity to propose that the OH service system should be extended to the entire labour market. In an attempt to meet demands from the employers' federation, the required staffing level was reduced by approximately 30 per cent. However, as the employers firmly opposed the proposal in general, it was passed by the Danish parliament in early 2001 only with votes from the left-wing parties.

The parliamentary decision was followed by an OH services order with a number of new clauses. New, important requirements included obligations to document any service provided and to secure contact with all affiliated companies. This was to be achieved through an annual plan for the use of OH resources, which was prepared by the OH service and its individual member companies working together. This change was a response to the refusal of a number of affiliated companies, particularly smaller ones, to use the service. The problem was highlighted in the evaluation and the ensuing political debate. New possible tasks – such as addressing absenteeism, health promotion, and the development of inclusive workplaces – were also added.

At the end of 2001, a Liberal–Conservative government replaced the Social Democratic administration. One of its first actions was to suspend any further expansion of the OH service system, which at that time covered approximately 40 per cent of the labour market.

The new government decided to base work environment law on just one of the parties in the labour market, namely the employers. And, this time, the reform was passed by the parliament in 2004 with only right-wing votes. The result was an extensive reform of the whole work environment system, with screening of all companies by labour inspectors[10,11] and a rejection of the compulsory OH service system. The compulsory system was replaced by a regulatory system, where labour inspectors were given the power to issue improvement notices to companies with deficiencies in their OH provision, specifying that they must seek advice from an authorised OH service unit. At the same time, the OH service units underwent great change.

The plan is to phase in the new OH system over a period of seven years. Companies with a mandatory affiliation to an OH service will be released from this requirement as labour inspectors screen them during the first four years. If the labour inspectors identify breaches of specified rules, they will issue the enterprise with an improvement notice. The improvement notice may require the company to seek assistance from an OH service, either to solve a specific work environment problem or to improve internal work environment activities (the establishment of a safety organisation or implementation of workplace assessment) over a period of two years (or for small enterprises only one year). After screening of the sectors with compulsory OH service affiliation is complete, the remaining part of the labour market will be screened in a similar way by the labour inspectors. A new provision is that it will also be possible for labour inspectors to issue improvement notices requiring the use of advisory services in those sectors that were previously not covered.

Companies that have acquired either a specific Danish certificate on work environment management or a certificate following the British OHSAS 18001 are exempted from both screening inspections and improvement notices, and thus from their obligation to use an OH service. Only approximately 1,100 enterprises were certified in 2005 (one year after the introduction of the new system), and the relatively complicated and expensive process of obtaining a certificate will limit the number of certified companies in the future.

A final new element is the establishment of a public system of four 'smileys'. A green smiley is given if the company holds a certificate for its work environment management system; a white (neutral) smiley signifies that an inspection has not uncovered any serious problems; a yellow smiley shows that an improvement notice has been issued requiring the use of advisory services to solve a specific problem; and a red smiley is used to identify companies that have received a notice requiring general improvement to work environment activities.

Structure and coverage of OH services

The original OH service system was established with three different types of OH service units:

- OH service centres covering different industries and sectors either in a specific geographical area or in the whole country
- sectoral OH service units providing services to a specific sector, such as slaughterhouses or car repair companies
- in-house OH service units integrated into a single company, but with a certain level of autonomy.

Table 1 shows the numbers of OH services in each category in the years after the system was set up.

When the OH service system began in 1979, a large number of fairly small OH service units were established. In accordance with demands for higher professional skills and a formal quality assurance system, a number of mergers have taken place, thereby reducing the number of independent units.

The sectoral OH service units were controlled by the social partners in the particular sector in question, but still owned by the affiliated companies. Some of the in-house company units were established in large municipalities or other large public institutions, serving only the staff employed in these undertakings.

The reform of 2004 removed the requirements of ownership and bipartite management of the units, and also the requirement for postgraduate education for OH professionals. The system of quality assurance has been replaced by a much simpler system for authorisation of units. The result is that all kinds of businesses, including traditional private consultancy companies, consulting engineers and even providers of chemicals and ventilation equipment, can qualify and be authorised as OH advisers.

There are now two types of authorisation:

- OH service units authorised to give advice on one or more specific work environment problems in the fields of physical, chemical, biological, ergonomic and/or psychosocial hazards

Year	1983	1989	1998	2001	2003	2005
OHS centres	61	54	45	35	24	17
Sectoral OH service units	7	9	10	9	7	6
In-house company OH service	52	58	45	26	23	17
Total	120	121	100	70	54	40

Sources: the Work Environment Authority and DANAK

Table 1
Numbers of Danish OH services by type, 1983–2005

	Original OH service units according to the old system	Units without a history in the old OH service system
Authorised as a multidisciplinary adviser	33	7*
Authorised to advise on specific hazards	0	4**

* Including three consulting engineers, one technology service institute, one environmental solution provider, one environmental consultant and one advisory company established by former professional OH service staff
** Including one technology service institute, two companies partly based on former OH service staff, and one company established by former labour inspectors

Sources: The Association of Preventive and Health Service Units in Denmark (2005) and the Work Environment Authority (2005)

Table 2
Numbers of OH advisers with authorisation according to the new system

- OH service units authorised to give multidisciplinary advice on all the above problems, and also advise on managing the work environment, co-operation and employee participation.

Table 2 shows the number of authorised work environment adviser units in November 2005 in relation to their original OH service status.

Relationship to health services

The OH service system has limited formal relations with general health services. The main reason for this is that all Danish citizens have free access to the primary healthcare system, based on general practitioners; in principle, the practitioners run private businesses but are fully funded by the state. Danish citizens also have virtually free access to both public hospitals and a network of specialised doctors, physiotherapists and psychologists.

Extensive access for all to both the primary and the secondary health system is also an important reason for the limited number of professional OH staff (Table 3). However, when the system was established in the late 1970s, the unions, among others, promoted a stronger emphasis on the prevention of hazards in the workplace than on medical check-ups and the treatment of workers.

The OH service units are allowed, though, to make referrals of employees with work-related health problems to the occupational medicine units in public hospitals – on equal terms with general practitioners. In addition, the OH service units also take a role in the placement of

Table 3
Distribution of
professionally
qualified OH
service staff by
year

	1983	1989	1994	1998	2002
Physio- and occupational therapists	33	31	30	28	27
Engineers, architects, machine technicians	12	16	25	24	26
Psychologists, other professional organisational consultants	0	0	7	10	20
Laboratory and environmental technicians	28	15	18	14	12
Physicians	7	6	3	5	4
Nurses	13	9	6	4	3
MScs in science and pharmacy	0	3	4	5	3
Environmental planners	0	0	4	5	2
Others	8	20	4	6	3

Sources: the Work Environment Authority and Jensen[12]

Table 4
Numbers of full-
time OH service
staff by year

	1983	1989	1994	1998	2002
Professional staff	238	369	586	603	650
Administrative staff	48	105	130	127	140
Management*	44	78	93	61	60
Total	330	552	809	791	850

* Many managers also function as professional advisers. The authors estimate that during the period 1983–2002 the amount of professional work for managers has been reduced from approximately 45 per cent to 15 per cent

Sources: the Work Environment Authority and the
Association of Preventive and Health Service Units in Denmark

employees with occupational disorders; this, however, is not a formalised role, and funding has to be negotiated between the individual company and municipality in each case.

The OH services' prevention strategy focuses on changes in the workplace, and has been segregated from the healthcare sector both professionally and structurally. Regional occupational clinics and general practitioners, which have very extensive coverage in Denmark, have taken care of diagnostics, referrals to curative services and health-related research. The relation between the healthcare system and OH services has thus been very restricted. European (EU) requirements for specific health examinations (eg of lead levels in the blood, or of shift workers) has been carried out to a limited extent by the few OH service units with medical staff. Otherwise, the workers have been referred to public health service clinics or practitioners. It is difficult to analyse the effect of these examinations, since they have not formed a part of the compulsory OH service system. It can be anticipated, in light of the increasingly liberal OH service market, that the number of private medical organisations offering services to larger private companies will rise.

The sickness absence compensation system in Denmark is based on municipal taxes and is separate from the regulation of OH services. Since 2005, however, companies have been obliged to include absenteeism in their workplace assessments, and an increase in demand for more OH advisory services in this field can be expected.

Staffing

Employment of professional staff in OH service units peaked in 2002 (Table 4). The number has gradually fallen since then – firstly as a result of the reduction in compulsory consultation time from 1.3 hours to 0.6 hours per employee per year, and secondly because of the gradual removal of compulsory OH service affiliation for designated industries from 2005 to 2009. The staffing level at the end of 2005 is not yet known, but an estimate would be a reduction of 20 per cent since 2002.

Ever since the establishment of OH services, the number of healthcare staff they employ has been fairly low in comparison to the number of other professionals, and it has recently been decreasing further (Table 3). The most important change has been a significant increase in staff with psychology training. The large increase from none to one-fifth of total staff in just over 10 years is clearly a reflection of a growing interest in psychosocial factors. This development was especially boosted by the healthcare sector, which was compulsorily affiliated to OH services from 1993; but since 2000, private industrial companies have also shown an increasing interest in OH advice on psychosocial factors.

Since 1998 OH service units have been required to employ a multidisciplinary staff qualified to give advice on physical, chemical, biological, ergonomic and psychosocial hazards. Since the liberalisation of the OH service system in 2004, the numbers of staff with qualifications related to marketing, health promotion and healthcare also seem to be increasing.

Development of professionals

Soon after the establishment of the OH service system in 1981, a voluntary postgraduate training course was developed and offered by the Work Environment Fund at cost. The 120-hour course was multidisciplinary and around 75 professionals (a quarter of the professional staff at the time) completed it. However, it was terminated after a few years because of limited uptake; this may have been due to a reluctance to pay for a voluntary course on the part of a number of unit managers.

In co-operation with OH professionals and social partners, the Work Environment Authority made a new attempt to launch a more comprehensive course in 1990. However, it was difficult to recruit participants; it was still a voluntary course, and many OH service units considered it too costly. The newly established Arbejdsmiljørådgiverne (Association of Health and Preventive Service Units) took responsibility for the training from 1994.[13] Training was made compulsory from 1998, and continued to be so until the repeal of the OH service system in 2005.[14] The compulsory training programme was based on the courses developed since 1990. It had three elements:

• in the first year of employment in an OH service unit: a nine-day introductory course, which focused on the work environment system, the labour market system, the role of the OH service system, and the internal company safety co-operation system
• during the first three years of employment: a seven-day methodology course, which focused on various aspects of OH service methods – multidisciplinary co-operation, process consultation, and support for the internal company safety co-operation system

- during the first three years of employment: 10 days of training in individual professional fields.

The introductory and methodology courses were both aimed at a multidisciplinary target group. The educational approach was problem-oriented, and included a combination of lectures and practical project work performed in multidisciplinary groups. Training in the professional field was organised in the form of three-week courses in industrial hygiene or in ergonomics developed by Arbejdsmiljøinstituttet (the National Institute of Occupational Health). OH service staff were not especially interested in following these training courses, and consequently there were long gaps between them.

Participation in the courses was expected to relate to a curriculum tailored to an individual, which was supposed to include a plan for further postgraduate training in a professional field. This was, however, rarely implemented, since both OH service unit management and the professionals themselves were reluctant to enter into pre-planned or binding training schemes.

An important reason for this is that none of the relevant educational institutions offered postgraduate education specifically aimed at work environment professionals. Newly employed engineers, physiotherapists, architects and employees with other educational backgrounds had to create a professional profile themselves through a combination of practical experience and diverse postgraduate training. As they had to plan this alongside their practical work, it generally developed into an individual jigsaw puzzle reflecting current priorities.

The lack of a formalised education system was, however, an important reason for the development of an extensive and informal experience-sharing network among professional staff. This developed rapidly from 1979 and peaked in the mid-1990s. The network included a number of groups with participants from several units, each covering specific issues, such as chemical hazards, ergonomic problems and the indoor climate. The groups were an important facilitator of both informal postgraduate training and of improvement in the quality of practice of advisory services. The flagship of the network was an annual OH service conference, which lasted three days and was attended by up to 250 participants.

The most important co-ordinator was the professional association of OH service staff, which organised several networking sessions as well as the annual conference. However, growing competition between OH service units evolved in the 1990s, and sharing experiences became more difficult. The number of participants at the conferences dwindled, and the association of OH service professionals essentially disintegrated after the millennium.

The annual conference was taken over by the Association of Health and Preventive Service Units in the late 1990s, and it was relaunched in co-operation with a number of other organisations in 2005, aiming at a broader target group.

This development demonstrates a creative and reflective culture of addressing new problems, skills and ideas, but also rather limited formalisation, although there was a short period of compulsory postgraduate education. The conclusion is, therefore, that the development of a professional standard based on a curriculum has never obtained a strong foothold in Denmark. However, extensive networking did provide for the development of an informal professionalism aimed at the specific qualifications required in OH. It is anticipated that, under the new system, Denmark will enter a period characterised by a much more diverse

Task area	%
Single-hazard tasks (eg noise, chemicals, indoor climate)	26
Ergonomic tasks	24
Multidisciplinary tasks	11
Teaching	11
Task concerned with behaviour, co-operation, supervision, reflection	6
Minor unidentified tasks	6
Tasks related to change in production	5
Tasks related to organisation of work	4
Health examinations	4
Advice on purchase of PPE	3

Table 5
Distribution of advisory tasks in 1998 (average for all OH service units)

Source: Aldrich et al.[9]

market of OH consultants, who will provide a very broad range of services but with varying quality. It is not likely that the market mechanism will be able to develop any quality code, and meeting a demand for formalised education and training within OH practice will hopefully be back on the stakeholders' agenda.

Main orientation of OH activities

The orientation of the activities of the OH service system has to a large extent been reflected in the development of the profession. As health-oriented tasks, such as medical examinations and health surveillance, were abandoned from the very start, technical and ergonomic staff had an important influence on the priorities of the advisory services.

The 1998 evaluation indicated the types of advisory tasks carried out by OH services (Table 5). It clearly shows that most tasks were of a technical nature, aimed at chemical, physical and ergonomic hazards.[15]

During the 1980s and the 1990s, there was extensive development of consulting practice and methods, which was to a large extent made possible by networking and the sharing of experiences. Among the key priorities was to find the right way to approach companies and to support the development of their internal health and safety organisation. The development is reflected in the types of presentation and seminar that had the highest priority at the annual conferences.[15]

The first wave of method development focused on how to present results effectively, in the form of training in report writing and oral presentation techniques. As it still proved difficult to 'deliver the message', the focus switched to the role of the consultant. In the late 1990s, the system engaged in comprehensive experiments with consulting skills. Inspired by organisational psychology and learning theory, different methods of process consultation and various participatory disciplines were introduced, and found their way into daily practice.

Special attention was paid to SMEs. Nevertheless, in the early 1990s, there was criticism of the services provided for SMEs from the social partners, who found that SMEs received only a very limited service. This was because, in OH service units' experience, advising small enterprises was time-consuming and difficult. On the other hand, a number of projects in various OH service units proved that positive results could be achieved by applying consulting strategies.[16,17]

This extensive development has resulted in a new standard of consulting practice, but – as was the case with the education programmes – it has been very difficult to sustain the practice and to assess its advantages and disadvantages.

Quality assurance

In 1998, the quality requirements for OH service units were tightened significantly, partly as a result of attempts by the then Social Democratic government to answer criticisms from employers' organisations.[18] The revised system of quality assurance included four minimum requirements:

- a written quality policy, including objectives, action plans and schedules
- a description of staff qualifications, including training plans and consultancy practice
- evidence of ongoing improvements in quality, including an annual evaluation
- at least five full-time qualified professionals in each OH service unit, with physical, chemical, biological, ergonomic and psychological qualifications.

In addition, each OH service unit had to pursue three general objectives:

- to be holistic and multidisciplinary
- to include a high level of preventive activity, as required by Article 6.2 of the European Union Framework Directive[19]
- to support the improvement of the internal capability of member companies to control their own work environment systematically.

A quality assurance system had to be documented and approved by Danmarks Nationale Akkrediteringsorgan (the Danish accreditation body, DANAK) in order for an OH service unit to be allowed to practise. Approval was based on a thorough audit, and was valid for five years. DANAK also carried out two or three inspections during this period to check how the units had implemented their quality systems. The inspections included participation in a company visit organised by the unit as part of its regular advisory services. The purpose of the visit was to investigate whether the unit's practice followed the guidelines of the quality system. Other important elements checked during the inspections were:

- the existence of a written agreement specifying the details of all consultations that lasted for more than 10 hours
- internal evaluation of methods and the level of prevention achieved for every case of consultancy that lasted more than 10 hours
- the companies' evaluations of how any advisory service was performed
- how quality improvements based on external and internal evaluation were implemented
- descriptions of the tasks and skills of all OH specialists.

Between 2005 and 2008, the former OH service system is being phased out and replaced by a system of authorised work environment advisers. One consequence of the new system has

Quality demand	The old OH system 1998–2005	The new OH system from 2005
Exchange of experience	Requirement to participate in cross-unit co-operation	Removed
Secure multidisciplinarity	Requirement to employ at least five full-time professionals (in case of an in-house OH service, two professionals)	Replaced by unlimited use of external consultants in order to meet professional requirements
Audits	Two inspections by DANAK, concerning eight specific topics, over a period of five years	One inspection by the Work Environment Authority, concerning two general topics, over a period of three years
Quality assurance system	Detailed requirements for a quality assurance system	A broadly defined general demand for the establishment of work procedures and methods
Quality improvements	A written annual action plan for quality development and one annual evaluation	One annual evaluation and no requirement for written documentation
Assurance of formal education	Three years of relevant education after high school	Three years of relevant education after high school
Assurance of OH competence	Nine-day introductory course, seven-day course in OH methods, and 10 days of professional postgraduate training for all OH service consultants	At least one single professional for each of the five work environment subjects must have more than one year's practical experience of advising on the work environment

Table 6
Quality demands on OH service units before and after the 2005 changes

already been a remarkable reduction in formal quality requirements (Table 6). The demand for a full-scale quality assurance system has been replaced by a limited number of rather broadly defined quality statements.

The new authorisation system seems to be designed to open the OH service market to a variety of advisory companies beyond the old OH service units in order to increase internal competition in the sector.

Discussion of the new system

The new Danish legislation represents a remarkable step away from the traditional Nordic reflexive regulation of the work environment, which replaced the traditional 'command and control' approach 30 years ago across Scandinavia.[1,2,20] The core of the reflexive system was the employer's duty, in co-operation with employees, to assess all potential risks in the workplace and to take the necessary steps to control them. This assessment was independent of whether specific rules or threshold limit values might apply, or whether labour inspectors had demanded any changes in the workplace. The rationale behind this approach was the complexity and rapid development of the work environment. In practice, it would simply be impossible for the authorities to issue rules on all potential hazards in the work environment because of interaction between multiple exposures and difficulties in finding threshold limit values for many types of exposure, especially regarding psychosocial factors.

The basic phrasing of the Work Environment Act has not changed, but the new inspection practice – with screenings of all companies – will almost inevitably turn the system back towards the command and control model. The reason for this lies in the screening of all companies by labour inspectors. If the inspectors do not find any immediate infringements, the company will in principle be released from inspections for the next three years, or even more. If infringements are found, a thorough inspection will be carried out, and the labour inspectors will issue improvement notices, which may include a requirement to use OH advisers. Seen from an employer's perspective, the company has received a clear signal from the authorities in either case. In case of exemption from further inspections, the conclusion must be that the workplace is officially approved by the authorities, and no further measures need to be taken. In case of improvement notices related to various infringements, it will be sufficient to fulfil the requirements in the notices. There will be no incentives for considering any further improvements to the work environment.

The tasks of OH services will also be clearly defined in accordance with the law, as indicated by improvement notices issued by the labour inspectors. It is likely that employers' demand for advice will be limited to the narrow context of improvement notices. This advice will, therefore, be quite different from that which prevailed in the former OH service system, which was based on a long-term relationship between adviser and company, and OH professionals who were obliged to give multidisciplinary and preventive advice.

The new OH service system will operate on traditional market terms, and in many cases the employer will terminate a contract as soon as they have received the advice necessary to gain the approval of the labour inspectors. The demand for continuous support based on long-term relations will be limited as long as the employers' only concern is to fulfil the demands of the Work Environment Authority. This situation will probably result in a significant reduction of interest in maintaining the experience of the more process-focused consulting strategies that have been developed within the framework of the new system. Consequently, there is a risk that skills relating to the improvement of safety practices within companies and to providing services to small enterprises will disappear.

On the other hand, it might be argued that a good work environment could be a competitive advantage, and that enterprises will be encouraged to request more comprehensive OH advice. But, so far, market demand seems to be limited to getting the right advice as fast as possible at the lowest possible cost. There may be several explanations for this market reaction, but it is most likely to be due to a lack of transparency concerning the relationship between OH advice, improvements in the work environment and economic benefits. It is, therefore, difficult to argue for raising the cost of advisory services. Another possible explanation is that Danish employers have the right to sack employees who are not able to work, even if their inability to work is caused by an occupational disease or a work-related accident.[21] This is a principal element of the Danish so-called 'flexicurity' labour market system,[22] in which companies can easily hire or fire employees, but where government social security systems are efficient. The employer has no obligation to be involved in rehabilitation plans for an injured person, and this may be a reason for employers' limited use of OH services in such cases.

Given this development, it is reasonable to assume that there will be a 'buyers' market' in the years ahead. The stable market for the current OH services will disappear, which will make downsizing necessary; at the same time, tough competition will probably evolve as new operators fight for a share of a shrinking market.

It is likely, though, that a number of the companies affiliated to the former OH service system will maintain some kind of affiliation to an OH provider because they are satisfied with the advisory services they have received so far. One possible constraint, however, may be the weak Danish tradition of purchasing optional advisory services from OH providers. The situation is different from that in Sweden, for example, where most companies are affiliated to an OH service unit at a higher cost per employee than in Denmark, even though it is not a legal requirement.[23]

Anticipated developments in OH services

It is difficult to discuss future needs and developments, since the whole Danish system is in the middle of a major transition with unpredictable consequences. The traditional multidisciplinary and long-term preventive approach will almost certainly be severely weakened, but it is hard to foresee what will happen to preventive activities. The authors are doubtful, but it is possible that the risk of a negative public image as a result of receiving improvement notices and a red smiley will motivate companies to make a preventive effort. This is the claim of the government. But it is also likely that the 90 per cent of companies that get a neutral (white) smiley will regard this as *de facto* approval of the work environment they offer. The most likely consequence is a weakening of the motivation for a high-level effort to improve the work environment.

One of the open questions concerns employee participation. This was guaranteed through the bipartite boards of the former OH service units. This influence has now vanished, since there is no provision for the management of authorised OH service units in the new system. There is a risk that employers will control the new units to a much greater extent, and that this may lead to distrust among employees. It is not certain how serious the problem will be, though, as there is a strong history of co-operation between the labour market partners in Denmark, and it will probably be important to many employers to maintain this tradition.

Finally, it must be concluded that the number of employees who have access to OH services will decrease in the future. After the first year with the new system, fewer than 10 per cent of the companies screened by inspectors received orders to use the expertise of an authorised adviser, which is less than 14 per cent of the level expected by the Danish parliament when the new legislation was passed.[24] If this rate applies to the whole labour market, after all companies have been screened over the seven years scheduled for the first complete period, the proportion of employees having access to OH services will fall from 40 per cent to 20 per cent.

References

1. Wilthagen T. Reflexive rationality in the regulation of occupational safety and health. In: Rogowski R & Wilthagen T. *Reflexive labour law – studies in industrial relations and employment regulation*. Deventer: Kluwer Law and Taxation Publishers, 1994; pages 345–376.
2. Lindøe P. Arbeidsmiljøregulering i de nordiske lande – et eksempel på refleksiv reguleringspraksis. *Tidsskrift for Arbejdsliv* 2002; 4 (4): 23–38.
3. Robens A. Report of the Committee of Inquiry into safety and health at work. Cmnd 5034. 1972. London: HMSO, 1972.
4. Arbejdstilsynet. *Bedriftssundhedstjeneste 1979*. Copenhagen: Arbejdstilsynet, 1979.
5. Korver T & Oeij P R A. 2005. The soft law of the covenant: making governance instrumental. *European Journal of Industrial Relations* 2005; 11 (3): 367–384.
6. Dankert H, Mærkedahl I, Nørregaard C & Bunnage D. *Bedriftssundhedstjenesten og virksomhederne – Rapport nr. 4 fra BST-undersøgelsern*. Publication no. 152. Copenhagen: Socialforskningsinstituttet, 1986.

7. Nord-Larsen M. *Bedriftssundhedstjenesten i udvikling 1982–1985. Rapport nr. 3 fra BST-undersøgelsen.* Publikation nr. 151. Copenhagen: Socialforskningsinstituttet, 1986.

8. Arbejdstilsynet. *Perspektivrapport om BST 2000.* Copenhagen: Arbejdstilsynet, 1991.

9. Aldrich P T, Forman M, Holm G & Mathiesen L B. *Evaluering af erfaringer med nuværende BST-ordninger.* Taastrup: DTI Arbejdsliv, 1999.

10. Jensen P L & Jensen J. *Developing inspection strategies to support local activities.* Canberra: National Institute of Occupational Health and Safety, 2004.

11. Kabel A. New occupational health system in Denmark. *Scandinavian Journal of Work Environment and Health* Suppl. 1, 2005b.

12. Jensen, U B. *BST og rådgivning af medlemsvirksomheder i 2002.* Copenhagen: BST Foreningen, 2003.

13. Limborg, H J. Qualifying the consultative skills of the occupational health service staff. *Safety Science* 1995; 20 (2/3): 247–253.

14. Arbejdstilsynet. *Arbejdstilsynets retningslinier om BST-uddannelser efer BST-bekendtgørelsens §15.* Copenhagen: Arbejdstilsynet, 2003a.

15. Limborg H J. The professional working environment consultant – a new actor on the health and safety arena. *Human Factors and Ergonomics in Manufacturing* 2001; 11 (2): 159–172.

16. Hasle P. *Health and safety in small enterprises in Denmark and the role of intermediaries.* Copenhagen: Center for Alternativ Samfundsanalyse, 2000.

17. Hasle P & Wissing P. *Workplace Health Promotion in Small Enterprises in Denmark.* Copenhagen: Center for Alternativ Samfundsanalyse, 2000.

18. Arbejdstilsynet. *Vejledning om godkendelse af bedriftssundhedstjenesten.* Third version. Copenhagen: Arbejdstilsynet, 2003b.

19. Council Directive 89/391/EEC of 12 June 1989 on the introduction of measures to encourage improvements in the safety and health of workers at work (the Framework Directive). *Official Journal* L183; 29 June 1989: 1–8.

20. Hasle P & Petersen J. The role of agreements between labour unions and employers in the regulation of the work environment. *Policy and Practice in Health and Safety* 2004; 2 (1): 5–22.

21. Bloch F S & Prins R. *Who returns to work and why? A six-country study on work incapacity and reintegration.* Newark, New Jersey: Transaction Publishers, 2001.

22. Andersen S K and Mailand M. *The Danish flexicurity model – the role of the collective bargaining system.* Copenhagen: FAOS, 2005.

23. Statskontoret. *Utnyttja företagshälsovården bättre* (Better use of occupational health services). Report 2001:29. Stockholm: Statskontoret, 2001. Available online at www.statskontoret.se/upload/Publikationer/2001/200129.pdf (viewed 23 April 2007).

24. Kabel, A. *Omfanget af påbudt rådgivning.* Hvidovre: Association af Preventive and Health Service Units in Denmark, 2005.

The Finnish occupational health system – challenges and approaches

Matti Lamberg, Finnish Ministry of Social Affairs and Health, Timo Leino, Finnish Institute of Occupational Health, and Kaj Husman, Finnish Institute of Occupational Health

Introduction

The system of occupational health (OH) services in Finland has been developed systematically since the 1960s, at first on the basis of collective agreements between labour market organisations, and later via legislative incorporation of the system into the Occupational Healthcare Act of 1978.

During the 1980s it became clear that, assuming a continuation of the economic growth that had already lasted a decade, the ageing of the population would inevitably lead to restricted availability of labour during the early years of the 21st century. Economic growth following the recession of the early 1990s transformed the labour market, intensified work processes, and required many workers to find new jobs and acquire new skills. In particular, older workers found it difficult to adjust to the new situation, and showed increasing interest in various early retirement schemes. The anticipated labour shortage initiated discussions on how work could be adjusted to suit the needs and working abilities of ageing workers, and prompted the reform of OH service legislation at the beginning of the new millennium.

Tripartite co-operation has played a key role at all stages of the development of OH services in Finland. Over the past decades, OH services have developed through consensus and collaboration between the authorities and labour market organisations in response to changes in working life. The need for change has been taken into account during each revision of OH service legislation. Systematic development and follow-up of OH services are carried out, in co-operation with various stakeholders, by the advisory committee on OH services at the Sosiaali- ja Terveysministeriö (Finnish Ministry of Social Affairs and Health).

Occupational disability has been a prominent problem in Finnish working life since 2000. The rate of disability pension claimants is high among workers aged over 55, especially in the 60–64 age group, in which fewer than 20 per cent are active in working life.[1] Priority is therefore given to maintaining and promoting work ability and preventing disability through appropriate OH measures and general health promotion.

In order to be successful, OH services require all parties to provide committed support to health and safety in the workplace, and to take notice of all the factors that influence whether people retain their full ability to work.

The OH service system in practice

The Finnish national development strategy in OH relies on high-quality expertise, products, labour productivity and competitiveness. Given that all citizens have a right to a safe working environment, improving OH is a fundamental part of the objectives of a welfare society.

OH services are an important part of health and social welfare policy, and of the health and social welfare service system. They support the maintenance of health and working ability, improve the quality of working life, and promote safety, as required by European Union (EU) legislation. They also support the full and prolonged participation of people in working life.

The Ministry of Social Affairs and Health has produced a development strategy for OH services to 2015.[2] The strategy is complemented by a detailed OH service implementation plan, which contains measures to:

- promote health and work capacity
- increase the attractiveness of working life
- prevent and treat social exclusion
- provide functioning services and reasonable income security.

The plan is based on and followed up by statistics, regular surveys and research on needs and trends, and assessments of the impacts of actions and improvements.

One target is that by 2010 employees should stay in work for two to three years longer than is now the case. This requires not only continuous improvement of work conditions and the work environment, but also measures to improve lifestyles and the general health and working capacity of the population (Figure 1). OH and other health services should invest more in both work-specific and general health promotion among the working-age population. These measures are also necessary for carrying out the pension reform that is currently under way in Finland.

Legislative basis for occupational health

The Primary Health Care Act of 1972, and the subsequent amendments of 1978, linked occupational healthcare to primary healthcare by allowing employers voluntarily to organise primary healthcare for their employees as a part of an OH service.

There have been further changes since, mainly as a result of the agreement concluded by the labour market organisations in the early 1990s concerning promotion of working capacity, and the consequent inclusion of activities to maintain that capacity in OH legislation. Good OH practice was defined as the main principle of OH services in the revision of the compensation system for the service in 1994.

According to the Occupational Healthcare Act (1383/2001), all employers are required to provide OH services for their employees. The financial compensation system of the Kansaneläkelaitos (Social Insurance Institution of Finland, SII) supports the attainment of the aims of the Occupational Healthcare Act and the provision of services to all employees in all workplaces. According to the Act, entrepreneurs and other self-employed people can provide themselves with statutory preventive and health-promoting OH services.

Four main laws form the basis of workplace safety and OH services: the Occupational Safety and Health Act (738/2002), the Occupational Healthcare Act (1383/2001), the Act on Occupational Safety and Health Administration (last amended in 1993), and the Act on the Supervision of Occupational Safety and Health (44/2006). The Sickness Insurance Act (1113/2005) provides detailed regulations on reimbursement and the follow-up of OH services.

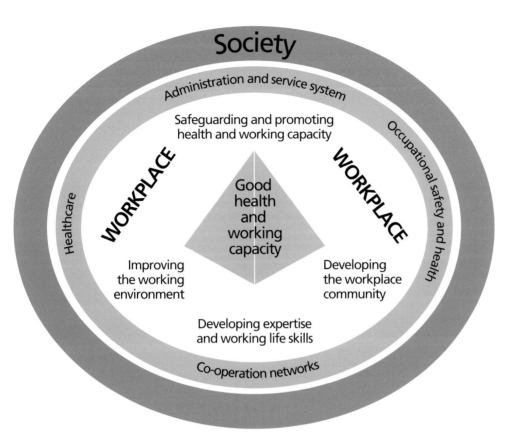

Figure 1
The domain of
comprehensive
OH services:
Finland's basic
approach[2]

The principle of comprehensive, planned and proactive occupational safety and health functions (according to the EU Framework Directive[3]) has been incorporated into the Occupational Safety and Health Act of 2002. The Act also requires that a documented health and safety policy be drawn up for every workplace. This policy document should contain a plan for maintenance of working ability. Articles 7 and 14 of the Framework Directive have been implemented and transposed through the Occupational Healthcare Act. The concept of the maintenance of work ability is included in both Acts and it creates a basis for quality development in OH services.

Implementation of OH policy

A government resolution on occupational healthcare to 2015 outlines the anticipated development of occupational healthcare.[2]

It is in the common interest of all stakeholders to develop services that are relevant, cost-effective and of good quality for the whole working population – healthier workers means more productive workers. The OH service system already exists. It is therefore necessary to focus on the content and functioning of the OH services so that they will better contribute to the maintenance of good health and working ability of employees throughout their work careers. An essential element is to improve collaboration between OH services and both employers and employees to achieve better results. The compensation system has been developed to allow new organisational models for OH services. Comprehensive OH services are now also available for the self-employed, on the basis of the equitable service principle. Extra budgetary funds have been made available to produce sufficient numbers of OH professionals and experts, and to improve and increase training. The number of graduate OH physicians has almost doubled over the past three years. A considerable number of OH experts, including psychologists, have been trained to meet a rising demand. The government's good practice guide to OH has been completely revised. It is complemented by a tool for self-assessment of the quality of OH services. Furthermore, the production of evidence-based clinical practice guides for OH services has been started.

Infrastructure

The Ministry of Social Affairs and Health supervises OH services and safety systems.[4,5] All important issues concerning legislation and the development of OH services are discussed in the advisory board on OH services at the Ministry by the social partners, the government, the service providers and Työterveyslaitos (the Finnish Institute of Occupational Health, FIOH).[4]

Under the Finnish Occupational Healthcare Act 2001, employers are required to organise and pay for preventive services for all workers regardless of the size, industrial sector or form of their undertaking.[5] Both the private and public sectors are covered. Curative services are voluntary, but they are included in 80 per cent of the service agreements. Using an OH service is voluntary for self-employed entrepreneurs (eg farmers) in Finland.

In Finland, OH services can be organised in several ways. An organisation can arrange cover through municipal healthcare centres, private medical centres, or by setting up an in-house service; alternatively, enterprises can collaborate to provide joint coverage. Of these, only the private medical centre model is profit-making. There were around 1,000 OH service units in 2003, serving some 1.8 million people. The coverage of OH services was highest among salaried employees (85 per cent), and lowest among self-employed individuals (20 per cent) and micro-undertakings employing fewer than 10 people.[6]

Employers are entitled to reimbursement from the SII for up to 50 per cent of approved OH service costs that they incur. In 2004, the reimbursement ceiling values per employee per year were €128 for preventive costs and €192 for curative services. The SII covers reimbursements from the sickness insurance fund, which is financed mainly by employers. Also, a small percentage of this fund is contributed by employees, which is justified by the fact that Finnish OH provision includes curative services that are wider in scope than stipulated in the Framework Directive. In 2003, the total OH service reimbursement costs of the SII were €167 million, and total OH service costs approximately €375 million. The average yearly cost per employee was in the range €114–€258.[7]

The four models of OH services are shown in Figure 2.

What is included in occupational healthcare

At workplace level, the Occupational Healthcare Act aims to promote co-operation between the employer, employees and the OH service provider in order to:

- prevent work-related illnesses and accidents
- raise the level of health and safety of work and the work environment
- maintain and improve the health, working ability and functional capacity of employees at all stages of their work careers
- promote the functioning of the work community.

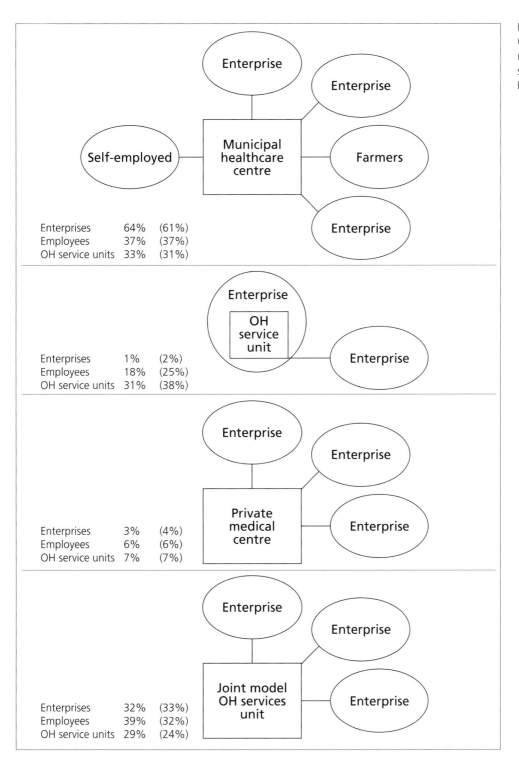

Figure 2
Organisational
models for OH
services in
Finland

OH processes must be based on the prioritised needs of the enterprise. OH service providers are asked to assess and monitor the quality and impact of their activities and continuously improve their performance. All actions taken by OH services should be based on good scientific and/or practical evidence. These principles are expressed in law in the form of good OH practice guidelines.[5]

The occupational healthcare that the employer must arrange in accordance with good practice in using OH professionals has to include the following duties (as stipulated by the Occupational Healthcare Act (1383/2001, section 12):

- surveillance of the health and safety of work conditions through repeated workplace surveys and other methods, paying attention to exposure to dangerous substances, workload factors, working arrangements, and the risk of accidents and violence. These factors are taken into account in the planning of work, work methods and work location, and in situations in which work conditions are changing
- investigation, assessment and monitoring of work-related health risks and problems, employees' health, working ability and functional capacity, including any risk of illness caused by work or the work environment, and undertaking medical examinations deemed necessary as a result, taking into account any special characteristics of the individual employee
- suggesting measures to improve health and safety at work, to adapt the work to the needs and capacity of the employee if necessary, to maintain and promote employees' working ability and functional capacity, and to monitor the implementation of proposals for action
- providing information, advice and guidance in matters concerning health and safety at work and the health of employees, including investigation of an employee's workload if requested by the employee on reasonable grounds
- monitoring and supporting the ability of a disabled employee to cope at work, considering the health requirements of the employee, giving advice on rehabilitation, and referring an employee for treatment or medical or vocational rehabilitation
- co-operating with representatives of other health services, labour authorities, educational authorities, social insurance, social services and the labour protection authority, and when necessary, with OH service providers for employers in a common workplace
- participating in the organisation of first-aid provision
- assisting in the planning and organisation of measures to maintain and promote work ability as a part of occupational healthcare, including any investigation into the need for rehabilitation where necessary
- assessment and monitoring of the quality and impact of OH services.

These duties must be carried out wherever applicable by OH professionals in co-operation with senior and line management, personnel administration and collaborative organisations in the workplace. To investigate factors giving rise to special risk, or with widespread health implications, in a common workplace, employers must co-operate with each other (as required in other legislation) in making use of OH expertise.

Human resources and competences

Where planning, implementing, developing and monitoring occupational healthcare are concerned, the employer is required to make sufficient use of OH service professionals and any experts that these professionals deem necessary for organising healthcare in accordance with good practice. The total number of posts in Finnish OH services is about 7,300. Some 1,700 physicians and 2,500 public health nurses work alongside other experts (Table 1).

OH professionals	OH experts
OH physicians OH nurses	Physiotherapists Psychologists Ergonomists Occupational hygienists Agricultural technicians Opticians Dieticians Technical experts Physical education experts Speech therapists

Table 1
OH professionals
and experts in
Finnish OH
services

Occupational healthcare professionals and experts must be professionally independent of the employer, the employees and their representatives. They are required to possess specified qualifications, and also to have knowledge and skills that have been maintained through adequate continuing professional development.

The employer of an OH professional or expert has a duty to ensure that he or she receives continuing training to maintain professional skills as often as needed, and in any case no less than once every three years. The duty to provide training also applies in respect of a general healthcare professional engaged in occupational healthcare as an independent provider.

According to a recent survey,[8] the availability of competent OH nurses is good. Around 90 per cent of OH service units have a public health nurse who has undergone at least seven weeks of study in OH. The availability of competent physiotherapists is poorer. In about one-third of the units, there is a physiotherapist trained in OH. As far as OH physicians are concerned, the objective of employing specialists is still far from being achieved, although a considerable proportion have specialised training. In 55 per cent of the units, there is a specialist or doctor who has attended at least a seven-week course in OH. Upgrading of the qualifications of psychologists has only just started, and therefore their training situation is still modest (but improving). Presently, only 10 per cent of units have a psychologist who has completed seven weeks of post-graduate training in OH. The Ministry of Social Affairs and Health has issued instructions on the content, quality, amount and organisation of extra education.

The FIOH is an important resource in the OH field. It has a staff of 800 researchers and other experts representing a multitude of fields. It produces evidence-based information, research results, surveys and statistics, recommendations for good practice, and practice guidelines. It also offers training and other services to occupational safety and health professionals, workplaces and the general public.

Monitoring
Monitoring of OH services is mandatory under Finland's Occupational Healthcare Act. It consists of three surveys and annual reimbursement statistics from the SII (Figure 3). The surveys are conducted at the FIOH every third year, and they are used at all levels to develop the OH service system.[6]

Figure 3
Surveillance of
OH services in
Finland

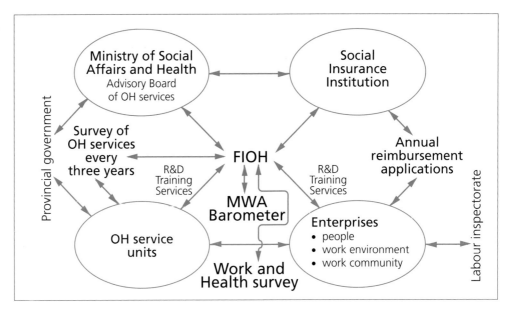

Strengths and weaknesses of OH services in Finland

Changes in Finnish society

Finland has the fastest ageing population in Europe,[1] which has many implications for working life and the provision and funding of social welfare. Even now, industry reports difficulties in recruiting trained employees. Rapid changes in how companies organise and run their businesses are taking place. Alongside traditional occupational hazards, risks and demands for workers' wellbeing, questions about competence and human relations skills are developing. These are related more to human factors than to the risks arising from technology.

Company size in Finland is small. Of 228,000 undertakings, 93 per cent employed fewer than 10 workers (24 per cent of the workforce) in 2003. At the same time, the number of SMEs is increasing. This is due to rapid growth in the service sector and downsizing and outsourcing by large companies. The leading sectors in Finnish industry are metal-working and engineering, information technology, and wood and paper. The private sector employs 73 per cent of the labour force. The proportion of women who work is high, at approximately 66 per cent in 2002. The unemployment rate was 7.2 per cent in August 2005.[1]

According to the survey *Work and health in Finland 2003*:[8]

- three out of four employed people were exposed to physical factors that could affect their health, including half to chemical agents and one in four to carcinogenic agents
- one in four found work to be physically 'somewhat' or 'very' heavy, and one-third had long-term or recurrent physical or mental symptoms, either caused or aggravated by work
- one in four suffered from at least mild work exhaustion symptoms
- one in 10 considered their accident risk at work to be 'extremely' or 'fairly' high
- there were 125,000 occupational accidents in Finland in 2001, of which 100 were fatal

- 12 per cent of employed men and 9 per cent of employed women had been involved in an accident at work or while commuting to or from work over the previous 12 months
- 4,807 cases of occupational disease were diagnosed in 2002. Repetitive strain disorders, skin diseases, noise-induced hearing loss and allergic respiratory diseases accounted for the majority of the cases
- the sick leave rate, as a percentage of the total number of working days available, ranged from 5.4 to 6.8 per cent among men, and from 5.8 to 9.4 per cent among women.

According to the 2004 'Working life barometer', the average number of days of sick leave taken per employee in 2004 was eight. If those employees who took no sick leave are excluded, that figure jumps to 13.[10]

Health behaviour and health surveys of the Finnish adult population[11] reveal that:

- obesity has been on the increase since the late 1970s
- physical activity in leisure time has increased since the early 1980s
- commuting as a means of physical exercise took a downward turn in the early 1990s
- consumption of alcohol has increased and daily tobacco smoking has remained the same (27 per cent of men and 20 per cent of women smoked daily in 2004).

Changes in working life

Factors influencing societal change include the development of the national economy, employment, long-term unemployment, the introduction of new technology, the ageing population, regional development and globalisation. The number of employees in primary production and manufacturing industries has decreased and continues to decrease. By contrast, the number of employees in the service industry is increasing. Specific growth sectors include care work, other services, and research and development. Mental and social strains on employees at work are increasing.

Small workplaces, micro-enterprises and one-man businesses are increasing, and are one of the few areas of employment where new jobs are being created. Small workplaces have considerably less potential for undertaking occupational safety and health work on their own account than larger companies.

Information technology is changing how people work and how services are structured, since it enables teleworking, networking and greater international co-operation. Changes in technology and production methods also require changes and reforms in work organisation. Highly computerised and automated production lines, and also a shift towards knowledge-based occupational activities, add to work intensity.

New materials and chemicals are being introduced. The risks involved in using them are identified and experiences of their use are gradually accumulated as they become more familiar. Despite positive developments, several sectors still have jobs and duties that involve severe physical strain, poor ergonomics and repeated movements.

Work organisations are changing in all sectors. Flexibility requires employees and workplace communities to be constantly attuned to change, to be able to manage and guide change, to improve expertise and professional competence, to learn continuously, to develop and to undertake new duties. New data are accumulating on the association between downsizing, poor management and 'just in time' working, and adverse health outcomes among employees.[12–14]

The diversity of employment relationships, accompanied by entrepreneurship, places challenges on the implementation of labour protection and occupational healthcare requirements. It creates a multitude of problems in collating and distributing information and monitoring and developing service systems. Atypical working hours have rapidly become more common, and total average working time has increased. Maintaining the health and working capacity of employees doing shift work and night work, and of self-employed people and others working long days, impose special demands on occupational healthcare.

At the moment, the age structure of Finland's working population of 2.5 million is advantageous, the average age being 39.5 years. However, this average will rise over the next two decades. By 2030, Finland is projected to have 26 per cent of its population over 65.[1] The smooth transition of young people from school to work is becoming increasingly important. Labour shortages will open job opportunities for foreign workers, who will also need occupational healthcare.

The potential for disabled people to participate in work will be supported through arrangements made at workplace level. The position of unemployed people involves special problems that make it difficult to maintain and improve their health and working capacity. Municipal health centres should be improved so as to support their health and working capacity, thereby helping them to find employment.

Harmonisation of work and family life has become a major challenge in developing the work environment. The increasing pace of working life and the ever greater demands of work have led to difficulties for the parents of small children in balancing work and family. More and more employees wish to – or find they have to – support and care for their sick or ageing relatives, which also requires more flexibility from employers and others in working life.

Conclusion
The Finnish OH system is characterised by strong political commitment and the willingness of the social partners, in tripartite collaboration, to discuss policies and the implementation of OH services. This can be seen in recent health and social policy programmes.

A higher employment rate in all population groups is needed for the maintenance and development of social welfare and economic growth in Finland. Both younger and older workers are needed in working life. An ageing workforce means a higher number of employees with chronic diseases, some of whom need adaptation at work. It is not enough to ensure a financial incentive for working if the attractiveness of working life cannot be raised. The Ministry of Social Affairs and Health in Finland has therefore launched several programmes and projects for:

• promoting health and functional capacity
• making work more attractive
• preventing and combating social exclusion
• providing efficient services and securing income
• promoting the welfare of families with children
• furthering gender equality.

The main aims are to prolong the occupational careers of the working population by two or three years by 2010, and to increase the retirement age from the present average of 59 years to 62.[15]

The coverage of OH services in Finland is high. The goal is full coverage of all working-age people in Finland. Self-employed individuals obtained entitlement to comprehensive OH services, including both preventive and curative services, at the beginning of 2006. Reaching small-scale and micro-undertakings is still a challenge. Special research and development projects for SMEs are under way.

There is still a need to decrease regional variation in the quality and accessibility of OH services. Especially in rural areas, OH service units are small and lack resources; also, the turnover of doctors is high, making it difficult to maintain high-quality expertise in the municipal centres. Large enterprises are outsourcing services to private OH service providers. It remains to be seen what the effect of this will be on the extent and quality of OH services. Restructuring of the municipalities in Finland has prompted new ways of organising OH services, in particular in small towns and in areas where it is difficult to find qualified OH professionals. A regional OH service model, a public enterprise model, and a joint venture model of public and private OH services are some of the recent developments. At the moment, it is too early to draw any conclusions on the advantages or disadvantages of these developments. However, even now it seems that a larger population base and unit size would make it easier to set up a feasible service with qualified experts. A recent survey shows, for example, that multidisciplinarity has already been achieved in OH service units serving more than 4,000 persons.[8] Work also has to be done to adapt the compensation system to meet the demands of the new OH service organisation models.

New forms of intensified collaboration between OH services and organisations are essential in order to improve primary prevention, especially in the maintenance of working ability and the prevention of work-related diseases and accidents. The advisory role of OH services will remain strong. Closer collaboration with inspection services is expected, particularly with regard to the planning and pre-inspection stages of production processes. The focus is on planning, implementation and following up actions to improve work, the work environment, and work communities within organisations.

Since OH services provide prevention, promotion and also medical treatment, they have proved to be an efficient and economical way of providing health services to employed people in Finland. They link together the stakeholders of a workplace and OH personnel. This allows the control of both personal and work-related factors in maintaining and improving people's health, wellbeing and ability to work. It also involves the public health approach, which is becoming as important as the control of hazards at work. The increasing tendency of the working population to become overweight may seem to be a minor problem at the moment, but in the long term it may be as big a health problem as workplace accidents. Depression and other mental health problems among the working-age population are increasing. Therefore, a special action programme to reduce mental problems among employees has been started at the FIOH and other expert organisations, and is being implemented at workplace level.

The workplace is a useful arena for health promotion. Health promotion at the individual and workplace level, the recognition of lowered work capacity and rapid diagnosis, treatment and rehabilitation are the strengths of OH services in Finland. Rapid and easy access to the services improve an employee's quality of life and earning potential, and save the costs incurred by more delays to a return to work. Special emphasis has therefore been placed on improving the early detection of lowered working ability and the building of seamless service chains between primary healthcare, specialist health services and rehabilitation. A centralised national electronic system for keeping health records is under construction for the whole healthcare system and will come into operation in 2007.

The state has allocated funds to double the number of physicians graduating in OH, to 50 per year. Core competence and minimum training requirements have been set for all OH professionals. In their curricula, both classical and emerging problems in working life have been considered. Special emphasis has been placed on the application of scientific knowledge, management of change, collaboration with companies, and co-working with experts in OH. Joint courses have been offered for a number of years now for OH physicians, nurses, physiotherapists and psychologists. A virtual university and research school for OH physicians was set up in 2005.

Content and practice in OH services need to be researched and developed continuously. A compendium called the Rainbow Project has been started to investigate and evaluate the core functions of OH services in Finland. Several handbooks and guides, covering subjects such as medical examinations in hazardous exposures and good OH practice, and a self-assessment tool called 'Quality key' have already been published. A series of systematic descriptions of evidence-based OH practices has been started, and the first sections – on work-related upper limb disorders and occupational asthma – are already available. The FIOH will continue to co-ordinate the work through the Cochrane Occupational Health Field,[16] and will be involved in the production of systematic reviews.

Surveillance of OH service activities, work conditions and activities related to the maintenance of work ability by the Ministry of Social Affairs and Health and FIOH, combined with the OH service statistics collected by the SII, will form a sound basis for the formulation of health policies and strategies for the future. In addition, the FIOH and other national research institutes complement statistics and survey data with the results of targeted research and action-oriented development projects. More data from these surveys will make the strong and weak aspects of Finnish OH services more transparent. A firm legal basis and long traditions of negotiation on occupational safety and health matters by the social partners, alongside the existing reimbursement system, have enabled the systematic and continuing development of OH services in Finland.

References

1. Tilastokeskus (Statistics Finland). Finland in figures. www.stat.fi/index_en.html (viewed 05 April 2007).
2. Sosiaali- ja Terveysministeriö (Ministry of Social Affairs and Health). *Government resolution on developing occupational healthcare*. Helsinki: STM, 2005. Available online at www.stm.fi/Resource.phx/eng/publc/publs/Julkaisu-2004-short.htx (viewed 10 April 2007).
3. Council Directive 89/391/EEC of 12 June 1989 on the introduction of measures to encourage improvements in the safety and health of workers at work (the Framework Directive). *Official Journal* L183; 29 June 1989: 1–8.
4. Sosiaali- ja Terveysministeriö (Ministry of Social Affairs and Health). *Occupational safety and health in Finland*. Tampere: STM, 2004. Available online at www.stm.fi/Resource.phx/publishing/store/2004/11/hm1101115401134/passthru.pdf (viewed 05 April 2007).
5. European Agency for Safety and Health at Work – Finland. See fi.osha.europa.eu/index.stm (viewed 10 April 2007).
6. Työterveyslaitos (Finnish Institute of Occupational Health). Occupational Health Services in Finland surveys 1992, 1995, 1997 and 2000.

7. Kansaneläkelaitos (Social Insurance Institution of Finland). See www.kela.fi/in/internet/english.nsf (viewed 10 April 2007).

8. Sosiaali- ja Terveysministeriö (Ministry of Social Affairs and Health). *Education and employment of occupational healthcare professionals and experts in 2003*. Helsinki: STM, 2005. Summary available online at www.stm.fi/Resource.phx/publishing/documents/3422/summary_en.htx (viewed 10 April 2007).

9. Työterveyslaitos (Finnish Institute of Occupational Health). *Työ ja terveys Suomessa 2003* (Work and health in Finland 2003). Helsinki: Työterveyslaitos, 2004. For an English summary, see pages 30–40 of the file at www.ttl.fi/NR/rdonlyres/FBFE8101-A608-4FB0-9564-8859AF302D66/0/yhtvet.pdf (viewed 10 April 2007).

10. Ylöstalo P. *Työolobarometri 2004* (Working life barometer 2004). Helsinki: Työministeriö, 2005. Available online in Finnish at mol.fi/mol/fi/99_pdf/fi/06_tyoministerio/06_julkaisut/10_muut/tyoolobarometri2004.pdf (viewed 10 April 2007).

11. Kansanterveyslaitos (Finnish National Public Health Institute). *Suomalaisen aikuisväestön terveyskäyttäytyminen ja terveys 1978–2006* (Finnish health behaviour and health surveys 1978–2006). Links to several years' surveys (in Finnish) at www.ktl.fi/portal/suomi/osastot/eteo/yksikot/terveyden_edistamisen_yksikko/tutkimus/elintapaseurannat/aikuisvaeston_terveyskayttaytyminen (viewed 10 April 2007).

12. Kivimäki M, Elovainio M, Vahtera J & Ferrie J E. Organisational justice and health of employees: prospective cohort study. *Occupational and Environmental Medicine* 2003; 60: 27–34.

13. Vahtera J, Kivimäki M, Pentti J, Linna A, Virtanen M & Ferrie J E. Organisational downsizing, sickness absence, and mortality: 10-town prospective cohort study. *British Medical Journal* 2004; 328: 555.

14. Vahtera J, Kivimäki M, Forma P, Wikström J, Halmeenmäki T, Linna A & Pentti J. Organisational downsizing as a predictor of disability pension: the 10-town prospective cohort study. *Journal of Epidemiology and Community Health* 2005; 59: 238–242.

15. Sosiaali- ja Terveysministeriö (Ministry of Social Affairs and Health). *Trends in social protection in Finland*. Helsinki: STM, 2003. Summary available online at www.stm.fi/Resource.phx/publishing/documents/2993/index.htx (viewed 10 April 2007).

16. Cochrane Occupational Health Field: see www.cohf.fi/index.htm (viewed 11 April 2007).

Occupational health on the rails: beware of oncoming reforms

Gabriel Paillereau, Centre interservices de santé et de médecine du travail en entreprise (CISME), Paris

Introduction

At the occupational health (OH) congress held by the Centre interservices de santé et de médecine du travail en entreprise (CISME) in October 2003, the author sketched out before several hundred OH professionals, chairmen, heads of department and physicians what the future of French occupational medicine might be, emphasising the necessary changes in a system that was running out of steam. This event followed more than 10 years of stormy discussions between employers' organisations, trade unions and the ministry of employment. Led by the Conseil supérieur de prévention des risques professionnels (Occupational Hazards Prevention Council), these discussions aimed to develop occupational medicine in France so that it fully meets the requirements of the European Union (EU) Framework Directive of 12 June 1989[1] and the needs of companies and employees. Meeting such an objective, it was argued, required the introduction of multidisciplinarity and the development of activities in the work environment.

The main obstacles to development were seen as:

- an over-abundant, unbending and unsuitable body of legislation
- the tendency of case law to become less rational and more unfair
- undermining by a few lobbies opposed to change of any kind
- delaying tactics by successive ministers.

The system of OH provision was caught in a pincer movement between the need to evolve – an objective apparently shared by unions and management – and the impossibility of doing so, caused by major disagreements on how change should take place. As a result, the system was condemned as unchanging, to the extent that its very existence was endangered. To avoid such an outcome, there was an urgent need for important decisions that would allow progress.

Many discussions took place and much pressure was exerted in the run-up to July 2004, when a decree to reform the organisation and operation of French OH services was published in the French government's official journal.[2] Given that this decree should have come as no surprise, the wave of outrage that followed it is hard to understand. The general tone of the opposing comments and articles revealed a complete failure to grasp the importance and the regulatory context of the reform. It seemed that any change would be rejected.

The consternation of supporters of the reform was understandable: at stake was this new decree, the result of interminable negotiations, that finally offered companies and employees a regulatory framework. This meant that the OH effects of the various changes that had occurred at the macroeconomic level over the previous 20 years could be taken on board. It would result in a renewed approach to OH problems at a microeconomic level, while giving multidisciplinary teams more scope for action.

The changes that the decree sought to address included:

- massive changes in companies
- significant demographic changes in the working population – it had become older, included more women, and was increasingly dominated by the tertiary sector
- changes in occupational hazards, typified by a trend away from 'traditional' risks towards psychosocial risks
- continuous improvement in working conditions, revealed by a large decrease in fatal accidents at work and of cases of occupational disease.*

While introducing innovative provisions into the regulations, based on the principles of the EU Framework Directive,[1] the decree also respected the traditions of French-style OH, historically characterised by the dominance of OH physicians and systematic yearly medical examinations. In this way the identity of French OH services could be preserved.

The French OH system before the reform

Born at the end of the Second World War, the French occupational medicine system opted for an approach that can be summarised in two basic principles, which are still in force today.

All private sector companies – whatever their activities, legal status or number of employees – were under an obligation to organise occupational medicine services for their staff. From the beginning, these services could cover either a single company or a group of companies, depending on the number of employees involved.

The 1946 Act[3] provided that employers would bear the cost of the implementation of occupational medicine regulations, represented in the main (80 per cent) by the salaries of OH physicians and the auxiliary staff (secretaries, nurses, technicians and so on) who contributed to the OH benefit. The cost of inter-company occupational medicine services would be shared among employers according to how many employees they had.

These principles show that the state decided to entrust to employers the responsibility for monitoring the health of their employees, but was still not prepared to withdraw from the arena itself. Indeed, the Act stipulated that government decrees would determine the organisation of occupational medicine services. Clearly, the state always considered occupational medicine as a 'common interest domain', while trusting private bodies under its control to provide it.

In practice, single-company services are simply part of the companies they serve. Inter-company services are non-profit-making associations, steered and managed by boards of directors, which in 90 per cent of cases are exclusively composed of employers' representatives. According to the Act, their presidents are liable to all the same prescriptions of the Act and subsequent decrees as employers are. Except for inter-company services in which there is equal representation on both sides (a situation found in around 10 per cent of services), employees' representatives are part of the control authorities, taking the form of 'supervisory committees', which must be organised in every inter-company service. They are informed, consulted or asked to comment on different aspects – medical and administrative – of the organisation and operation of the services.

---

* Against this trend must be recorded an increase in fatal road accidents and a large rise in cases of musculoskeletal disorders.

The general philosophy of the system is summarised in Article L241-2 of the Labour Code,[4] an essential part of the 1946 Act. According to this Article:

> Occupational medicine services are carried out by one or several physicians called occupational medicine physicians whose role, exclusively preventive, consists in avoiding any deterioration of workers' health due to their work.

This Article, unchanged until the Social Modernisation Act of 2002, reveals several other characteristics of the French system. The most important concerns its purpose, which only relates to workers' health problems due to their work and not to health problems in general. This observation is particularly important because – with the exception of the immediate post-war years, during which occupational medicine participated widely in the 'reconstruction' of the workforce via systematic medical examinations – 'avoiding any deterioration of workers' health due to their work' has for nearly 60 years been the only justification for occupational medicine. In particular, the objectives of occupational medicine were not considered as belonging to 'public' health, which until very recently was regarded by employers' organisations and employees' trade unions alike as the business of the state.

It may be observed that the implementation of occupational medicine is entrusted to specialised OH physicians, whose role is exclusively preventive, and who are the employees of occupational medicine services. Unlike other countries, France opted for a strict separation between occupational and general medicine. An important reflection of this is that the ministry in charge of occupational medicine is the Ministry of Employment, not the Ministry of Health. This separation strengthens the independence of occupational medicine in comparison to other forms of medicine, and of OH in comparison to health in general.

OH in the private sector

In 2004, private sector OH services involved:

- 15 million employees
- 1,068 OH service units (724 single-company units covering 1 million employees and 344 inter-company units covering 14 million employees)
- 7,359 OH physicians (specialists) – 3,557 full time and 3,802 part time
- 5,515 medical secretaries
- 3,824 nurses
- 313 engineers and technicians.*

Public sector employers, with the exception of hospitals, tend to lag behind their private sector counterparts, and they often call in inter-company services to enable civil servants to benefit from preventive medicine. The agricultural sector has its own system, which is organised on the basis of specific rules. This is because the Mutualité Sociale Agricole (the agricultural social insurance system) is responsible for both social security and preventive medicine (for employees working in farms and in the food-processing industry in particular).

Furthermore, the role of an OH physician consisted, on the one hand, in managing measures to address the work environment, especially by promoting improvement in work conditions, by giving advice on adapting workplaces, techniques and working patterns, and by protecting

---

* Social scientists, psychologists and occupational hygienists are not included in these figures.

employees against all dangers and risks of work accidents or handling dangerous products. On the other hand, it involved performing medical examinations to assess employees' working ability.

During the period just before the reform, the system was no longer meeting the requirements of employers or employees. This was partly because an excess of 'medical time' was being dedicated to medical examinations and partly because of the inadequacy of measures taken in the work environment. With regard to the latter, in quantitative terms just 20 per cent of the working time of OH physicians was spent on the work environment (compared to the 33 per cent intended by legislation), and in qualitative terms there were insufficient individuals with technical competences in ergonomics, toxicology and other matters related to OH.

The apparent consensus on diagnosing problems, which had been established with difficulty at national level more than 10 years earlier by the state, employers' organisations and the trade unions, was not enough in itself to develop the system further. Despite the urgent need for profound change, discussions had been bogged down for a long time as the government's search for a compromise was rendered impossible by mutually exclusive interests.

Reflections by employers' organisations and the trade unions on the inadequacies of the system resurfaced at the end of the 1990s, under the pressure of a European injunction accusing France of transposing the EU Framework Directive wrongly and unsatisfactorily. The injunction finally allowed progress to accelerate, despite all the difficulties inherent in questioning a system that was criticised on all sides but in which some people nevertheless found qualities precluding change.

The obligation to meet European requirements and the need to consider changes in the workplace and in occupational hazards are shared by all countries in the EU. However, two interdependent factors specific to France justified the reform. There was a shortage of specialist OH physicians and there were obstacles to opening up the system to other OH professionals. All this is directly connected with the 'hyper-medical' nature of the system set up in 1946, and helps to understand why it was so important for France to reform its OH system.

Shortage of specialist OH physicians

The French system has always been characterised by the special role played by OH physicians. Their number, more than 7,300 in 2004, has always been very high in comparison to other European countries. Just before the EU enlarged to 25 members, there were as many OH physicians in France as in all the 14 other member states put together.

It seems somewhat illogical under these circumstances to talk about a shortage; nevertheless, such a shortage had existed for nearly 20 years, because of the difficulties in training enough specialist physicians and the diversity of their tasks. The shortage of specialist OH physicians was (and still is) a structural feature of French occupational health:

- in 2004, 5,000 full-time equivalent (FTE) OH physicians were providing occupational medicine to 15 million employees, ie 3,000 workers for each FTE OH physician
- by 2010, 4,000 FTE OH physicians will be providing occupational medicine to 16 million employees, ie 4,000 workers for each FTE physician
- within a few years there will be 5,000 workers for each FTE physician, as a result of the retirement of many physicians currently in service.

Given these figures, it is difficult to argue that the future of OH provision belongs to OH physicians alone, or that it is possible to reduce the average number of tasks covered by a physician, while still maintaining yearly medical examinations and developing activities in the workplace, without sharing the tasks with other specialists.

To argue in this way would be to claim that it is possible to provide a wider range of services in less time, individually and collectively, in a context where the perennial complaint of most OH physicians is that they cannot complete their work for lack of time.

Given that all OH physicians are obliged to comply strictly with a code of medical practice, which forbids any practice leading to an excessive increase in the number of employees to be monitored, the problem had become insoluble by 2004. How could the system do more work in less time when it could not even manage less work in more time?

Obstacles to the development of multidisciplinarity

The enormous changes in companies seen in recent decades, notably in techniques of production and work organisation, have had effects on the physical and mental health of workers. These changes and their effects will inevitably continue. It is therefore advisable to consider improving the skills available as one of the major requirements of a reform.

The purely medical solutions of yesterday are unsuitable today and will become more unsuitable tomorrow. But some of the problems can be solved by using the skills of OH professionals who are not physicians. Continuing rapid changes in all companies and in all sectors, and the development of multidisciplinarity in all OH services (made compulsory by the Social Modernisation Act of 2002[5] and the Decree relating to the generalisation of multidisciplinarity of 2003[6]), have made reform an absolute priority.

The need to involve other professionals was, apparently, widely accepted in principle by both employers' organisations and trade unions before the reform, but unfortunately there were considerable differences between the principle and its application.

The new requirements were carefully worded so as not to appear to be a regression by some or an intolerable imposition by others. Among other measures, they created the post of 'occupational hazard prevention operative' (OHPO). OHPOs are intended to oversee a precise statement of the needs to be covered and determine the regulatory context of interventions, the content and level of training and, in general, the conditions needed for the reforms to take root.

The first OHPOs were appointed in 2004 by committees specially created by legislation at inter-regional level, just before publication of the Decree to reform the organisation and operation of OH services. All of them were either engineers or technicians holding at least a bachelor's degree in OH. They were to be employed by OH services or practise as independent professionals within various private or public systems that must themselves be licensed.

The professional independence of OHPOs and the conditions for their activities within multidisciplinary teams are determined by law. The law also provides means of dealing with questions concerning these issues, but they have not always been addressed with the required degree of objectivity. A kind of 'protectionism' could be detected on the part of OH physicians, who, steeped in the traditions of their medical culture, could not imagine that the system might be shared with other specialists. As a result, a kind of 'closed shop' has developed, which results in restrictive thinking. For example, most of the trade union representatives who sit on the Occupational Hazards Prevention Council and have to pronounce on ministerial decrees and orders are OH physicians.

Thus, comparing the activities of the OH physician in the workplace to anthropometry or ergonomics is 'reductive' and leads to a double error. Some claimed that the introduction of a multidisciplinary approach simply meant adding the services of ergonomists or anthropometrists to the many remaining domains, which the OH physician, 'multidisciplinary' by definition, would continue to take care of. Others went to the opposite extreme, fearing that recourse to these professionals would progressively remove the substance from the work of OH physicians in the workplace, and would rapidly leave them stranded in purely clinical activity.

OH physicians and OHPOs – professionals with complementary skills

The structures for OH and preventing occupational hazards need to be provided with sufficient resources. This means bringing together and co-ordinating medical, technical and organisational skills to provide a high-quality health service at work that meets the needs of both organisations and employees.

OH physicians cannot reasonably claim the ability to take on everything; they have objectively nothing to fear from the arrival of ergonomists or technicians, since their training, and also the regulations in force, guarantee them a unique position and role. Though fewer in number than in the past, they retain a key role in the system because of the specific nature of their remit. They have access to all employees in every company, right down to the very smallest organisations; they are irreplaceable players in the French concept of OH.

The OH physician acts as adviser to employer and employee, as a specialist with free access to the workplace, protected by the codes that govern his or her practice, and as a protector, thanks to the ethics and professional standards attached to his or her position. As a result, the OH physician can always be considered as the health mediator within an organisation.

Even if some have no hesitation in criticising, on occasions violently, certain shortcomings of occupational medicine and the physicians themselves, nobody is able to propose a credible alternative to what they do. The hypothesis that OH services could be set up without specialist OH physicians is unimaginable because, as Uitti *et al.* assert, 'occupational medicine is the very essence of all occupational health services'.[7]

Nevertheless, the need to enrich medical resources is incontestable. The appearance of OHPOs, and to a certain extent occupational nurses, demonstrates this. They are already present in the largest companies, but the authorities intend to introduce them more widely into the system, particularly in inter-company OH services.

Recourse to all these complementary skills – medical, technical and organisational – should cover the whole field of OH and the prevention of occupational hazards. If the actual outcome is to match aspirations, occupational medicine services need to take on board these new skills rapidly and prove their real ability to reform, and become OH services, meeting the new expectations of employers and employees.

A choice between two visions of the future

Although no-one has ever sought to dispute the legitimate concerns of both sides of industry about OH and the prevention of occupational hazards, neither side has treated OH and hazard prevention as a priority for many years. The economic difficulties since the mid-1970s have led employers to focus on growth, and employees to concentrate on employment.

Only quite recently have health and prevention reappeared at the centre of negotiations between employers' organisations and trade unions. They were the first themes examined as part of the 'social recasting' launched by the Mouvement des entreprises de France (the employers' association, MEDEF) in 1998. They led to the management–union agreement of 13 September 2000,[8] which at least partly legitimised the policy of the authorities on OH, as did the Decree of 28 July 2004.[2]

Thus, at the moment of the reform, symbolised by the Decree, there were two conflicting visions.

The conservative vision

The first vision favoured the status quo, aiming to satisfy some of the employers and trade unions and not to offend some of the practising OH physicians. This conservative option would have meant maintaining or even strengthening the existing regulatory and administrative straightjacket, symbolised by the compulsory yearly medical examination for all. It would also have had negative fallout, such as the practical impossibility of monitoring all employees (through clinical examinations and action in the workplace); this would have led to many of them being 'abandoned' in practice – 1.5 million by 2004, 4 million by 2010, and nearly 8 million in 10 years' time.

Such a choice would have had two other consequences: on the one hand, a failure to meet the needs of companies and employees; on the other, an inequality of treatment among different employees.

The reformist vision

The second vision was to look to the future by making access to 'appropriate' OH monitoring a priority for all employees. This option challenged two dogmas. The first concerned the sacrosanct annual medical examination for every employee. The need for this had been beyond dispute in 1946, but by 2004 had become an anachronism. No serious scientific study showed it to be of value. Therefore, there was growing interest in reducing the frequency of examinations, using the medical time freed up to strengthen action in the workplace.

The second dogma to be challenged concerned the *de facto* monopoly of the OH physician in OH services. While this was an undeniable source of progress in earlier years, it was now in danger of hampering the integration of new players into future multidisciplinary OH teams.

If the principles of total health cover at work and of equality of treatment among employees are seen as fundamental, the second vision must prevail.

The Decree of 28 July 2004[2]

After the *a priori* assessment of workplace hazards and the implementation of a multidisciplinary approach, the reform of occupational medicine meant the rapid application of new rules on the definition of 'strengthened' medical supervision, on the frequency of regular medical examinations, and on the provision of 'appropriate' skills. All these provisions were designed to encourage the re-establishment of a balance between needs and resources.

The provisions of the Decree of 28 July 2004 were characterised firstly by changes in the way the number of workers to be monitored by OH physicians is calculated, the abolition of the compulsory yearly medical examination for all, and its replacement by an examination every two years for employees who are deemed not to need heightened medical surveillance. This was followed by more action on the work environment, thanks to 150 dedicated half-days a year and to the general application of multidisciplinarity. Finally, changes were made to the operation of OH services. These corresponded fairly closely to the reformist vision of the future, and satisfied some stakeholders while displeasing others – this explains the 'media fever' of the summer of 2004.

In the minds of their detractors, the changes were not simply a reform but rather a revolution, in a country where the myth had developed and become accepted that a purely medical conception of OH would lead to the greatest benefit.

The Occupational Health Plan 2005–2009 – the heart of the reform

Most of the overseers of the changes would have been content with the programme described. But they did not count on the enthusiasm of a minister who wanted a wider reform, in which OH would form part of an sector that had been partly abandoned for years – public health – or one that had previously been regarded as quite different – environmental health.

The *Plan de santé au travail 2005–2009*[9] (Occupational Health Plan 2005–2009) was published by the government in February 2005. It was the result of consultations with many experts and bodies in the field of occupational safety and health, and was discussed by unions and management in the Occupational Hazards Prevention Council. It goes far beyond the measures enacted by the Decree of 28 July 2004; it is being incorporated into legislation and brought into force gradually. Under its provisions, new regulations are being produced, a precise schedule announced, new resources assigned and measurable objectives determined for the five years the plan covers.

Objectives and actions of the plan

The aims of the plan and the means of reaching them can be summarised as follows:

- to develop knowledge of dangers, risks and exposures in the workplace by:
  - introducing OH into the health and safety system
  - structuring and developing research into health and safety at work
  - organising access to knowledge
  - developing and co-ordinating funding bids for research projects in OH
  - developing the training of health professionals in OH
- to strengthen the effectiveness of monitoring by:
  - creating regional multidisciplinary cells
  - adapting the technical details of monitoring to local requirements
  - developing local knowledge and strengthening the monitoring system
  - reinforcing the training of health and safety monitoring teams
- to reform steering bodies and remove barriers between administrations by:
  - setting up structured inter-departmental co-operation on the prevention of occupational hazards
  - reforming the Occupational Hazards Prevention Council
  - creating regional consultative bodies
  - improving and harmonising technical regulations
- to encourage companies to play their part in occupational health by:
  - modernising and strengthening the preventive actions of OH services
  - mobilising OH services to prevent psychosocial risks

○ reconsidering aptitude and ability to work
○ transforming the structure of how compensation for workplace accidents and occupational diseases is paid, providing an incentive for preventive action
○ encouraging the development of in-company applied research
○ helping companies to develop *a priori* risk assessment.

The plan symbolises the current 'revolution' much more effectively than either the suppression of the yearly medical examination or the generalisation of a multidisciplinary approach. This historic movement of OH towards public health and environmental health, combined with the move from occupational medicine to OH, is what really defines the audacious 'big upheaval' that the French OH system is currently undergoing.

The plan aims to start a new impetus to improve the prevention of occupational hazards over the next five years. Occupational hazards are the cause of human tragedies and economic handicaps. The purpose of the plan is to reduce them, and to encourage the spread of a genuine culture of accident prevention.

It has to provide for collaboration and enable all players to share objectives, at both national and local levels. Thus, it is an 'organisational plan', the aim of which is a better structure for the French system of preventive activities. It will increase knowledge of occupational hazards through the creation of an agency in charge of their scientific assessment. The aim is to reconcile social progress and economic prosperity, sustainable growth and social cohesion.

The plan is much more than a 'wish list'. By tracing the outline of tomorrow's OH provision, it represents the real framework of the reform, its 'road map'. All the partners have to buy into the implementation of a long-term policy, which at present is only partly operational. Several key measures have already been taken, including:

• the creation of regional multidisciplinary research centres and regional support committees for health and safety executives
• the recent setting-up of regional occupational hazards prevention committees
• the launch of regional OH plans with which OH services will be necessarily associated.

The far-reaching changes introduced by the plan have obviously provoked questions, controversy and opposition among a significant number of people and organisations dealing with occupational safety and health. Nevertheless, closer examination of these reservations shows that they mostly do not concern the aim of the plan but rather the resources required for its implementation.

The way to success – a complex equation with many unknown factors
In its Occupational Health Plan, the government has presented OH authorities and workers with an ambitious programme. The breadth and complexity of the tasks to be accomplished are daunting, and this may cause some stakeholders to opt for passivity or refusal. Others may see them as positive challenges.

Then come the questions of whether the system can survive and on what basis. Can the old foundations still support a stable edifice or does everything need rebuilding?

The answers to these questions lie first in the existing legal and regulatory framework, profoundly reworked in recent years to comply with the EU Framework Directive. Secondly, they lie in the political, economic and social environment. Finally, they lie in the response given by politicians, as well as by employers and employees via their representative organisations.

It is difficult to tackle these questions without also taking account of other players and factors whose roles and impacts may prove to be decisive. For example, there may be fears about the consequences of a new health catastrophe, whatever its cause. The results of the 2007 presidential and parliamentary elections in France, with their entourage of commitments and promises, must also be considered. The increasingly influential power of victims' defence associations (for example in the case of asbestos) must also be acknowledged. Finally, it is essential to remember the crucial role of the media, which are capable of rapidly popularising – and polarising – any question relating to health. This is all the more so since public opinion in this field is quick to react and to mobilise, and is no longer prepared to accept the least compromise, automatically seeing it as a defeat, a retreat or a denial. Professor William Dab speaks of:

> ... an urbanised population ... in which individualism became a dominant value, with an omnipresence of media capable of arousing an invading emotion and a distance to disease and death which turns any untimely death into an object of indignation and of scandal.[10]

Without denying the importance of a possible pandemic of avian influenza, it is quite disturbing that public opinion can be traumatised by the suspect death of one wild duck, yet forget about 20,000 deaths caused by accidents in the home, 7,000 deaths caused by road accidents or the 1,000 people who drown each year.

In the process of reforming the French system, the tasks to be undertaken are numerous; this means that the possible snags are even more plentiful. Discussion here will be limited to some of the more delicate tasks concerning the organisation and financing of OH services, the role of the state, and the position of OH in the general health system.

The legal status and financing of OH services

The government has always distinguished between prevention of occupational hazards on the one hand and compensation for occupational accidents and diseases on the other by entrusting them to different authorities – occupational medicine and social security respectively. From the outset, non-statutory bodies took full responsibility for administration. Therefore, inter-company occupational medicine has always been organised in the form of non-profit-making associations financed, administered and run by employers.*

None of the statutory instruments issued since 1946 cast doubt on this principle. It is true that the Decree of 28 July 2004 did introduce the presence of employee representatives on the boards of the associations, but this did not challenge the predominance of the employers' representatives. It seems unlikely that anything will upset an order established 60 years ago. Witness the view of the present minister that the response of the government in deciding the content of the reform was to 'trust occupational medicine'.

---

* As a result of the 2002 'asbestos crisis', France expanded its concept of employer's responsibility. Previously an employer had a general obligation to ensure safety to the best of his or her endeavour; this case added an additional absolute duty.

And yet nothing is decided for certain, since elected representatives of all shades of political opinion have proposed, among other things, 'to create a public OH service'. This proposal obviously created a general outcry, but it also gained the support of those who work on the principle that a 'public' OH service would offer better guarantees to employees exposed to occupational hazards than the present system, which they see as having been incapable of preventing the asbestos catastrophe.

The proposal to bring OH under state control therefore reveals a renewal of interest in the subject on the basis of dramatic circumstances disputed by no-one, but using arguments that are at least debatable.

The debate is far from over, especially if exceptional circumstances prompt the government – anxious not to trail behind a public opinion worried by the succession of dramas or catastrophes that call the management of health or the environment into question – to alter the rules of the game without being sure that this will contribute to better prevention. This last doubt seems only too plausible, judging by the mediocre performance of the various forms of preventive medicine under the responsibility of central government. According to most observers, the doubt applies whatever the branch of preventive medicine in question.

This issue is fundamental to the organisation and functioning of OH services. Since the 1946 Act, the governing principle has been that 'expenses relating to occupational health services are to be charged to employers; in the case of services common to several companies, these costs are shared in proportion to the number of employees'.

The financing of OH is subsidised by employers, in the form of contributions paid to the OH service of which they are a member. The amount varies according to the expenses the service incurs in meeting regulatory obligations. Over the years, this principle has been widely amended, leading to two major types of contribution: per capita contributions, representing the individual proportion of the total annual expenses of the services (roughly €70 on average per year, per employee), and contributions calculated as a percentage of salaries (generally 0.38–0.40 per cent of 'capped' salaries). Many variants exist, leading to great diversity in price.

All in all, the system in force for 60 years has been satisfactory, although disputing voices have been raised against it demanding modifications. Employers have criticised the wide variation in prices charged, and costs which they feel are too high for the contents of the 'health–work provision'. Employees have felt that employers' contributions are insufficient, and have argued for an increase to provide extra resources which they see as an essential precondition for high-quality 'health–work provision'.

This debate on the 'health–work provision' naturally combines with that on the financing of compensation for accidents at work and occupational diseases. The Occupational Health Plan gives both issues joint priority for discussion.

The future of OH will depend on the choice of how to finance it tomorrow. The nature of the services, the price to be paid, how it is calculated, the method of recovering the cost, and the redistribution or use of the resources collected are all relevant characteristics. Which of these elements are changed depends on the authorities' preferred philosophy. Although the balance leans in favour of the status quo at the moment, there is no guarantee that it will always prevail.

The state – the main actor in the reform

Like all countries in Western Europe, France adopts a liberal economic and social approach, but this does not mean that liberalism rules unchallenged.

Historically, France was one of the first nation-states in the world. This expresses itself in the centralisation of power in the hands of a ubiquitous administration.

The power, even virtual omnipotence, of the state – founded in the economy of the 17th century through royal monopolies and 'Colbertisme' – admittedly declined with the first Industrial Revolution and the development, throughout the 18th century, of a middle class that had grown rich through trade. The Revolution of 1789, which put an end to absolute monarchy, might have sounded the death knell of centralism. But this was not what happened; the victory of the Jacobins and then the Napoleonic Empire both ensured the revival of the tradition and gave back to the state all its past prerogatives.

The second Industrial Revolution, during the 19th century, changed nothing in the long term. Even though the state, hesitating between empire, monarchy and republic, gave the impression of being shaken to the point of tottering, it recovered its power in the end.

The 20th century, whose politics were marked by the two world wars, the wars of decolonisation, the Cold War and the fall of the Soviet empire, and whose economy was characterised by the depression of the 1930s, post-war reconstruction, the advent of the consumer society and the beginnings of globalisation, did nothing to undermine the prerogatives of the state. Indeed, it even reinforced them by allowing the state to be more involved than ever in the economic field and to invest in the social field, thanks to the affluence that marked the closing decades of the century.

The state – a major player in the health field

The emergence of the Welfare State – or to put it in a more derogatory way, the 'nanny state' – should therefore have come as no surprise. The modern 'homo egonomicus', a successor to the 18th-century 'homo economicus', relies on a centralising and egalitarian vision shared by the majority of his fellow citizens to demand the state to work for the common good and meet the needs of all (via the redistribution of wealth and, in particular, the provision of public services). At the same time, without really admitting it, this ambivalent character wishes a liberal and individualist vision to prevail where his own interests are concerned, in contradiction to his first demand. The population demands that the state use its resources with enough generosity and tolerance to satisfy individual, even egocentric, aspirations (through education, culture and leisure, of course, but also by a huge range of laws guaranteeing the preservation of particular advantages and acquired rights).

The demand for an interventionist state to defend the French social model remains very strong, simply because it is engrained in the minds of many that 'the state will provide'. In fact, the state has always fought against the effects of uncontrolled liberalism, at the risk of occasionally damaging companies' economic performance by its interventions in the employment field.

The French state, buoyed up by its responsibilities and its prerogatives, and wanting and needing to respond to the expectations of the people, set up years ago a system of health protection considered until recently as one of the most elaborate and efficient in the world.

Although the state's activities in the field of health and safety at work have been much less visible, it has always had, since 1946, the objective of limiting threats to the health of employees from their work through increasingly precise regulations. The result is a system that places the human being at the heart of its concerns. But, for all that, is this system keeping pace with the world of the 21st century? Probably not, in that it has remained fossilised for too long. Hence, an OH system that in many respects has been rightly referred to as anachronistic, has been retained.

The modifications to the legal and regulatory framework introduced through government decrees of 2001[11] and 2004 and the Occupational Health Plan constitute a great step forward. The state has admitted the need in the medium to long term for work that will no longer be solely based on state administration, and instead is bringing together as broad a range as possible of leaders and players in OH to define objectives and then achieve them.

Occupational health, public health and environmental health

For 60 years, occupational medicine has been practised in an ambivalent way – as if it existed in a world of its own – belonging admittedly to the world of medicine but at the same time somewhat detached from the health system.

No-one has ever doubted the vital contribution of occupational medicine to reducing, and even eliminating, certain diseases. The case of tuberculosis is an excellent example but, at the same time, could also be the worst example, since no other case has ever superseded it. The simple fact that it is still referred to in praise of occupational medicine demonstrates, at best, a major breakdown in communication and, at worst, blatant inadequacies in the system.

Occupational medicine has played an important role in improving work conditions, notably in reducing accidents at work, but there is no assessment of the share it has contributed to these advances.

The fact that improvement in work conditions and a reduction in accidents at work are cited as the only indisputable examples of success that can be credited to occupational medicine nevertheless reveals the historic isolation of occupational medicine in France. This isolation derives from the marginal nature of preventive medicine compared to curative medicine, from the somewhat diffident attitude of OH physicians themselves, from their relative marginalisation by self-employed colleagues belonging to private medicine, and from their image among employees and employers.

As was noted by Professor William Dab, public health has for a long time been misunderstood in France, because it has been viewed above all in connection with interventions by the authorities. This vision was also reductive, because only professionals with a public status were recognised as actors in public health, and because physicians in private practice are currently the main actors in the health arena. The state is responsible for the health of the population, but nevertheless it is not the only actor in public health. So – even if this assertion may be considered iconoclastic – companies are full players in public health too, insofar as they influence the health of employees through their work conditions and the occupational hazards to which they are exposed. In fact, as Dab asserts:

> ... since a sanitary action applies to the public – and not only one person – or since it arouses a public debate, we are in the field of public health.[10]

Such a definition of public health is bold and even risky; it can actually blow some health problems out of all proportion,* under the influence of a very widespread confusion between the 'precautionary principle' and preventive measures. On the other hand, its major merit is to allow no-one responsible for a health problem to shirk their responsibility by transferring it systematically to the state.

France is still some distance from laying to rest some widespread clichés, held by many including some health professionals. It is true that, during the last 20 years, important events have widely altered approaches to health. The asbestos crisis, the rise in the death rate during the heat wave of 2003 and the catastrophic explosion at AZF in Toulouse in 2001 prove not only that occupational medicine cannot be considered as a 'combat area' but also that occupational health is an integral part of public health. They also prove that it is impossible to talk of either without also referring to environmental health.

The Occupational Health Plan notes:

> Ministries in charge of employment, health and the environment deal with subjects which are linked (risk assessment) or widely convergent (risk management). These three ministries, to which the Ministry of Research is associated, are engaged in an interdepartmental approach dynamics, particularly established by the elaboration of the Health and Environment National Plan. These dynamics, which can only continue to increase, allow these ministries and the actors who manage them to meet on subjects and approaches common to the national and local levels.[9]

This interdepartmental approach explains the evolution of occupational medicine towards OH. This movement is also enshrined in a number of laws and regulations, including the Framework Directive, the Occupational Health Plan, in the Public Health Policy Act of 9 August 2004,[12] and in the impressive arsenal of plans that now frames the management of sanitary risks (the health and environment national plan, the social cohesion plan, the national cancer plan and so on).

Nobody can challenge the Occupational Health Plan without the risk of causing irreparable damage to the system as a whole and, in consequence, to all its beneficiaries. This was also the gist of a speech by Gérard Larcher, deputy minister for social relations, in which he said:

> [The Occupational Health Plan] is simple in its objectives: better understanding, better leadership of occupational hazard prevention policies, better controls and greater involvement from companies. With this plan and the Public Health Act of 9 August 2004, occupational health has become an essential element of public health.

Towards a new deal
Bringing OH and public health closer together is the reason for strengthening the role of the occupational hazards branch of the Caisse nationale d'assurance maladie (National Fund for

---

* An example of this over-reaction is the claimed connection, widely reported in the media, between the contamination of oysters by toxic algae in Arcachon (which was energetically disputed anyway) and the death of two people in the same city after eating oysters. A careful examination of the situation proved quickly and happily that neither death had anything to do with oysters, but in the meantime and even for a long time afterwards, many people stopped eating oysters.

Health Insurance) and its regional representatives, which are associated with a generalisation of the multidisciplinary approach.

It also provides the justification for restructuring the Occupational Hazards Prevention Council, which from now on will be available in every region as a Regional Occupational Hazards Prevention Council. The mission of the councils is to ensure better co-ordination at a local level between all the public officers and private operators in the fields of OH and occupational hazard prevention, by sharing information, highlighting common areas and leading partnership activities. The co-ordinating authority will specify priority activities in regional OH action plans.

The decisions to link all the players together, to make better use of their skills, to improve work conditions and to increase the prevention of occupational hazards also justify calling on the services of the Institut national de recherche et de sécurité (National Research and Safety Institute) and the universities in research and the development of knowledge. Bodies, equal or tripartite, such as the Agence nationale pour l'amélioration des conditions de travail (National Agency for the Improvement of Working Conditions), its regional representatives and the national organisation for prevention in the public buildings and works sector, are also parties to the generalisation of multidisciplinarity.

Finally, it is important that OH should take its full place within the public health system and play a full role in health monitoring and warning – hence the reinforcement or creation of new bodies, such the Institut de veille sanitaire (Health Monitoring Institute) and the Agence française de sécurité sanitaire de l'environnement et du travail (French Agency for Health and Safety of the Environment and Work). It is through these bodies that 'knowledge networks' will progressively be organised, with particular responsibility for the surveillance of occupational hazards, based on the key idea that – because of the unique position of the OH physician – occupational medicine's contribution to epidemiological knowledge is irreplaceable.

In future, these networks will have to be used more, and also more effectively, to achieve one simple aim: to reduce in a concrete, measurable and sustainable way the number of accidents and cases of disease at work.

To be accepted as a major player in reforming the OH system, OH service units need effective administration as well as a highly skilled OH physician. This is why actions aimed at raising the quality of the administrative organisation began in 2004 within inter-company OH services, through the deployment of a 'progress approach' or 'quality improvement approach' that goes beyond the administrative procedure of qualification that enables OH services to practise.

If, while implementing the reform, the state has to maintain – or even strengthen – its control, that is not a problem in itself, as long as it respects the 'liberal' framework that, in the main, still characterises the French system. Without denying any of its prerogatives, the state will then give everyone a real chance to support improvements in OH and to improve the prevention of occupational hazards.

The reform at a glance

Figure 1 shows the organisation of occupational medicine at the time when OH physicians played the main role under the 1946 Act and the Decree of 28 December 1988.[13] By the time

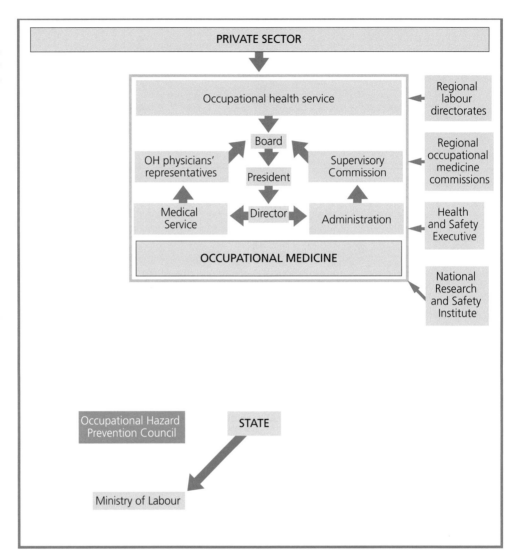

Figure 1
Occupational
medicine
yesterday
(1946–2004)

of the reform of 2004, the model no longer met the requirements of employers and employees, owing to both the excess of 'medical time' spent on medical examinations and the inadequacy of preventive action in the work environment.

Figure 2 shows the new organisation of OH, according to the Decree of 28 July 2004.[2] The OHPOs have now appeared – their role is to support the actions of OH physicians through the development of multidisciplinarity in all OH services. This was made compulsory in the Social Modernisation Act of 17 January 2002[5] and the Decree on the generalisation of multidisciplinarity of 25 June 2003.[6]

Figure 3 shows the organisation which is being implemented under the Occupational Health Plan 2005–2009. The plan aims to set up a new framework for improving the prevention of

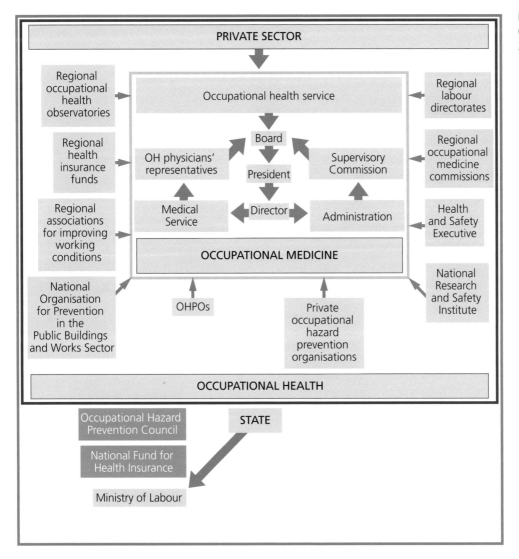

Figure 2
OH today (since 2004)

occupational hazards over the next five years. It has to reconcile social progress and economic prosperity, sustainable growth and social cohesion. With this plan and the Public Health Act of 9 August 2004,[12] OH is becoming an essential element of public health.

Conclusions

France is at the very start of the process of challenging the models that have applied since the end of the Second World War. Alongside this, the incontrovertible structural facts that the working population is ageing and includes more women are bound to lead to significant changes in work organisation within companies and in the nature of work tasks.

These changes will have great consequences for OH and the prevention of occupational hazards. They will mean changes to many tools. 'Working ability', 'disability' and 'evaluation of

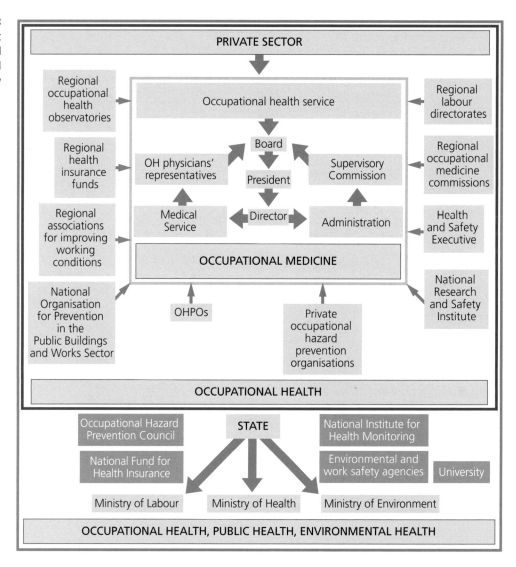

Figure 3
OH, public health and environmental health tomorrow

professional practices', for instance, are some of the topics that will soon have to be discussed. Demographic changes also justify the investigation of new ways of looking at OH provision.

Debate will continue among the professional elements of OH provision – this is the most appropriate level of negotiation between unions and management, since it is closest to the real problems. In quite a different context, the sudden (and very new) interest of insurance companies in OH, apparently considered as a new market, deserves more extensive examination.

These examples of topical issues and the figures above (which fit around one another like Russian dolls) show that the reform of occupational medicine as a result of the new legislation passed between 2002 and 2004 is just one element in a radical transformation of the system, mainly based on the Occupational Health Plan 2005–2009. It falls within the framework of a revolutionary policy; yesterday's restricted 'occupational medicine' approach has expanded into today's OH provision, which in turn will expand to include public and environmental health tomorrow. These continuing changes have been reported further by Paillereau.[14,15]

So, the present big upheaval is not intended to breathe new life into an outmoded system, but rather to build a completely new one. Each action completed, each objective reached in the coming months and years, will be another building block in the whole, and will give access to a tool that fits the needs and concerns of the present day.

Nevertheless, although the Occupational Health Plan is the real heart of the reform, it is not an end in itself. It will only make sense if, beyond the state and despite all the uncertainties, it improves the health of employees and contributes to better health policies in companies, while beginning a process to which all professionals and bodies involved in OH can subscribe without any biased ulterior motives.

References

1. European Commission. Council Directive 89/391/EEC of 12 June 1989 on the introduction of measures to encourage improvements in the safety and health of workers at work (the Framework Directive). *Official Journal* L183; 29 June 1989: 1–8.
2. Décret no. 2004-760 du 28 juillet 2004 relatif à la réforme de la médecine du travail et modifiant le Code du travail. *Journal Officiel de la République Française* no. 175, 30 July 2004. Available online at admi.net/cgi-bin/affiche_page.pl?lien=./20040730/ SOCT0411143D.html&requete=2004-760#debut (viewed 11 April 2007).
3. Loi no. 46-2195 de l'11 octobre 1946 relative à l'organisation de la médecine du travail. *Journal Officiel des lois et décrets*, 12 October 1946, page 8638.
4. Article L241-2 du Code du travail. Loi no. 73-4 du 2 janvier 1973. *Journal Officiel de la République Française*, 03 January 1973. Available online at www.legifrance.gouv.fr/ WAspad/UnArticleDeCode?commun=CTRAVA&art=L241-2 (viewed 11 April 2007).
5. Loi no. 2002-73 du 17 janvier 2002 de modernisation sociale. *Journal Officiel de la République Française* no. 15, 18 January 2002, page 1008. Available online at www.legifrance.gouv.fr/WAspad/Visu?cid=586486&indice=2&table=JORF&ligneDeb=1 (viewed 11 April 2007).
6. Arrêté du 24 décembre 2003 relatif à la mise en œuvre de l'obligation de pluridisciplinarité dans les services de santé au travail. *Journal Officiel de la République Française* no. 302, 31 December 2003, page 22704. Available online at www.legifrance.gouv.fr/WAspad/Visu?cid=634896&indice=1&table=JORF&ligneDeb=1 (viewed 11 April 2007).
7. Uitti J, Sauni R, Verbeek J & Antti-Poika M. Occupational medicine – the essence of occupational health. *Työterveyslääkäri* 2006; 24 (2): 6–8. Available online at www.terveysportti.fi/ltk/ltk.koti?p_artikkeli=ttl00343 (viewed 12 April 2007).
8. Accord du 13 septembre 2000 sur la santé au travail et la prévention des risques professionnels. Available online at www.vie-publique.fr/documents-vp/ani_ 13-09-2000.pdf (viewed 12 April 2007).
9. Ministère de l'emploi, du travail et de la cohésion sociale. *Plan de santé au travail 2005–2009*, February 2005. Available online at www.travail.gouv.fr/IMG/pdf/PST.pdf (viewed 12 April 2007).
10. Dab W. Santé, peurs, incertitudes : un nouvel univers de risques. *Préventique Sécurité* January–February 2006; 85: 6–10.

11. Décret no. 2001-1016 du 5 novembre 2001 portant création d'un document relatif à l'évaluation des risques pour la santé et la sécurité des travailleurs, prévue par l'article L. 230-2 du Code du travail et modifiant le Code du travail. *Journal Officiel de la République Française* no. 258, 07 November 2001, page 17523. Available online at www.legifrance.gouv.fr/WAspad/UnTexteDeJorf?numjo=MEST0111432D (viewed 09 May 2007).

12. Loi no. 2004-806 du 9 août 2004 relative à la politique de santé publique. *Journal Officiel de la République Française* no. 185, 11 August 2004, page 14277. Available online at www.legifrance.gouv.fr/WAspad/Visu?cid=712996&indice=1&table= JORF&ligneDeb=1 (viewed 13 April 2007).

13. Décret no. 88-1198 du 28 décembre 1988 modifiant le titre IV du livre II du Code du travail (deuxième partie : Decrets en Conseil d'État) et relatif à l'organisation et au fonctionnement des services medicaux du travail. *Journal Officiel des lois et décrets*, 30 December 1988, page 16668.

14. Paillereau G. From occupational medicine to occupational health: the 'new French revolution'. Paper presented at the International Congress on Occupational Health Services, Helsinki, January 2005. *SJWEH Supplements* 2005; 1: 31–34.

15. Paillereau G. From occupational medicine to occupational health: status and future tasks of OH services in France. In: Muto T, Higashi T & Verbeek J. *Evidence-based occupational health. Selected papers presented at the International Congress on Evidence-based Occupational Health, Utsunomiya, Japan, December 2005.* Amsterdam: Elsevier, 2006.

Occupational health services in Germany

Brigitte Froneberg, Federal Institute for Occupational Safety and Health, Germany

Background and legislative development

The legal framework for occupational safety and health in Germany has its roots in the Bismarckian social policy of imperial Germany, which – while substantially modified and broadened in scope – still provides the basis for current legislation. The first occupational health (OH) services were introduced in the late 19th century, often on private initiatives and where they were most needed, eg in mining, large-scale chemical industries and steel production. These early OH services were usually provided as a company bonus to ensure a healthy and stable workforce, as, too, were subsidies for meals and housing. In line with the available knowledge at the time, the services were primarily curative and, not least, intended to ensure job fitness and an early return to work in case of sickness absence.

The growing body of knowledge in occupational medicine, industrial safety and prevention – alongside an increasing stakeholder interest, as voiced for example by the Hauptverband der gewerblichen Berufsgenossenschaften (HVBG, the umbrella organisation of the various German accident insurance funds), by trade unions, and by the Verband deutscher Betriebs- und Werksärzte (VDBW, the association of German company doctors) – led in 1973 to the formulation of the Gesetz über Betriebsärzte, Sicherheitsingenieure und andere Fachkräfte für Arbeitssicherheit (ASiG, Act on company doctors, safety engineers and other safety specialists).[1] In accordance with international labour law (ILO conventions C155 on occupational safety and health,[2] and C161 on OH services[3]), the Act confirmed employers' responsibility for occupational safety and health, obliged the employer to contract occupational physicians and safety specialists at the company's cost, and also specified in general terms the complementary duties of all the professionals involved.

Therefore, occupational physicians and safety specialists alike have the task of supporting the employer in the field of occupational safety and health, on all aspects of health protection and occupational safety, including how work activities are structured around workers. In particular, they have to:

- advise the employer and any person responsible for occupational safety and health and accident prevention, especially when:
  - planning, constructing and maintaining company-owned installations and social and sanitary rooms
  - procuring technical equipment and introducing new work processes and working materials
  - selecting and testing full body protection
  - dealing with questions of work physiology, work psychology and other questions of ergonomics and work hygiene, particularly working rhythms, working time and breaks, the structuring of workplaces, and the organisation of work and the work environment
  - organising first aid in the company
  - questions arise related to changes of job as well as the integration and re-integration of disabled people into work

- inspect plant premises and technical equipment (especially before first use) and working procedures (especially before their implementation) from the point of view of safety
- observe the implementation of occupational safety and health and accident prevention regulations, and in this context:
  - inspect places of work regularly, report on deficiencies made known to the employer or to the person normally responsible for occupational safety and health and accident prevention, and propose measures for the elimination of such deficiencies and work towards their implementation
  - pay attention to the use of full body protection
  - investigate the causes of occupational accidents and diseases, collect the results of such investigations, and propose to the employer measures for their prevention
- work towards a situation where every employee conducts himself or herself in accordance with the requirements of occupational safety and health and accident prevention, instruct them in particular on the accident and health risks to which they are exposed at work and on installations and measures for the prevention of such risks, and participate in the training of safety officers.

Occupational physicians have the additional tasks of medically examining employees; evaluating their health from an occupational medicine point of view and giving them advice; collecting and interpreting the results of examinations and evaluations; and participating in the scheduling and training of employees in first aid and of auxiliary medical staff. Occupational physicians can apply curative measures in response to acute need, but the law does not provide for ongoing treatment of employees.

More detailed supervision was provided by the individual accident insurance funds,* in the form of Unfallverhütungsvorschriften (UVVen, accident prevention regulations), as foreseen under the dual system of inspection and legislative control of the German occupational safety and health system. Inspection is legally performed by state labour inspectorates and by the technical inspectorate of the Berufsgenossenschaften; the two inspectorates are legally obliged to co-ordinate their tasks. Both inspectorates also have to ensure that employers comply with their legal obligation to contract an OH service organisation, as specified by the applicable UVV. While the legislative power in occupational safety and health rests with the federal government, the Berufsgenossenschaften are authorised to issue binding accident prevention regulations. Compliance with both types of regulation is supervised equally by the state labour inspectorates and by the Berufsgenossenschaft's inspectorate. The UVVen also specify in detail the annual amount of time an appointed health and safety specialist has to spend on company premises, taking into account the number of employees in the company and the risk categories of their work.

---

* Until recently, there were approximately 75 statutory Berufsgenossenschaften (accident insurance funds) operating in Germany – 35 for industry and commerce, 20 for agriculture and 20 for the public sector. There was an umbrella organisation for each sector, and the funds operated under private law and with equal employer and employee representation on the supervisory board. Their number has recently decreased because of mergers; there are currently 27 for the industry and commerce sector. The Berufsgenossenschaften are supervised by the Federal Ministry of Labour. The employer must by law be a member of a Berufsgenossenschaft, while for historical reasons the employee is not, although his or her status as an insured person is essentially equal to that of the employer. The Berufsgenossenschaften for industry and commerce are financed exclusively by employers through annual contributions in line with their claims on the fund for coverage of insured events (occupational accidents and diseases, commuting accidents) in the previous year. The public sector Berufsgenossenschaften are financed through the public budget; those in the agricultural sector also receive a public subsidy.

Although the declared goal of the ASiG and the UVVen was the prevention of occupational accidents and diseases through complementary action by health and safety professionals, enterprises with fewer than 30 employees were originally exempted from the obligation to contract an occupational physician and a safety engineer under the regulation concerning the Berufsgenossenschaften (the exemption remained until 1995). At the time of the enactment of the AsiG, the necessary resources in terms of specialised professionals were not available, and they had still to be trained.

Ultimately, it was the translation of European Union (EU) regulations into German legislation, notably the implementation of the Framework Directive[4] in 1996, that paved the way for the general provision of comprehensive multidisciplinary OH services to all employees in undertakings of all sizes, excepting only the self-employed. The Framework Directive was adapted in a direct transposition as the Arbeitsschutzgesetz (occupational safety and health act),[5] albeit with inclusion of the essentially unchanged ASiG. The UVVen, however, needed considerable adaptation in order to provide for surveillance of the entire workforce. With a view to allowing for a realistic timeframe to reconcile logistic and resourcing problems, a protracted lead-in time was envisaged, with full coverage to be achieved by 2004.

However, it soon became clear that adequately trained health and safety professionals, particularly occupational physicians, were not available in sufficient numbers at that time; nor could they possibly be trained or otherwise acquired in the near future.[6,7] Medical OH services until then were provided by in-house company doctors, by occupational physicians (Facharzt für Arbeitsmedizin) or by other specialists with limited additional training in occupational medicine (specialists with Zusatzbezeichnung Betriebsmedizin) either in private practice or employed by a supra-regional service. It became apparent that other OH service models or adequate alternatives would have to be developed if 'full coverage' were to be attained. Ultimately, the most promising model proved to be the so-called 'employer model'. Employer models make use of the opening clause of Article 7.7 of the Framework Directive where it is stated:

> Member states may define, in the light of the nature of the activities and size of the undertakings, the categories of undertakings in which the employer, provided he is competent, may himself take responsibility for the measures referred to in paragraph 1.[4]

The model, allowing for OH services on demand as contracted by the 'motivated, informed and trained' owner or manager of a micro-enterprise, was evaluated in its various forms for qualitative adequacy, efficacy, effectiveness and acceptance by the employers, employees and health and safety professionals concerned. In a detailed nationwide project,[8,9] it was found, in small enterprises, to compare favourably with the more traditional service options, such as various pool models and supra-regional services.

So far, more than 25 Berufsgenossenschaften, with a large number of small enterprises among their clientele, have developed employer models for occupational safety and, albeit less often, for OH as a legal care option for enterprises with fewer than 10 employees. Requirements for participating in the employer model option are stipulated by the Berufsgenossenschaften:

- participation of the employer in motivation, information and training measures organised by the accident insurance fund in question
- good occupational safety and health practice in day-to-day company work as assessed by the Berufsgenossenschaft in charge
- identification and contracting of the necessary OH support as suggested by risk analysis.

Amendments to previous regulations include the abolition of the annual minimum time requirement for OH services, which related to the number of employees and the risk categories of their work. The old requirements had resulted in impractically short periods for OH service provisions to low-risk micro-enterprises. The details of all service options are now available from the new accident prevention regulations on occupational physicians and safety specialists (BGV A2),[10] approved by the Ministry of Economy and Labour in 2005. The HVBG plans further evaluation of the various employer model variants and, if necessary, modifications.[11] Virtually all butchers (19,864 enterprises with 317,123 employees) and bakeries and small caterers (401,559 enterprises with 2,951,222 employees) in Germany have already selected the employer model, since it allows for flexible adaptation of legal health and safety requirements to randomly arising needs for advice and care.

OH services and the changing world of work

Legislation is not all that has changed in occupational healthcare over the last 100 years and most noticeably in the last two decades. Various interrelated processes, most of them connected to what is generally termed globalisation, have prompted concern, critical debate and finally constructive adjustment in the German OH community, most prominently among occupational safety and health professionals themselves.

The change processes can be outlined as follows:

- shifts from agriculture to industry to services, leading to new forms of work and exposure to new risks
- better recognition and containment of classical hazards, resulting in a constant decrease in occupational accidents and classical occupational diseases (classified as such in the official list of occupational diseases[12])
- a rise in absenteeism and early retirement due to diseases with a multifactorial etiology, such as musculoskeletal disorders and stress-related disease
- fragmentation of work as a result of 'corporatisation' and increased competition on the global market – highly visible in huge increases in small enterprises, atypical employment, self-employment, informal sector work and migration, and also in a worrying rate of unemployment
- deregulation, a shift from a control role to an advisory role in public services, and privatisation
- development of integrative and systematic strategies in occupational safety and health (management systems for quality assurance of products and services, for environmental issues, and for health and safety itself)
- voluntary adoption of a 'safety culture' philosophy, especially by larger enterprises, which has positive reach-out effects on smaller companies via the supply chain, and of corporate social responsibility as a marketing instrument
- impending demographic change and anticipation of an ageing working population, including more chronic medical conditions
- a broadening of the professional scope of OH professionals and a shift in their professional role and self-understanding (the rise of the 'health manager')
- availability and use of new instruments such as Workplace Health Promotion and the Work Ability Index
- client orientation and a focus on evidence-based methods and instruments
- the need for closer co-operation with general healthcare professionals with a view to improving the prevention of diseases with a multifactorial etiology and for better case management and rehabilitation

- efficient information management (national and supra-national health and safety internet portals, campaigns, good practice, prizes and so on) and initiation of a public debate on health and safety matters (eg the New Quality of Work Initiative[13]) as a means to bring health and safety into the mainstream and improve general awareness.

While some of these developments already indicate response and adaptation to the primary challenge, hardly any of them were part of the formative education and training of occupational physicians and safety professionals just a few years ago. German health and safety professionals have therefore had to cope with a number of major changes.

Firstly, these professionals suddenly found that they had to compete within the framework of the Single European Market, and hence had to develop standards and instruments for auditing the quality of their OH services. They also had to learn to market their services in a transparent and client-oriented way – where 'clients' are not only the employees, but also the SMEs which contract their services and whose managers often have little health and safety knowledge and are often unfavourably inclined towards new European health and safety regulations. Most also had to discard the vision of their future as corporate medical directors of large companies and instead content themselves with service to a multitude of small firms, along with the extra challenges that brings (such as time spent travelling between clients).

Secondly, they had to broaden their professional scope in response to modern hazards resulting from poor work organisation, from psychologically demanding work (such as that performed in call centres), from sedentary work, or from an ageing working population.

Finally, they had to improve their team work and management skills and to make best use of electronic resources, often at the same time as suffering a reduction in staff. They had – and often still have – to learn how to network more efficiently across professional borders (eg between occupational physicians and safety specialists, or between occupational physicians and physicians in primary healthcare).

In general, German occupational safety and health professionals have responded to these changes in a very positive way.

Quality assurance and management of services

In 1995 the Federal Ministry for Labour and Social Order opened a discussion on quality assurance in OH services, with the broad support of all sectors of the German occupational safety and health community. The initiative led to the development of quality criteria, a quality assurance audit instrument, the training of auditors, and the foundation of two audit associations, the Gesellschaft zur Qualitätssicherung in der betriebsärztlichen Betreuung (Association for Quality Assurance in Occupational Healthcare, GQB)[14] and the Gesellschaft für Qualität im Arbeitsschutz (Association for Quality in Occupational Safety, GQA).[15] The GQB was founded in 1999 by the Verband Deutscher Betriebe- und Werksärzte (Association of German Company Doctors, VDBW).* The GQB quality assurance concept, audit and criteria were developed in co-operation with the VDBW, the Bundesärztekammer (Federal Chamber of Physicians, BÄK) and the Bundesanstalt für Arbeitsschutz und Arbeitsmedizin

---

* The VDBW has a current membership of around 3,300 occupational physicians, corresponding to approximately one-third of all occupational physicians in Germany.

(Federal Institute for Occupational Safety and Health, BAuA), and were modelled on approved international examples from Canada, the United States and Australia. The audit consists of the assessment of structure, process and outcome quality in OH services according to 85 criteria applied by a trained and experienced external auditor. If there is a positive audit result, a quality seal, valid for three years, is granted, which is also useful for marketing. Participation in the audit is voluntary. The association is supervised by a board on which all relevant stakeholders are represented. The GQB instrument has now acquired international recognition. The GQA has evolved along similar lines, and the two instruments are comparable.

Modernisation of education and training

The course for specialisation in occupational medicine has been extended from four to five years' postgraduate training and now comprises the following:

- 60 months of clinical training on the premises of a recognised institution supervised by a recognised specialist, consisting of 24 months' internal medicine and general medicine, and 36 months of occupational medicine, some of which can be replaced by up to 12 months in surgery, anaesthetics, psychiatry and so on
- 360 hours' theoretical training in a recognised training institution (an academy for occupational and environmental medicine) to be completed during the five years of postgraduate training.

The training is usually financed by the trainee; the employer will normally grant paid leave if the trainee is already employed, within the framework of the right to continuous professional development which all employed physicians enjoy.

The scope of the specialism training includes:

- knowledge, experience and competency in:
  - prevention of work-related health problems and occupational diseases, their causation and basic epidemiological concepts
  - health counselling, including vaccination
  - workplace health promotion, including individual and group counselling techniques
  - counselling and planning in matters of technical, organisational and individual health and safety
  - accident prevention and safety at work
  - organisation and provision of first aid and emergency treatment in the workplace
  - participation in medical, occupational and social rehabilitation
  - occupational re-integration and integration of the chronically ill and of vulnerable persons at work
  - assessment of working ability and capacity, including occupational physiology
  - occupational and environmental hygiene, including occupational toxicology
  - occupational psychology, including psychosocial aspects
  - OH examinations for the purposes of prevention, assessing job fitness and placement, including traffic medicine
  - the basics of hereditary diseases, including indications of the need for genetic counselling
  - indications, adequate sampling techniques and treatment of samples for laboratory examinations, including biomonitoring and evaluation of results in an OH context
  - providing expert opinions on occupational diseases and assessment of working ability and employability, including changes in job assignments

- ○ assessing environmental factors and their relevance to health
- ○ developing enterprise strategies for prevention
- knowledge, experience and competence in defined examination and treatment procedures, including:
  - ○ health examinations according to regulations
  - ○ risk assessment and risk analysis
  - ○ ergonomic workplace counselling
  - ○ ergometry
  - ○ spirometry
  - ○ audiometry
  - ○ optometry
  - ○ evaluation of various measurement results in an OH context for factors such as noise, climate, light or hazardous chemicals.

A diploma consisting of condensed specialism training is also available and requires the following:

- completed postgraduate education in a clinical specialism involving patient care
- 36 months of practical training on the premises of a recognised institution supervised by a recognised specialist, consisting of 12 months of internal medicine and general medicine, and 24 months of occupational medicine
- 360 hours of theoretical training in a recognised training institution (an academy for occupational and environmental medicine) to be completed during the 24 months of occupational medicine training.

In this case, the training is usually financed by the trainee, who more often than not already works as a general practitioner or similar in the public healthcare system, and therefore has to take leave in order to study. He or she may even have to find and finance a locum to cover absences for study.

The basis for the theoretical training in occupational medicine is the new curriculum (Kursbuch Arbeitsmedizin),[16] developed in collaboration between the seven responsible training institutions (Akademie für Arbeitsmedizin und Umweltmedizin), and approved by the Bundesärztekammer in 2000 as a further instrument for quality assurance. Corresponding course units, developed and tested in project work at BAuA, became available to all academies in 2004, and adapted textbooks are on the market.

There are guidelines for occupational physicians on a large variety of professional topics and for all occupational diseases. They represent the 'state of the art', are continuously updated, and are available from various sources, among others the website of the Deutsche Gesellschaft für Arbeitsmedizin und Umweltmedizin (German Society for Occupational and Environmental Medicine, DGAUM).[17,18]

Modern vision of the profession

The intense discussion on how best to adapt the profession and professionalism to the changing world of work prompted the VDBW in 2003 to formulate Leitbild Arbeitsmedizin,[19] which presents a vision of the modern occupational physician and his or her role in the present social context. The two-page paper refers to the current demographic, technological and economic challenges to society at large and emphasises the increasing need for prevention. In describing the traditional and modern core activities of occupational physicians, the 'considerable impact of the profession on health and work ability of the working population' is related to the individual, the enterprise and society at large.

Co-operation with the primary care system for better prevention

Close co-operation between occupational physicians and general practitioners, although always considered important for prevention, care and rehabilitation, has never been formally established. It is, in fact, hampered rather than promoted by the special status of the occupational physician, who is not part of the general healthcare system with its referral and consultation modalities, and also by the considerable competition between both groups of professionals. The degree of co-operation is therefore largely dependent on the 'chemistry' between individual colleagues of different disciplines.

There are, however, positive regional initiatives, such as the Netzwerk Betrieb Rehabilitation (Network Enterprise Rehabilitation).[20] The network was formed in the mid-1990s by occupational physicians and physicians in primary care, medical and professional rehabilitation and other institutions in northern Germany. It is a collaborative network designed to improve transparency, mutual understanding and better case management in the best interests of patients, enterprises, and accident and health insurers. The initiative was begun with the support of a broad range of stakeholders and with state and federal funding. It is still in operation.

The current situation and outlook

Since 2004, all German enterprises have been covered by OH services, contracted and financed by the employer. OH services are provided continuously by in-house services in larger enterprises, by contracted external services from the Berufsgenossenschaften, by other local, regional or nationwide services in private ownership, or by independent occupational safety and health professionals. All operate in accordance with the minimum time specifications of the Berufsgenossenschaft in charge of the firm, and exclusively on demand in the case of micro-enterprises where the employer model option is used by the Berufsgenossenschaft in question. Data on the market share of the various service arrangements are not available.

Apart from contract services provided by a single independent health and safety professional, OH services are usually multidisciplinary, offering specialist interventions from an increasing number of professions. The range of the services on offer increases with the size of the enterprise. All major OH service organisations employ at least an occupational physician, a safety engineer and a psychologist. The four largest German units are, or are part of, extensive service undertakings with staffs ranging from several hundreds to several thousands. They offer a wide range of services to all sectors and sizes of industry, and have a presence in all German regions, in some or many neighbouring countries, and in some cases even beyond. Their business volumes were reported to be in the range €34 million to more than €1 billion for 2005. They are also active in research and training. Even the smallest of these large OH service organisations serves more than a million employees.

Their usually very detailed health and safety-related service catalogue typically includes the following items:
- preventive health and safety measures as required by ASiG and the Arbeitsschutzgesetz
- health examinations according to statutory legislation by the Berufsgenossenschaften
- integrative multidisciplinary health management and case management
- emergency medicine and first aid
- travel

- traffic medicine
- traffic psychology
- assessment of fitness to work
- voluntary health check-ups
- environmental medicine examination and counselling
- risk analysis and management
- safety advice in the development and planning of machinery, processes and so on
- technical surveillance of machinery, processes and so on
- management of toxic chemicals
- safety management
- safety audits
- construction safety
- fire protection
- development of efficient system structures
- integrated management
- environmental protection
- environmental hazards (including counselling, management, assessment and training)
- transport safety for hazardous chemicals
- occupational and food hygiene (including counselling, management, assessment and training)
- hospital hygiene (including counselling, management, assessment and training)
- crisis management
- environmental hygiene (including 'sick building syndrome')
- microbiological examinations for hospital equipment, drinking water, legionella
- workplace and environmental measurements
- emission measurements
- communication and conflict management
- courses for client-oriented behaviours
- moderation techniques
- health promotion
- health circles
- coping techniques
- time management
- psychological analysis of the enterprise, work situation and counselling
- expert opinion on people, processes, machinery and so on
- training and continuous education.

While many of these services relate to current legislation in various sectors (eg health and safety, public health, environment), others clearly represent responses to a growing industry demand for improvements in work organisation and human resource management.

As mentioned above, by law companies have to contract an OH service. However, OH service organisations operate entirely on their own account under free market conditions, and do not form part of a public health scheme or a national health service of any kind. Thus, information on the number of the various groups of OH professionals – occupational physicians, safety counsellors, occupational hygienists, psychologists, physiotherapists, trained assistance staff and so on – is scanty or lacking. However, the number of safety counsellors – approximately 15 per cent specialised engineers, 85 per cent trained technicians – far exceeds the number of all other specialists. It was estimated in 1999 by the HVBG and BAuA – the major training institutions at that time – to be around 105,000 specialists (or 1 per 361 employees).

Occupational physicians are registered with the BÄK after they have finished their training. By the end of 2003, 12,236 occupational physicians were registered in the BÄK database;[21] around one-third were full specialists, while two-thirds were specialists in other fields – usually general or internal medicine – and had completed additional minor training in occupational medicine. Overall, between 200 and 450 occupational physicians are trained and registered annually, which is more or less equivalent to the number of retirees from the profession.[8] The numerical ratio of occupational physicians to active workers was 1:2,566 in 2004, as compared with 1:2,911 in 1999. However, estimates for 1998 from a regional data subset suggest that only around 60 per cent of all registered occupational physicians actually provide company services, and many only part-time.[22]

The activity spectrum of OH services has broadened considerably over the last 20 years, and the once justly criticised predominance of health examinations – which occupied up to 90 per cent of working time in 1978[23] – in company doctors' activities is no longer a real issue, largely due to their improved training and competence. A regional survey of 1998 gives a proportion of 46.8 per cent on average for health examinations, with an inverse relationship between time on health examinations and degree of formal specialisation.[8] A BAuA-initiated nationwide survey for 2001 on the professional activities and role interpretations of company doctors[24] reports less than 30 per cent of working time spent on performing health examinations for 24 per cent of physicians; of 31–50 per cent for 37 per cent of physicians; 51–70 per cent for 27 per cent of physicians; and 70 per cent for 12 per cent of physicians. Company doctors spending comparatively less time examining workers' health tend to be employed by only one company or to serve almost exclusively large enterprises, and generally work full-time; company doctors still engrossed in health examinations tend to work on a contract basis, more often only part-time, and tend exclusively to serve SMEs.

In 2004, the clients of OH services constituted an active workforce numbering 31.4 million employees, out of 40.6 million employable persons of working age in Germany. A total of 35.7 million persons were actually at work, but 4.3 million had no obligation to contract OH services because of their status as self-employed people or employed family members.[25] The gender gap in employment persisted, with a male employment rate of 71.1 per cent (of employable men) and a female employment rate of 59.3 per cent (of employable women).[26] Roughly 70 per cent of the active workforce were employed in SMEs (as defined by the EU). SMEs represented approximately 90 per cent (around 3.3 million) of all German enterprises, 40 per cent of gross investments, and 49 per cent of business transactions, and provided 80 per cent of all vocational training.[27] Of all German SMEs in 2001, 43.3 per cent were in services, 25.7 per cent in crafts, and 21.0 per cent in trade.

The downward trend on classical occupational safety and health indicators, such as accident and disease rates, is continuing, and can reasonably be related to both successful prevention and a steady decrease in traditional hazards in the work environment.[28] In 2004, occupational accident rates reached an all-time low, with rates of fewer than 30 severe accidents and fewer than three fatal accidents per 100,000 workers. The number of compensated occupational diseases further decreased to 17,413, with 5,217 newly recognised cases in 2004. The vast majority of new cases are caused by noise, followed by asbestos-related diseases.*

---

* Skin diseases constitute the leading notified cause; however, they are only compensated for when the victim cannot work, although preventive/rehabilitative measures are immediately initiated.

Of major concern, however, are absenteeism and early retirement on health grounds and their costs to industry and the public. For 2004, BAuA estimated that around 1.2 million working years were lost to sickness absence, corresponding to a €40 billion loss in production (ie lost labour (wage) costs – 1.8 per cent of gross national product) and a €70 billion loss in productivity (ie lost gross value creation (products and services) – 3.1 per cent of gross national product). The leading cause of absenteeism (24.3 per cent) is musculoskeletal disorders (MSDs). While 29 per cent of German employees perform heavy physical labour, which is perceived in 94 per cent of cases as a burden, another 57 per cent of employees work continuously in an awkward position or either exclusively sitting or standing, giving rise to complaints in 95 per cent of cases. Absence from work is more frequent among young workers (144 events per 100 insured workers aged 15–20, as compared with 105 events for workers of all ages). However, the duration of absence periods is far longer among older workers (26 days per event for workers aged 60–65, as compared with 12 days per event for workers of all ages).

In 2004, 169,390 employees retired early for medical reasons (male average age 50.4; female average age 49.1). The main causes were psychological disorders (31.1 per cent), MSDs (18.7 per cent), cancer (14.7 per cent) and cardiovascular diseases (11.4 per cent). At present, younger and older age groups are less well represented on the labour market. While, among the young, prolonged education may partially account for a lower labour market participation rate, the causes among the higher age groups include available transfer benefits, inadequate training and poor health. While 80 per cent of 50–54-year-olds participate in the labour market, the rate drops to 66 per cent for 55–59-year-olds and goes down to 27 per cent for those aged 60–64.

Despite political desire, employment of older workers still has to become an everyday reality in German enterprises. Occupational physicians are generally well aware of the increasing importance of promoting health and employability throughout one's working life, in the best interests of individual employees and society; they are, in general, also well prepared to deal, for example, with ergonomic problems at work and with MSDs, as is demonstrated by their education, their participation in related continuing professional development, and the availability of relevant professional guidance.[29] However, taking note of workers' complaints on ergonomic conditions at work, as quoted in the current annual occupational safety and health report of the federal government, it seems that the advice of occupational physicians could be taken more seriously, especially in light of the progressively ageing workforce. Simply relying on good practice examples available on the Internet and the general healthcare system alone may not always translate well into the necessary adaptation of work to the individual worker.

Stress and stress-related health impairments probably top the agenda of most occupational safety and health stakeholders. However, the rather complex etiology of such disorders – more often than not involving an interplay between individual characteristics, personal lifestyles and life events as well as negative workplace influences – makes successful intervention from a workplace perspective in isolation a challenging task. The work-related elements of this interconnectivity include irresolvable supervisor or colleague conflicts, demanding work schedules, overload and other features of a flawed work organisation, often aggravated by a general loss of purpose, motivation and meaning in the face of diminishing perspectives and increasing uncertainties in a world of precarious work.[30] Enterprises and health and safety professionals alike sometimes seem rather doubtful of the efficacy of the instruments so far at their disposal, and hence of their ability to prevent ill health due to factors that owe less to controllable workplace influences than to the realities of daily life.

With its Initiative Neue Qualität der Arbeit (New Quality of Work Initiative, INQA), the German federal government has successfully launched a nationwide debate, inviting occupational safety and health stakeholders and large sections of the public to join forces in developing a vision of the future world of work, *Wie wollen wir morgen arbeiten?* (How do we want to work tomorrow?).[31] Eleven working groups have been established on the following topics:

- life-long learning
- new quality of office work
- 30, 40, 50 plus – ageing at work
- traumatic events
- safety in the use of new products
- body, mind, work – a holistic approach to counteracting psychological and physical strain
- new quality of construction work
- healthy nursing
- design of work systems
- fit for competition – new ways for SMEs
- integrated prevention in the world of work – new ways for the prevention of chronic obstructive lung diseases.

INQA hopes to find a universally acceptable way of effectively facing the challenges posed by globalisation and impending demographic change to working life, and of paving the way for a healthy and productive workforce of the future. However, although the all-inclusive participatory effort continues, results are not yet quite tangible and threads of discussion still have to be woven into a viable strategy.

References

1. Bundesministerium der Justiz. Gesetz über Betriebsärzte, Sicherheitsingenieure und andere Fachkräfte für Arbeitssicherheit. 1973. Available online at bundesrecht.juris.de/asig (viewed 13 April 2007).
2. International Labour Organization. Convention concerning occupational safety and health and the work environment, C155. Geneva: ILO, 1981. Available online at www.ilo.org/ilolex/english/convdisp2.htm (viewed 13 April 2007).
3. International Labour Organization. Convention concerning occupational health services, C161. Geneva: ILO, 1985. Available online at www.ilo.org/ilolex/english/convdisp2.htm (viewed 13 April 2007).
4. Council Directive 89/391/EEC of 12 June 1989 on the introduction of measures to encourage improvements in the safety and health of workers at work (the Framework Directive). *Official Journal* L183; 29 June 1989: 1–8.
5. Bundesministerium der Justiz. Gesetz über die Durchführung von Maßnahmen des Arbeitsschutzes zur Verbesserung der Sicherheit und des Gesundheitsschutzes der Beschäftigten bei der Arbeit (Arbeitsschutzgesetz). 1996. Available online at www.gesetze-im-internet.de/arbschg (viewed 13 April 2007).
6. Barth C, Glomm D & Wienhold L. *Betriebsärztliche Kleinbetriebsbetreuung – Bedarfsabschätzung, Strategien, zeitgemäße Betreuungsmodelle.* Schriftenreihe der Bundesanstalt für Arbeitsschutz und Arbeitsmedizin: Fb 904. Dortmund and Berlin: Bundesanstalt für Arbeitsschutz und Arbeitsmedizin, 2000.
7. Froneberg B, Wienhold L & Glomm D. Occupational health care in small and medium sized enterprises – how many doctors do we need and how do we ensure good care? *International Journal of Occupational Safety and Ergonomics* 1999; 5(4): 585–590.

8. Kliemt G, Wienhold L, Barth C, Dörr R, Glomm D, Khan A, Korus H C, Scheuch K & Voullaire E. *Effektivität und Effizienz der betriebsärztlichen Betreuung in KMU – vergleichende Bewertung von alternativen Betreuungsstrategien und Regelbetreuung.* Schriftenreihe der Bundesanstalt für Arbeitsschutz und Arbeitsmedizin: Fb 998. Dortmund and Berlin: Bundesanstalt für Arbeitsschutz und Arbeitsmedizin, 2003.

9. Froneberg B, Kliemt G, Wienhold L, Glomm D & Scheuch K. Modern strategies for occupational health care – effective, efficient and according to need. In: *Work in the global village. Proceedings of the international conference on work life in the 21st century, 15–17 October 2001.* People and work – Research report 49. Helsinki: Työterveyslaitos (Finnish Institute of Occupational Health), 2002; pages 105–111.

10. Hauptverband der gewerblichen Berufsgenossenschaften. *Berufsgenossenschaftliche Vorschrift A2: Unfallverhütungsvorschrift Betriebsärzte und Fachkräfte für Arbeitssicherheit,* 2005. Available online at www.bgfe.de/bilder/pdf/bgv_a2_a08-2005.pdf (viewed 13 April 2007).

11. Strothotte G. Neues BG-Konzept für die betriebsärztliche und sicherheitstechnische Betreuung kleiner Unternehmen. *Die Berufsgenossenschaft* 2004; 7: 281–284. Summary available online at www.lvbg.de/lv/arbeitssicherheit/downloads/pdf_files/strothotte.pdf (viewed 13 April 2007).

12. Hauptverband der gewerblichen Berufsgenossenschaften. List of occupational diseases as contained in the Appendix of the German ordinance on occupational diseases (05.09.2002). HVBG, 2002. Available online at www.hvbg.de/e/pages/statist/bklist/index.html (viewed 16 April 2007).

13. Bundesanstalt für Arbeitsschutz und Arbeitsmedizin. *Safe, healthy, competitive – the New Quality of Work Initiative in Germany.* Available online at www.inqa.de/Inqa/Navigation/english.html (viewed 16 April 2007).

14. See www.gqb.de/gqb/de/index.php?navid=0 (viewed 16 April 2007).

15. See www.gqa.de/zertifikat.php (viewed 16 April 2007).

16. Bundesärztekammer. *Kursbuch Arbeitsmedizin.* Köln: Bundesärztekammer, 2002. More information available online at www.bundesaerztekammer.de/bestellung_fortbildung.asp?his=1.102.155.183 and www.vdbw.de/de/arbeitsmedizin/kursbuch_arbeitsmedizin.php (viewed 16 April 2007).

17. Deutsche Gesellschaft für Arbeitsmedizin und Umweltmedizin. *Leitlinien der DGAUM für arbeitsmedizinisch relevantes ärztliches Handeln,* 2005. Available online at www.dgaum.med.uni-rostock.de/leitlinien/leitlin1.htm (viewed 16 April 2007).

18. Deutsche Gesellschaft für Arbeitsmedizin und Umweltmedizin. *Merkblätter für die ärztliche Untersuchung bei Berufskrankheiten gemäß Anlage 1 der BKV und wissenschaftliche Begründungen für neu aufzunehmende Berufskrankheiten,* 2006. Available online at arbmed.med.uni-rostock.de/bkvo/mb_list.htm (viewed 16 April 2007).

19. Verband Deutscher Betriebs- und Werksärzte. *Leitbild Arbeitsmedizin,* 01 June 2003. Available online at www.vdbw.de/de/documentpool/leitbild_arbeitsmedizin.pdf (viewed 16 April 2007).

20. See www.netzwerk-betrieb-reha.de/index.html (viewed 16 April 2007).

21. Bundesärztekammer. Statistik 'Arbeitsmedizinische Fachkunde' der Bundesärztekammer, October 2004. Available online at www.vdbw.de/de/themen/Stat.pdf (viewed 16 April 2007).

22. Nauert T *et al.* Qualitätssicherung in der betriebsärztlichen Betreuung in Schleswig-Holstein. *Arbeitsmedizin Sozialmedizin Umweltmedizin* 1998; 33 (7): 289–293.

23. Borgers D & Nemitz B. Bedingungen werksärztlicher Tätigkeit und das Arbeitssicherheitsgesetz. *Jahrbuch für kritische Medien* 1978; 3: 116.

24. Kliemt G & Voullaire E. *Tätigkeitsspektrum und Rollenverständnis von Betriebsärzten in Deutschland.* Schriftenreihe der Bundesanstalt für Arbeitsschutz und Arbeitsmedizin: Fb 1000. Dortmund and Berlin: Bundesanstalt für Arbeitsschutz und Arbeitsmedizin, 2000.

25. Deutscher Bundestag. *Bericht der Bundesregierung über den Stand von Sicherheit und Gesundheit bei der Arbeit und über das Unfall- und Berufskrankheitengeschehen in der Bundesrepublik Deutschland im Jahre 2004* (Report of the Federal Government on the Current Level of Safety and Health at Work in Germany 2004). Drucksache 16/319, January 2005. Available online at www.osha.de/statistics/statistiken/suga/suga2004/suga2004 (viewed 16 April 2007).

26. Eurostat. Labour market latest trends, second quarter 2005. *Statistics in Focus* 2005; 20. Available online at epp.eurostat.cec.eu.int/cache/ITY_OFFPUB/KS-NK-05-020/EN/KS-NK-05-020-EN.PDF (viewed 16 April 2007).

27. Enquête-Kommission Globalisierung der Weltwirtschaft – Herausforderungen und Antworten. Schlussbericht, 2002. Available online at www.bundestag.de/gremien/welt/glob_end/3_1_5.html (viewed 16 April 2007).

28. Deutscher Bundestag. *Sicherheit und Gesundheit bei der Arbeit 2005. Bericht der Bundesregierung über den Stand von Sicherheit und Gesundheit bei der Arbeit und über das Unfall- und Berufskrankheitengeschehen in der Bundesrepublik Deutschland im Jahre 2005* (Report of the federal government on the current level of safety and health at work in Germany 2005), October 2006. Available online at de.osha.europa.eu/statistics/statistiken/suga/index_html (viewed 16 April 2007).

29. Hartmann B, Spallek M, Liebers F *et al.* Leitfaden zur Diagnostik von Muskel-Skelett-Erkrankungen bei arbeitsmedizinischen Vorsorgeuntersuchungen. Anhang zum Berufsgenossenschaftlichen Grundsatz G 46, 'Belastungen des Muskel- und Skelettsystems'. *Arbeitsmedizin Sozialmedizin Umweltmedizin* 2006; 41 (1): 5–15.

30. Launis K & Gerlander E M. Worklife changes challenge the object formation of occupational health services. *SJWEH Supplements* 2005; 1: 19–22.

31. Thiehoff R. *Wie wollen wir morgen arbeiten?* Initiative Neue Qualität der Arbeit, 2004. Available online at www.inqa.de/Inqa/Redaktion/Zentralredaktion/PDF/Publikationen/inqa-de-pdf,property=pdf,bereich=inqa,sprache=de,rwb=true.pdf (viewed 16 April 2007).

Developments in occupational health services in the Netherlands: from a professional to a market regime

André N H Weel, Mediforce and the Netherlands Society of Occupational Medicine, and H Nico Plomp, Free University of Amsterdam

Introduction

Occupational health (OH) services – as organisations providing advice and support for employers to promote the health and safety of their employees – were first seen in the first half of the 20th century. During the second half of the century there was an increase in OH services – in number and size – in many Western European countries, including in the Netherlands. However, coverage of OH services in the Netherlands was never higher than 40 per cent of the labour force.

Since 1994, the Dutch OH service system has seemed to be in permanent change. After a sudden increase in coverage to almost 100 per cent of the workforce, accompanied by the start of many new OH service units, there was a period of severe competition and insufficient quality of service (judged by professional criteria). New types of service provision outside certified OH services have arisen.

This chapter describes the processes of change and tries to answer questions about their causes.

The processes are described in their societal and political context. The chapter focuses on aspects such as the legal foundation of OH services, their coverage, professional composition, financing and quality. The objective is to contribute to discussion about the identity, competence and strategy of OH services.

The conclusion of this chapter is that government policy, as translated into a permanent stream of legislation, has been a major determinant of the changes. Nevertheless, political viewpoints have shown profound changes since the early 1990s. OH services and the professionals who provide them have been reactive rather than proactive in these developments.

The origin of OH services in the Netherlands

In the Netherlands, the Industrial Revolution started about 1850, later than in many other European countries. Political attention to health and safety at work is said to have started in 1874, when the Dutch parliament adopted a law restricting child labour. In 1889, the first Labour Act regulated and limited working hours, night work, and the work of women. The Safety Act 1895 contained stipulations concerning how factories and workshops should be fitted out, while 1893 saw the start of the Labour Inspectorate. In 1903, the first physician was appointed at the Labour Inspectorate. As a medical inspector, he would pay particular attention to the OH aspects of factory work.

The Occupational Accidents Act (Ongevallenwet) of 1901 regulated financial compensation for people suffering accidents at work. In later years, some occupational diseases were defined as occupational accidents in the sense of the Act.

The first medical inspectors encouraged companies and employers to arrange their own medical services. In 1919 the Shipping Union South, a co-operative association of companies in the port of Rotterdam, appointed a physician to pay special attention to dock workers absent from work. Other large companies, such as Dutch State Mines (1923),[1] Philips (1928),[2] Royal Dutch Airlines (1933),[3] Stork and De Schelde (a shipyard company) started their own in-house medical services. A preventive approach to work and health was adopted.

The nature of medical involvement in enterprises in the inter-war era has been accurately described by Kuiper as involving five streams: accidents, medical examinations, sickness absence, occupational hygiene, and the prevention of tuberculosis.[4]

Expansion of OH services

After the Second World War, further large companies, such as Dutch Railways and Shell, created their own services for health and safety at work. Physicians were employed as well as nurses and psychologists, the latter for special function tests in the framework of pre-employment medical examinations.

Only large organisations could afford their own company-based medical services. But within medium-sized companies there was a growing awareness of the importance of occupational safety and health. These companies were not able to hire their own medical staff, so they formed associations of companies within a particular region to establish and manage so-called combined OH services. The oldest is OHS Dordrecht, founded in 1941. Most regional OH service organisations started between 1950 and 1980. This was a time of genuine expansion and a pioneering period. The Dutch construction industry was supportive of the spread of regional OH services all over the country. The medical department of this branch set up initiatives and provided money for the establishment of new regional OH service units that met the needs of various companies from different branches. By 1980 complete geographic coverage of the Netherlands had been achieved: every company and employer had an OH service organisation in their neighbourhood. In that year, there were about 40 regional OH service organisations, but coverage measured as the proportion of workers receiving occupational healthcare did not exceed 40 per cent until 1994.

In 1982, the regional OH service bodies formed a federation for better co-operation. The working area of each provider was precisely defined. One advantage was that there was one central point for customers or organisations active in more than one region. The construction sector, an important contract partner in regional OH services, could make a single agreement on occupational healthcare for all Dutch construction workers.

In 1959, a firm legal foundation was laid for OH services in the Act on Occupational Health Services. The Act included an overview of the many tasks OH services had to fulfil. However, there was no general obligation for employers to secure an OH service contract. Only companies with 750 or more employees and, specifically, lead-processing companies had such an obligation.

Until 1980, OH service staff consisted almost exclusively of occupational physicians and OH nurses. This was considered to be insufficient for comprehensive occupational safety and health care. The opinion that professional enlargement of OH services was needed emerged from debates about the then-forthcoming Working Conditions Act (Arbowet) of 1983, which was to bring about fundamental changes in the structure of OH services. In the course of the 1980s new kinds of professional entered OH services: safety engineers, occupational hygienists, ergonomists and 'organisational advisers'. The latter were mostly psychologists or sociologists, who became active in advising employers about issues such as working relationships, work stress and conflicts at work. The Working Conditions Act of 1983 proved to provide a strong incentive for a preventive and multidisciplinary approach to health and safety at work.

Government policy on social security and OH services, 1990–1997

The law concerning occupational accidents from 1901 was abolished in 1967. New social insurance legislation came into force that year, in the form of the Disability Insurance Act (Wet Arbeidsongeschicktheid, WAO). The Act guaranteed a disability pension to any employee who had become disabled 'by disease or infirmity', without distinguishing between causes of disability. Thus, the *risque professionnel*, which existed in most industrialised countries, was replaced by the *risque social*, which provided financial compensation to disabled workers irrespective of the cause of their disease.

In the 1970s and 1980s, broader interpretations were given to the concepts of 'disease' and 'infirmity', not only by employees making a claim but also by employers and insurance physicians. As a result, the prevalence of work disability increased from year to year, reaching a peak of almost 14 per cent of the working population in 1990. One in seven Dutch workers was incapacitated from work. The financial obligations of the social funds had become so high that payment problems were anticipated. In the same year the Dutch prime minister, Ruud Lubbers, uttered his famous statement: 'The Netherlands are ill'. In the autumn of 1990, ministers, trade unions and employers' organisations convened to find solutions to the problems. A parliamentary committee started work. One of the solutions was found in far-reaching adjustments to social insurance legislation.

Until 1994, employers were reimbursed for the sickness absence of their employees out of collective funds. The employer contribution to these funds was largely independent of current sickness absence figures in specific companies or branches of industry. The Act for Reduction of Sickness Absence (Wet Terugdringing Ziekteverzuim, TZ) privatised a part of the social security system by creating a financial risk for employers. The first two (for small companies) to six weeks (for larger ones) of any absence period were no longer reimbursed; employers had to pay the costs themselves. This created a big financial incentive for employers to invest in the prevention of sickness and disability. In 1996, a second Act (Wet Uitbreiding Loondoor-Betalingsverplichting bij Ziekte, WULbZ) had even more far-reaching consequences. Employers were now obliged to continue to pay absent workers 70 per cent of their wages for 52 weeks. At the same time, the duration of disability pension benefits was made dependent on the length of a person's employment.

In 1994, there was a fundamental revision of the Working Conditions Act. The principle of direct or 'command and control' regulation, which had prevailed in government health and safety policy since the late 19th century, was abandoned. Instead, a principle of self-regulation by stakeholders was introduced, to be guided by means of 'target or performance' regulations, and stimulated by financial incentives. This reform can be regarded as an attempt to create more rights and responsibilities in the public domain, in combination with new obligations for stakeholders. Thus, the objective was not the abolition of regulations, but an adjustment of government interventions in relation to self-regulatory capacities. The government adopted a participative role in the regulatory process.

The ultimate goals of the legislative reform were:

- more flexible and effective OH services, able to anticipate new technologies and the internationalisation of business and industry
- a healthier and safer work environment
- a reduction in the high rates of absenteeism and disability, which were among the highest in Europe at that time
- to bring national legislation into line with the European Union (EU) Framework Directive on health and safety.[5]

The legal reform of 1994 also introduced the obligatory affiliation of all employers to a certified OH service organisation. In practice, however, the introduction of formal certification of OH services and affiliation of companies was spread over the period 1994–1998, starting with the high-risk industries.

The reform precisely followed the recommendations of the Molitor Group, set up in 1994 by the European Commission, which advocated an extensive programme of action that would result in the simplification of community and national regulations, a decrease in administrative expenditure on trade and industry, and a strengthening of the competitive position of businesses within the EU. The Netherlands was the first EU country to carry out a health and safety reform that was consistent with the Molitor recommendations.

The Working Conditions Act of 1994 was also designed to reform the OH service system in order to support high-quality professional services. The employer was now obliged to formulate policies on absenteeism, rehabilitation and the work environment. Moreover, the previous ban on profit-making by OH services was lifted so as to promote a competitive market. The number of tasks of any OH service supplier was reduced to four, which were obligatory for all companies. The employer must hire or establish a professional (certified) OH service unit for at least the following activities:

- management of absenteeism and prognosis of recovery (after 13 weeks of absence, a reintegration plan should be made)
- professional approval of risk assessments generated by the company
- health surveillance of workers, based on work-related risks; it is obligatory for companies to offer this, but employee take-up is voluntary
- freely accessible consultation times for employees to discuss work and health issues.

In 1997, a further legislative measure (Arbo-besluit) was taken to promote self-regulation in occupational safety and health. About 1,200 detailed health and safety regulations, dating from the 1920s and 1930s, were replaced by 38 more global ones.

The OH service certification procedure is described below.

Consequences

Expansion of OH services

The obligation on all employers to contract a certified OH service unit led to an explosion of provision in the market. Until 1994, 40 per cent of the workforce (mainly workers in the larger industrial companies and civil servants) was covered. By 1998, coverage had risen to 95 per cent, an increase of 117 per cent. New players entered the OH service market, which originated mainly from the institutions that controlled funds for sickness absence, disability and unemployment in the different branches and sectors of industry. These branch funds had been abolished after the privatisation of 1994. Physicians and support staff had started new OH service units, sometimes with financial support from private insurance companies. The packages offered by these new OH services focused on the management of workers' absenteeism. Due to heavy competition, prices had to be kept low to keep a substantial market share. In contrast to the 'old' OH services, the new providers were organised at a national level from the beginning, which made them attractive to branch organisations and private insurance companies. By 1998, 'old' providers had 43 per cent of the market, OH services originating from social insurance institutions 41 per cent, and other newly established commercial services 16 per cent. Old OH services as a whole had scarcely been able to enlarge their market share.[6,7]

Some striking switches were observed. Several large in-house OH service organisations (including those of Dutch Railways, Philips and the Dutch government) were outsourced and continued as new commercial services, or were bought by other providers, mainly those from social insurance institutions. In 1994, 40 old regional OH service suppliers, already co-operating in a federation, had merged and established their own national OH service – Arbo Unie, still the largest OH service organisation in the Netherlands.[8]

In 1995, the largest OH service providers started a national OH branch organisation. It was involved in issues such as quality assessment and certification of OH services, vocational training for OH professionals, agreements with private insurance companies, and agreements with professional organisations such as the Nederlandse Vereniging voor Arbeids- en Bedrijfsgeneeskunde (Netherlands Society of Occupational Medicine, NVAB). An agreement on the professional independence of the occupational physician, the Professional Charter, was reached in 1997.[9]

In practice, this branch organisation turned out to be powerless, due to a lack of unity among its constituent OH service units about goals and strategies. Competition has proven to be stronger than the desire for co-operation.

Insurance companies

Dutch OH service units are self-supporting. They do not receive any funding from the government, but are dependent on the contributions of affiliated employers. For insurance companies, the units became attractive partners. In selling sickness absence insurance policies to customer organisations, absence management and control of customers became important issues for insurance companies. In some cases, they bought OH service organisations so as to have more direct supervision and control of sickness absence management. For OH services, ownership of this kind could be attractive, because the service became part of the insurance company and gained better access to the insurer's other customers. The circumstances provided a financial guarantee.

The tendency for insurance companies to become more and more prominent in the ownership and management of OH services caused tensions and conflicts. It is useful to examine one of these conflicts in some detail because it is illustrative of the new situation.[10]

A private insurance company, REAAL, obliged its client companies to agree to a statement determining what data their OH services should collect in a case of sickness absence. Medical data – eg concerning diagnosis and prognosis – was included in this package. The OH service – as representative of the employer – had to transfer the data to an executive appointed by REAAL. The NVAB questioned this practice. Together with the Royal Dutch Society of

Medicine (Koninklijke Nederlandsche Maatschappij tot bevordering der Geneeskunst, KNMG), a press report was issued in which the practice was deemed 'unacceptable'. An insurance company is not allowed to require confidential medical data concerning sick employees. Moreover, the handover of confidential data from employees by OH services undermines the position of the occupational physician. The NVAB's opinion was supported by the OH service organisation involved. Stricter agreements should be made with insurance companies, and politicians were informed about the case.

Impact on client companies

Larger companies tend to take a more structural approach to preventive policy with regard to occupational safety and health. In comparison with the situation before the legislative reform, they are more likely to invest in preventive measures (99 per cent of them do so, compared with 32 per cent for micro-undertakings with fewer than 10 workers). They have also developed a systematic approach to the management of absenteeism and disability in conjunction with the OH service (99 per cent do this, compared with 49 per cent for micro-companies). While larger firms try to reduce the risks of absenteeism and disability, small and medium-sized enterprises (SMEs) place greater emphasis on avoiding them. SMEs tend to impose financial sanctions on employees in cases of absenteeism, and to select according to health status and risk of absenteeism when hiring personnel. A large majority of the SMEs (78 per cent, compared with 20 per cent of companies with more than 500 workers) opt for private insurance schemes to control the risk of paying salaries for 52 weeks to sick employees. Moreover, SMEs usually contract the minimum OH service package required by law, while the larger firms often prefer a package that includes specific additional preventive services.[6]

Additional legislation

Shortly after the legislative reform of 1994, it was found that additional regulations were needed to compensate for the negative impact of the reform on chronically sick people. In 1998, the Disabled Rehabilitation Act (Wet Reïntegratie Arbeidsgehandicapten, REA) had the aims of promoting the rehabilitation of the chronically sick, and – in particular – of compensating employers for the risk of payment of wages in cases of absence of chronically ill employees.

In 1998, following a further Act on medical examinations, pre-employment medical examinations were greatly restricted, being allowed only under very strict conditions for jobs with specified high demands or exposures. In this way, the government tried to eliminate the use of pre-employment medicals to reject people with high absence risks.

Effects on absence and disability

Notwithstanding the radical reforms and the high expectations of all stakeholders, the figures for absenteeism and disability did not drop substantially after 1994. Between 1993 and 1995 there was a decrease in disability claimants, but in 1997 this returned to its 1993 level. These disappointing results prompted the government to intervene again, this time to promote prevention at work and return to work in cases of sickness absence.

Over the period 1999–2004, clear decreases in the absenteeism rate (from 6.1 to 5.4 per cent) and the disability claim rate (from 1.7 to 1.3 per cent) were observed.

Effects on vocational training and education

In 1994 and subsequent years, many insurance physicians entered the new OH services to start working as occupational physicians. Special 15-day programmes were developed to train them in occupational medicine. The occupational physicians were required to follow continuous medical education courses in accordance with social insurance legislation. Moreover, postgraduate training in occupational medicine was adjusted to the new requirements of OH services regarding sickness absence and rehabilitation strategies. New competences and learning objectives for occupational medicine were determined and officially assessed by the Dutch College of Social Medicine in 1996.[11]

Quality systems for OH services

In the Netherlands, the supervision of work conditions and health and safety policy in enterprises is organised in two ways. In the first instance, any OH service provider needs a certificate before being allowed to make a contract with an employer. Second, the government supervises work conditions through the Labour Inspectorate. There is no government body that directly supervises the activities of OH services. Thus, the only avenue of quality control is indirect, ie through certification. Both internal (in-house) and external (combined) OH services have to be certified. In 1993, a quality certification system was introduced that was supposed to guarantee high quality in a competitive market.

From 1994 to 1998, the government carried out the certification process itself, largely based on the concepts and procedures of the International Organization for Standardization (ISO). Accordingly, a special bureau was set up at the Ministry of Social Affairs and Employment. Government auditors travelled all over the country to visit OH service providers, interview management and staff, read quality manuals, and contact customers.

Since 1998, certification has been in the hands of an independent foundation, the Foundation for Management of Certification of Occupational Health Services (Stichting Beheer Certificatie Arbodiensten, SBCA), in which employees, employers and OH services are represented. Although set up by the government, the SBCA operates free from government pressure.

Certification of OH services is carried out by specific bodies, which are commercial bureaux usually involved in different forms of certification, such as ISO audits. A certification bureau checks whether the quality manual of an OH service unit complies with its requirements. This check is carried out on the basis of a document issued by the SBCA, which contains around 100 requirements and 'verification points'. The quality manual is designed to reflect how well OH services meet these requirements, which can be divided into three groups. The first group concerns the structure of the OH service. For instance, the mission statement of an OH service unit should stipulate the provision of health services as its main product. Another requirement in this group concerns the necessary level of expertise embodied in the services. The second group of requirements concerns the quality assurance system. Each unit should have a quality handbook describing all its products and explaining how the quality of these products is guaranteed. The third group of requirements is directed at the actual products, by offering a detailed description of the products an OH service unit should deliver. This third group has since been abolished, as it was found to be too expensive to control.

Approval of the quality manual by a certification bureau is followed by an audit of the unit's internal organisation. Certain aspects of an OH service require annual recertification, while extensive recertification takes place every four years.

In 2001, an evaluation study was carried out into the effectiveness of the certification process in terms of guaranteeing the desired quality and complying with the needs of stakeholders.[12]

The main conclusion was that the certification system of 1998 did not have the kind of influence on the quality of OH service in the Netherlands that had been anticipated. The regulations are so detailed that OH service managers felt compelled to comply with the numerous prescriptions rather than provide the services requested by their customers. This situation was partially caused by the influence that employer and employee representatives have had on the certification system. If one party requires a change or addition, the other party feels obliged to counter it with changes and additions of its own. While both parties aspired to a simple certification system, in practice the system became more complicated, largely because it was essentially a compromise.

In recent years, ideas about quality in OH services have been developed further (Figure 1). The latest thinking is to reach agreement on the effects of the services and to check whether objectives have been realised. Under such an arrangement, employers, employees, the government and OH services jointly define the purposes of care – eg the management of sick leave – and qualitative objectives are formulated. The next step is to define parameters for levels of quality to be achieved. In practice, employers and employees find it easier to agree on the objectives to be achieved (ie the desired effects) than on the products needed to achieve these objectives (ie the methods to be applied). If objectives are clear at enterprise level, employers and employees can jointly define what is needed to achieve them. The latter case represents a step closer to real quality: satisfaction of clients and customers with the contribution of OH services towards realising their own objectives. OH services are, in fact, fuzzy commodities: their effectiveness cannot be demonstrated as a stand-alone characteristic, but depends highly on the context in which they operate, such as the efforts of the enterprise itself.

These recent ideas and opinions have not yet been incorporated into the certification process.

Service provision outside OH services

Second-line services

Since 1994, alongside certified OH services, many specialised or so-called 'second-line' services have appeared on the OH market. These deliver special services for companies for the management of absenteeism and the prevention of disability, and include physical training, psychotherapy, stress management, conflict management, pain-control training, and different forms of employee training to strengthen coping strategies. The services often offer management support in preventive or sickness absence control policy. In most cases, clients are referred to these second-line services by their OH physician. The services are paid for by the employer or his or her private insurance company.[6]

Rehabilitation (reintegration) companies have also appeared, offering services such as mediation, outplacement, career counselling, referral to specific training, and training in job applications. By 2003, 133 certified independent reintegration companies had been registered.[13]

Self-employed professionals

Since 2000, an increasing number of occupational physicians have left OH services because of their dislike of the bureaucracy that is characteristic of many units. They have preferred to work more closely with customer companies than traditional OH service providers permit, and have started to work as self-employed or freelance professionals. In 2003, these self-employed occupational physicians constituted a working group within the NVAB. The growth

Figure 1
Three aspects of quality in OH services

```
┌─────────────────────────────────────────────────────┐
│   Quality = complying with well-defined requirements  │
│   Testing focused on organisations and products       │
└─────────────────────────────────────────────────────┘
                         │
                         ▼
┌─────────────────────────────────────────────────────┐
│   Quality = doing what you have promised to do (ISO·2000) │
│   Testing focused on safeguarding internal processes  │
└─────────────────────────────────────────────────────┘
                         │
                         ▼
┌─────────────────────────────────────────────────────┐
│              Quality = good services                  │
│              Testing focused on effects               │
└─────────────────────────────────────────────────────┘
```

of this method of offering a service to companies has received a boost from the legislative changes of 2005, usually referred to as the 'Made to measure' regulation for OH services (see below). The working group stressed the importance of quality assurance in OH services. In 2004, the working group, which had 110 members at that time, was transformed into an association with close links to the NVAB.[10]

Recent government policy (1999–2006)

OH service covenants

In 1999, in a memorandum to the Dutch parliament, the government launched the idea of negotiating so-called 'OH service covenants', with the objective of bringing about greater involvement of employers and employees at branch level in matters of health and safety at work. Shortly afterwards, the Ministry of Social Affairs and Employment started an extensive programme of OH service covenants, defined as 'agreements between employers, trade unions and the government at branch level about an action plan to achieve specified goals in the field of health and safety at work'. Co-operation between social partners should start with a statement of intention that sets clear (quantitative) targets. All the parties should be engaged in the implementation and evaluation of the interventions. The financial contribution of the social partners should be at least 50 per cent. The main aim of the covenants was to create an infrastructure for co-operation at branch level between employers and employees (trade unions) on matters of health and safety. Other aims of the covenants were to improve working conditions, and reduce absenteeism and the number of cases of work-related disability. Initially, 20 branches with specific health risks (heavy lifting, high work pressure, repetitive strain, noise, solvents, allergenic agents, quartz) were selected. By 2003, covenants had been created in 55 branches, encompassing 3.7 million workers. The contribution from government amounted to €125 million in 2002. Since 2003, new covenants have also included goals in terms of sickness absence and return to work.

OH services did not play a significant role in these covenants. The NVAB became involved at a rather late stage.

Ongoing social insurance legislation

An Act called Wet Verbetering Poortwachter[14] (literally 'Law for the improvement of the gatekeeper') of 2002 requires that all stakeholders adopt a comprehensive approach aimed at rehabilitation during the first year of disability, and before a claim for a disability pension. The Act creates the possibility of applying sanctions to both employers and employees in cases of failure to comply with the procedure. After six weeks of absence, a rehabilitation record is started, containing an analysis of the problem causing the absence, a prognosis for return to work and a plan for its realisation. Employers and employees should be committed to the plan. If there is no work available in the company itself, the employer is obliged to look outside for appropriate work. If rehabilitation outside the company is necessary, a private rehabilitation service is often involved.

In 2004, the waiting time for a state disability pension was prolonged from one to two years. Accordingly, employers nowadays have to continue to pay wages for two years. Once again, the government has tried to lower the increase in disability pensions.

Another government intervention in the disability problem was the Work and Income according to Work Ability Act (Wet Werk Inkomen naar Arbeidsvermogen, WIA) of 2005. In parliament there was much resistance to this Act: it was felt to be superfluous after previous legislative measures and the impressive decrease in disability figures since 2002. After a tough political and parliamentary debate and protests from the trade unions, the government succeeded in passing the Act, which means that the threshold for receiving disability pension has been raised considerably. Positive features are the Act's emphasis on the retained abilities of sick employees, and the incentives it provides for employers to achieve effective sickness absence guidance and return to work for their employees.

The 'Made to measure' regulation

This regulation is the direct consequence of a ruling of the European Court of Justice in 2003, in which it was assessed that the Netherlands had not interpreted the EU Framework Directive correctly during the process of adjustment of national legislation to European Directives.[15] In particular, the legal obligation for all employers to have a contract with a certified OH service unit was judged to be in conflict with the Framework Directive, since the direct responsibility of the employer was neglected in compulsory outsourcing of this kind. As a consequence, the obligation on employers to hire an OH service unit was partly abolished in 2005. Employers are no longer obliged to contract external OH services for legally required preventive activities. In the first instance, they should arrange these activities themselves, with their own employees or hired external experts. If this is not desirable, they may hire an external OH service provider. The 'Made to measure' regulation is commonly expected to have far-reaching consequences for OH services and the employment of professionals. In 2005/06 many OH professionals lost their jobs in OH service units and a considerable number have since become self-employed.

Withdrawal of the government

There are clear signs that the government, and the Ministry of Social Affairs and Employment in particular, are of the opinion that the programme of legislation on social security and health and safety at work is complete. The Ministry is leaving the initiative more and more to the social partners – employers and employees – and no new laws or programmes are expected. The OH service covenant project will expire in 2007, and it has been made clear that no funds will be available to extend it. Employers and trade unions will have to maintain the co-operative infrastructure themselves.

We even see a tendency towards what has been called 'national decapitation'. In the legislative fever of the 1990s, more obligations for employers were introduced than were required by EU Directives. In 2005 and 2006, there was a wave of deregulation, in which some of the rules were repealed. One example is the repeal of the obligation of the employer to organise a free consultation hour with OH experts for problems of work and health. Another is the very liberal regulation of hazardous chemicals, under which the employer must now define his or her own threshold limit values for some categories of chemicals (albeit supported by scientific advice). These measures have been heavily opposed by experts, not only in occupational safety and health circles but also on government committees.

Latest market developments

Over the period 1999–2004, the OH service market became more stable. Strong price competition subsided and some units developed and sold more preventive products, such as stress training, employee assistance programmes for mental health problems, training for managers in communication with workers on sick leave, career consultation, and company physiotherapy programmes. Others continued to focus on sickness absence packages. Market research showed that price was not the most important criterion for choosing an OH service.[16] The main reasons were found to be quality and the price–quality ratio; for large companies, tailor-made services were also important, while SMEs were more interested in the contract that their branch organisations had negotiated with the service provider. Thirteen per cent of SMEs stated that their contract with an insurance company included a contract with an OH service unit. It became clear that SMEs were using the infrastructure created by the branch organisations and the insurance companies.

In 2004, 10 per cent of companies changed their OH service provider; among the largest firms, the proportion was as high as 17 per cent. Large companies complied better with regulations than small ones; they carried out risk assessments more frequently, and invested more in safety measures. Employers appeared to be becoming more satisfied with OH services in several respects: in 2003, 84 per cent said they saw clear positive effects from using the services; in 2002, the corresponding percentage was 52 per cent.

During this period, 1999–2004, the process of mergers between OH services continued. In 2004, the seven largest OH service organisations covered 85 per cent of the market; in-company services had 10 per cent; and the remaining 5 per cent was covered by small units.

SMEs increasingly used the regional or branch offices set up by insurance companies for absence management. Often, an office would indicate the need for a referral to an occupational physician or a second-line service, or would look for the possibility of providing rapid medical treatment if the absent worker was on a waiting list. For insurance companies, these offices became tools for limiting the costs of absenteeism through referring cases to the chain of 'their' contracted and preferred providers of OH, rehabilitation and second-line services. By directing the offices and providing case management, insurance companies have come to exert a considerable influence on the referral and financing of OH services.[17] In fact, a kind of managed care has developed in OH.

In recent years, complaints about OH services and their approach to company and employee problems have been reported to the so-called 'broad platform of insured people and work' and to the NVAB. Many of the complaints deal with the way people are treated by OH service staff. The treatment is often felt to be impolite, and problems are not always taken seriously. Sometimes, the complaints are concerned with a lack of confidentiality in handling clients' medical and personal data.

Evaluation of the current OH service system has been carried out by an employers' panel (the ZARA/SZW).[18] At present, TNO Work and Employment monitors the performance of OH services annually.

Discussion and conclusions

This chapter has described processes in the origin and reform of OH services in the Netherlands in the context of the societal and political environment. The emphasis has been on the most recent period (since 1994).

Four periods may be distinguished. The main aspects of each period are summarised here as a means of approaching the basic question posed in this chapter: what factors have driven the processes of change?

First period: 1920–1980 – medical OH services

Medical personnel from the Labour Inspectorate were very active in stimulating employers to arrange medical services for their workers. Medical treatment of occupational diseases and accidents was the main activity. After the Second World War, there were more and more initiatives in large and national enterprises to establish in-house medical services. In the 1960s and 1970s, the so-called 'Great Eight' (Philips, Postal Services, Dutch State Mines, Shell, Dutch Railways, AKZO, the Government Medical Service, and Hoogovens) was a powerful body, even forming its own club of managers within the NVAB. In summary, there was a kind of coalition between government and captains of industry to establish and expand OH services.

Second period: 1980–1994 – multidisciplinary OH services

The nature of OH services changed during this period. From monodisciplinary services with medical doctors as managers, the services became multidisciplinary advisory bodies. Lawyers and economists entered the boards of management. The process was stimulated to a great extent by the introduction of the Working Conditions Act of 1983. The Act required that four types of professional be employed in all OH service units: occupational physicians, safety engineers, occupational hygienists and organisational advisers. In summary, legislation was the driving force during this period.

Third period: 1994–1999 – commercial OH services

This period is characterised by a fundamental change in the OH service market. Units were transformed into business organisations, mostly operating at a national level. Management of OH services was now taken over by businessmen. Private investors and insurance companies bought up existing units. New commercial OH providers and second-line services appeared. There was intense competition: the struggle was mainly about the price of services, and quality was put under pressure. In OH packages, sickness absence control played a predominant role. Nevertheless, the absence and disability figures did not drop substantially.

It is reasonable to conclude that the commercial transition of Dutch OH services was triggered by the stream of legislation introduced after 1994. 'A free market of services in healthcare' was a political target, not a policy advocated by OH experts and their professional associations.

Fourth period: 1999–2006 – lost monopolies

During the fourth period there were clear reductions in absenteeism and disability rates. Furthermore, many aims of the earlier reforms were gradually achieved, and companies' investments in prevention and rehabilitation increased. It is obvious that the Wet Verbetering Poortwachter made a positive contribution to these outcomes – by assigning clear obligations to employers and employees in the process of returning to work, and by imposing clear sanctions in cases of non-compliance with the rules. Employers became more active in health and safety, and independent OH services became almost superfluous in some respects.

OH services concentrated their efforts on sickness absence guidance, and the administrative procedures surrounding it, to an even greater extent than during the third period, and in general neglected preventive strategies. Second-line services had to fill the gaps in knowledge and skills of OH services. Much less workers' health surveillance was performed, and its quality was generally insufficient.[19] In fact, OH services had lost the incentive to adopt a preventive approach. As a consequence, many units even lost their experience in prevention. The Labour Inspectorate was unable to carry out an effective maintenance strategy, and inspection was largely limited to a paper check on companies' OH service contracts. The prevailing bureaucratic certification system could not counteract these developments. During this period, there was a shift in OH competences from prevention to sickness absence guidance.

The reforms eventually brought about the results that politicians had intended 10 years before. Financial incentives alone were not sufficient to achieve the success. Only after the development of an effective infrastructure created by private insurance companies and branch organisations, targeted at quick help and the limitation of damage risks, did most companies seriously start to develop a policy for the management of absenteeism and disability.[13] Proactive stakeholders included the government, some branch organisations and private insurance companies. Employers, employees and their traditional health and safety advisers, the OH services, were mainly reactive during this period.

Societal and political factors appear to have been the major determinants of the design of professional care for work and health and of the OH service organisations providing the care. The main causes of the profound changes in service structure and functionality since 1994 are to be found in the societal developments and changing political viewpoints that influenced legislation and created obligations for employers.

New opportunities for OH services?

If we extrapolate these recent developments into the future, the end of traditional OH services may be expected over the coming decade. The present structures of the services in the Netherlands, built in the 1990s and supported by detailed legislation, will fade away. Having a certificate is no longer a guarantee of survival for a service, because the employer is free to look for other solutions. The OH services' role is being taken over by enterprises themselves, with support for particular tasks only from external (often self-employed) experts or branch institutions. Employers have learned a lot over the last decade. They prefer to do things on their own. In a way, they have become experts themselves, and use critical judgment in composing their package of professional OH support from a broad range of providers in the free market. Large companies buy priority care for their employees to avoid waiting times for medical treatment. The latest legislative changes push them further in a 'do-it-yourself' direction. Occupational physicians refer patients directly to clinical specialists.

The positive aspect of these developments lies in the increasing involvement of employers in health and safety issues. However, questions remain. How and by whom can the public health aspects of OH services be guaranteed? In the current situation, this seems to be nobody's concern.

For enterprises and OH professionals, the challenge is to create an interface that meets the needs of both parties. In this interface, a balance between professionalism and working for profit has to be found. Experts look for space to deploy their competences, whereas employers expect to get cost-effective answers to their well-selected questions regarding health and safety.

OH service organisations often keep their strategies and solutions to themselves, and do not share insights and experiences. They arrange training and continuous professional development for themselves. This is due to competition in the shrinking market for their services.

A more creative approach lies in the further professionalisation and specialisation of OH services. There is a growing field of opportunities. Evidence-based guidelines on lower back pain and adjustment disorders have changed approaches to these common medical problems, in both OH services and general healthcare. Due to these guidelines, better treatment and guidance are being provided by OH services. Scientific evaluation studies have proven the positive impact of new guidelines and approaches on return to work, and sometimes also on health complaints. Similar developments are detectable for a range of other common health issues, such as depressive disorders, hearing impairments, rheumatoid arthritis, cancer survival, and diabetes.

The challenge for OH services is to maintain and improve their identity, competences and strategies. These are the conditions for survival on a free market.

References

1. Bakker J G. *De verbandkamer. Geschiedenis van 80 jaar verbandkamers, longinstituten en Arbo-zorg in mijnbouw en petrochemie.* Geleen: DSM, 1999.
2. Maurik G van, Netelenbos W J, Wely P A van & Zuidema H. *Philips occupational health 1928–1978.* Eindhoven: Philips Medical Service, 1978.
3. Koninklijke Luchtvaart Maatschappij. *Meegroeien met de vloot. 50 jaar KLM Geneeskundige Afdeling.* Schiphol-Oost: KLM Geneeskundige Afdeling, 1983.
4. Kuiper J P. *Bedrijfsarts en arbeidende mens. Dissertatie.* Assen: Van Gorcum, 1968.
5. Council Directive 89/391/EEC of 12 June 1989 on the introduction of measures to encourage improvements in the safety and health of workers at work (the Framework Directive). *Official Journal* L183; 29 June 1989: 1–8.
6. Plomp H N, Wal G van der & Weel A N H. Privatisering van de Ziektewet: uiteenlopende effecten bij zowel bedrijven als Arbo-diensten. *Nederlands Tijdschrift voor Geneeskunde* 1999; 143: 1369–1373.
7. Plomp H N, Wal G van der & Weel A N H. Marktwerking in de sociale zekerheid en Arbo-dienstverlening. *Nederlands Tijdschrift voor Geneeskunde* 1999; 143: 1374–1378.
8. Bruins Slot J H W & Spreeuwers D. *Kleine historie van Arbo Unie.* Nieuwegein: Arbo Unie, 2003.
9. Plomp H N, Weel A N H & Wal G van der. Professionele integriteit binnen commerciële Arbo-dienstverlening. *Nederlands Tijdschrift voor Geneeskunde* 1999; 143: 1379–1382.
10. Vernooy A I F & Weel A N H. '*Laten de bedrijfsartsen hun tijd verstaan en hun taak in dien tijd begrijpen*'. *Zestig jaar Nederlandse Vereniging voor Arbeids- en Bedrijfsgeneeskunde (NVAB) 1946–2006.* Eindhoven: NVAB, 2006.
11. Weel A N H, Beek A J van der, Kroon P J, Verbeek J H A M & Dijk F J H van. Recent changes in occupational medicine in the Netherlands. *International Archives of Occupational and Environmental Health* 1999; 72: 285–291.

12. Marcelissen F H G & Weel A N H. Certification and quality assurance in Dutch occupational health services. *International Journal of Occupational Medicine and Environmental Health* 2002; 15: 173–177.
13. Plomp H N. The introduction of market incentives in the field of occupational safety and health: its impact on occupational health services and companies: experiences from the Netherlands. Submitted for publication, 2006.
14. Wet van de 29 november 2001 tot verbetering van de procesgang in het eerste ziektejaar en nieuwe regels voor de ziekmelding, de reïntegratie en de wachttijd van werknemers alsmede med betrekking tot de loondoorbetalingsverplichting van de werkgever (Wet Verbetering Poortwachter). Staatsblad 2001, 628. Available online at www.st-ab.nl/1-01628-wvp.htm (viewed 11 May 2007).
15. European Court of Justice. European Commission *v* The Netherlands, ruling 2003.
16. Market Concern. *Overzicht omzet en marktaandeel Arbodiensten 2001–2004*. Bunnik: Market Concern, 2005.
17. Plomp H N. Ontwikkeling van de tweedelijns-Arbo-dienstverlening: naar geïntegreerde ketens van verzekeraars en zorgaanbieders. *Nederlands Tijdschrift voor Geneeskunde* 2000; 144: 1165–1170.
18. Veerman T J, Schellekens E I L M & Duvekot J A. *Werkgevers over ziekteverzuim, Arbo en Reïntegratie: eindrapport ZARA/SZW-werkgeverspanel*. Doetinchem: Elsevier bedrijfsinformatie, 2001.
19. Weel A N H & Duijn J C M. *Het kind en het badwater*. Utrecht: NVAB, 2004.

Occupational health services in Norway – legislative framework, trends, developments and future perspectives

Arve Lie and Odd Bjørnstad, National Institute of Occupational Health, Oslo

Introduction

The history of occupational health (OH) services in Norway goes back to company physicians in the silver mining industry in Kongsberg during the 17th century.[1] The first modern OH service unit is usually regarded as having been founded at the Freia Chocolate Company in Oslo in 1917 by Professor Schiøtz. A public health approach, based on prevention by hygienic inspections and health surveillance, was adopted. It was not until 1977, when the Work Environment Act was passed, that there was a major expansion of OH services, starting in particular with the emergence of external, multidisciplinary units providing services to many enterprises.

Structure of services, distribution and coverage[2]

Today, OH services in Norway consist of around 400–500 units and cover approximately one million employees. This is equivalent to 50 per cent of the total workforce. The units are widely distributed all over the country. The average cost of OH provision amounts to €150 per employee per year, which gives a total cost of €150 million per year. The monetary value of services purchased by enterprises varies considerably – from less than €50 up to more than €1,000 per employee per year.

The average size of the units is small compared to those in many other European countries. On average, four full-time professionals cover just over 2,000 employees, which is equivalent to two OH professionals per 1,000 employees.

About 40 per cent of total OH service provision consists of internal services owned by enterprises. The rest is provided by external services, of which about half are owned by the participating enterprises, and half are privately owned.

Legislative foundation

The legislative foundation for OH services derives partly from work environment legislation and partly from health legislation. This means that two ministries are currently involved: the Ministry of Labour and Social Inclusion, and the Ministry of Health and Welfare.

The legislative basis for OH services was first stated in the Work Environment Act of 1977; it is also included in the revised Work Environment Act of 2005. A regulation on OH personnel states which types of services the employer should request from an OH service unit. The responsibility for having an OH service is put on the employer, who is also responsible for making sure that OH personnel have the right competence.

There is also legislation specifying which trades and industries are obliged to have an OH service unit. Examples include mining, forestry, food production, construction work, transportation, oil, metal, chemical and wood processing, and hotels and restaurants. Ideas about the role of OH services are essentially similar across Europe, as the European Union (EU) Framework Directive[3] of 1989 lays down the general direction. However, OH practice varies a great deal between the countries and even within them.[4]

Relationship to primary healthcare

Most of the tasks of OH services referred to in the legislation are preventive by nature. The general understanding of OH personnel is that they should not get involved in health problems unrelated to the work environment. Nevertheless, many OH service units also provide some types of curative services in areas not related to the work environment, and become engaged in the improvement of healthy behaviour and in lifestyle issues. In a recent study, a large majority of responding OH service units were found to be involved in promotional activities with regard to physical exercise (92 per cent), alcohol reduction (87 per cent), smoking reduction (86 per cent) and nutrition (72 per cent).[5]

It may be difficult, and also possibly meaningless, to differentiate between work-related and non-work-related issues – especially when it comes to rehabilitation work, where OH services, according to the legislation, should play an important supportive role within the enterprise. One major challenge, therefore, is to improve co-operation between OH services and other health professionals, in particular general practitioners. Major steps to improve co-operation are currently being taken as part of the national campaign 'Inclusive Working Life' (IWL), with the objectives of reducing sickness absence and early retirement on health grounds, promoting an early return to work, and aiding employment of the functionally impaired.[6] OH services are expected to be an important expert contributor to IWL because of their knowledge of and contact with the workplace, and their tradition in assessing work capacity.

Although some general practitioners question the impartiality of OH services, most do not. But since the services operate more and more on a free-market basis, there may indeed be grounds for questioning their impartiality. Of course, this may limit co-operation between OH services and other health professionals, but – in the first instance – it represents an ethical challenge to OH services in the grey zone between business and ethics.

OH services in Norway are becoming increasingly market-led, and therefore must sell their products to enterprises. This means that services that tend to improve companies' finances may receive greater attention than activities beneficial to society at large. In an IWL setting, this means that OH service units will be more engaged in the reduction of sickness absence than in preventing early retirement and the taking of disability pensions. A recent study[7] has found this to be the case – this suggests that the future contribution of OH services to public health may become limited.

Staffing and competence

OH services in Norway are essentially multidisciplinary. According to official records, they employ nurses (660), physicians (340), ergonomists (340), safety engineers (380), psychologists (30) and other staff (460), giving a total of 2,200 full-time employees. But the actual number of OH staff is much higher, since there are many small units, and many professionals work part-time. Although there is a registry of OH service providers[2] at Statens Arbeidsmiljøinstitutt (National Institute of Occupational Health, NIOH), it is virtually impossible to give exact numbers. The register is based on voluntary reporting. Many units choose not to be recorded, and there are no strict, official criteria for the resources and competences an organisation requires in order to call itself an OH service unit.

A typical unit consists of one physician, one nurse, one ergonomist and one safety engineer or occupational hygienist. There are specialisms within all their working areas. Most OH service personnel have been through basic training programmes, but the amount of training varies a great deal. At present, 30–40 per cent of occupational physicians are specialists in occupational medicine, and 25 per cent of the hygienists and 10–15 per cent of the occupational nurses and ergonomists are specialists within their fields.

The basic training, and much of the advanced training, of OH personnel is managed by the NIOH. In addition, some training is carried out by professional associations and the universities. The training programmes are being developed to meet the needs of modern working life, with a focus on factual knowledge, process understanding and skills.

Main orientation and focus of programmes

Norwegian legislation stipulates that OH services should focus on areas such as workplace risk assessment, surveillance of the work environment and health of the worker, evaluation of work ability, rehabilitation and workplace adaptation, education and training of employers and employees, and curative services targeted at work-related disorders.

The present focus on IWL has received considerable attention in Norwegian working life in general, and among OH personnel in particular.[6] A new public body, consisting of Working Life Centres (WLCs), with more than 400 employees, has emerged from the national insurance system. The main task of the centres is to give support to enterprises and OH services on issues such as sickness absence and rehabilitation. They now seem to have become increasingly involved in health, environment and safety issues, and are giving their services free of charge to enterprises. In this sense, they are acting more and more as competitors to OH services. Many OH service units are in a worrying financial situation and strongly dislike this development.[6]

In addition, OH services are involved in workplace health promotion programmes and other types of public health intervention, such as healthy eating, physical exercise and anti-smoking campaigns.

Quality in OH services

There are no formal quality regulations for OH services in Norway. The employer is responsible for assessing service quality.

In 1998 the Ministry of Local Government and Regional Development began an evaluation of OH services.[8] A random sample of enterprises obliged to have an OH service unit was studied. Managers, safety representatives and representatives of the OH service received a mailed questionnaire with questions about the types of OH service delivered and aspects of their assessment. In addition, in-depth interviews were performed in eight enterprises. The study revealed large differences in opinion between the respondents. To give an example, 71 per cent of the OH service respondents stated that they had been involved in policy development and work on health, environment and safety in their enterprises. The corresponding figures for managers and safety representatives were just 28 per cent and 55 per cent respectively, which indicates that the contributions of the OH service tended to be invisible to them.

These were the major conclusions of the study:

- OH services have a positive impact on safety, health and environment work in the enterprises, but significant improvement is still possible
- 80 per cent of customers are generally satisfied
- OH services should focus more on quality issues
- OH services should be better adapted to and focused on customers' needs.

As a result of these findings, OH services in Norway, together with the NIOH, the social partners and Arbeidstilsynet (the Labour Inspectorate), have developed a quality system called 'Good occupational health service',[9] which is an evaluation tool based on auditing principles. The tool is now part of the basic training programme for OH service personnel in Norway, and is being widely used by the services.

Financing structure

Generally speaking, employers cover all OH service costs. Recently, a small reimbursement has been provided to OH service units that are doing work under the IWL agreement. But this is of minor importance, since it amounts to only 1–2 per cent of the total costs of the average unit. Although OH services, according to legislation, should have a free and independent professional role, this role is being challenged by having to sell services on a free market with increasing competition between service providers. The lack of public funding may lead to services being offered that are more focused on what is advantageous for enterprises and not always on what benefits society. For example, a strong focus on reduction of sickness absence may lead to a greater use of disability pensions. This will be financially beneficial to enterprises, since the costs of disability and early retirement are largely borne by society, whereas the costs of sickness absence are evenly shared between enterprises and society.

Public surveillance

The Labour Inspectorate is responsible for surveillance of the work environment. Its inspections are directed at employers, concentrating on whether they adopt a systematic approach to health, environment and safety, and not at OH services. The inspectors may question the work and quality of an OH service unit, but usually they do not, often due to lack of competence with regard to the work of OH services.

Helsetilsynet (the Health Inspectorate) is formally responsible for the examination of compliance with health service legislation. So far, it has paid little attention to OH services. This lack of public surveillance and attention, alongside a lack of public funding, may add to the free-market development of OH services in Norway. In reality, the services can sell what the enterprises are willing to pay for, with practically no interference from the public authorities.

Developmental trends and future perspectives of OH services in Norway

Currently, there is a trend towards the development of larger OH service units. Two new OH service chains have emerged, the largest covering almost 200,000 workers and owned by one of Norway's large insurance companies. Small units are being bought by large ones. Other units respond to the increasing competition by forming various types of formal or informal network. The situation is very similar to what has been seen in the Netherlands, Sweden and other European countries. There is reason to hope that the trend towards larger units may lead to higher quality. On the other hand, rising competition and lack of attention on the part of the Labour and Health Inspectorates may lead to the provision of new types of services, well out of line with the intentions of OH legislation. Personal massage and aromatherapy are examples of such services. Nowadays, they are easy to sell, but they scarcely accord with the reason for obliging certain types of enterprise to have an OH service.

Thus, many OH professionals are worried about the future of OH services in Norway. This is a consequence of both major, ongoing structural changes, and a lack of interest in OH on the part of the public authorities. There were great expectations among OH service personnel of the recently revised Work Environment Act, in particular in terms of hopes for public signals in favour of the certification of OH services and the provision of services to all workers. Once again, they were disappointed. In a small survey about OH services,[10] covering 300 OH professionals in 2004, the following question was asked: 'Will you be working in an OH service five years from now?' Thirty per cent replied 'yes', 50 per cent 'maybe' and 20 per cent 'probably not'. Many highly skilled OH professionals have left their jobs during the last five years, and there is at present a pessimistic feeling about the prospects for Norwegian OH services.

There are further difficulties with a free market in OH services in Norway. Virtually anyone can now be called an OH service provider. The authors' experience is that enterprises in Norway today are, unfortunately, not able to distinguish between good OH service providers and the charlatans who offer a product that is fundamentally divergent from what the Norwegian legislature regards as good OH practice.[9] Accordingly, many people in OH services feel that the present situation in Norway makes it necessary to have an obligatory certification system.

In the OH services survey of 2004 mentioned above,[10] 91 per cent of respondents were in favour of a certification system, even though they knew that they would have to pay for it themselves. Denmark has had a certification system for some years. Their system, which is inexpensive and easy to operate, may be a good model for OH services in Norway. Indeed, a similar system was proposed during the preparation of the recent revision of the Norwegian Work Environment Act. But no decisions have been taken so far.

Another question is who should be covered by OH services. Today, coverage is regulated by a Labour Inspectorate provision,[11] which stipulates the types of enterprises obliged to have an OH service unit. Many traditional health, environment and safety problems, such as chemical and physical exposures, are being taken care of better than ever before.

However, the psychosocial work environment, the problem of an ageing workforce, and rehabilitation and work capacity issues are tending to become ever more important. Accordingly, it is difficult to connect the need for OH services to certain specific trades or businesses. In the survey of 2004, 83 per cent of the professionals were in favour of providing OH services for all workers.[10] There is also a growing understanding among Norwegian politicians that OH services should be expanded to cover all workers over the long term. And a prerequisite for providing OH services for all is some type of quality control, such as an obligatory certification system.

The problem of OH services in relation to small and medium-sized enterprises (SMEs) is one that is shared across Europe. It also represents an increasing challenge, since more and more employees will work in SMEs in the future. Nordic experiences indicate that ensuring that SMEs have a contact person at an OH service with generalist OH competence and trouble-shooting ability may be one way of facilitating co-operation between SMEs and OH providers.[12] Giving financial support to SMEs to enable them to have basic OH services, with a main focus on risk assessment (as in Austria and Germany) may be beneficial.

Conclusions

There are good indications that OH services are an important contributor to health, environment and safety work in enterprises. They also seem to be a prerequisite for good rehabilitation work, which will be increasingly important given the ageing of the Norwegian workforce. There is, however, a need for more hard evidence on the outcomes of OH services, and this is a challenge for scientific OH environments. A Cochrane Collaboration[13] study for OH services is urgently needed and has recently been initiated.[14]

The present authors' view is that OH services in Norway should be expanded to cover all employees on an obligatory basis. A prerequisite for compulsory OH services is some type of quality assurance, eg a certification system. Otherwise, the service would be made obligatory without any demands in terms of content. Quite simply, market mechanisms do not seem to work when it comes to OH services. The certification system should be easy to implement at a low cost, creating as little bureaucracy as possible. Certification, however, only deals with a small part of the quality issue. National guidelines also seem to be beneficial, and are now available for OH physicians on the internet[15] and on CD-ROM as a part of the Norwegian electronic medical handbook. The guidelines are as evidence-based as possible.

Last but not least, customer orientation in OH services is important. Services should engage in discussion with their customers (managers and workers' representatives), and decide what to focus on in the coming years. OH services should refrain from activities that do not meet the professional and ethical standards of good OH practice. Integrity and evaluation of the services is a fundamental part of good ethics.[16] Health, environment and safety work requires the joint efforts of the employer, the employees and highly professional and multidisciplinary OH personnel. A consequence of customer interaction should be a more skilled and satisfied customer – who then asks for the right types of service.

References

1. Natvig H & Thiis-Evensen E. *Arbeidsmiljø og helse. Yrkeshygienens og bedriftshelsetjenestens frembrudd og utvickling i Norge* (Work environment and health. The rise and development of industrial hygiene and occupational health services in Norway). Oslo: Norsk Bedriftshelsetjeneste, 1989.
2. Fagsekretariatet for Bedriftshelsetjenesten. *Oversikt, bedriftshelsetjenesten i Norge* (Occupational health service register in Norway). Available online at apps.didac.no/bht (viewed 19 April 2007).
3. Council Directive 89/391/EEC of 12 June 1989 on the introduction of measures to encourage improvements in the safety and health of workers at work (the Framework Directive). *Official Journal* L183; 29 June 1989: 1–8.
4. Hämäläinen R M, Husman K, Räsänen K, Westerholm P & Rantanen J. *Survey of the quality and effectiveness of occupational health services in the European Union, Norway and Switzerland.* Research Report 45. Helsinki: Työterveyslaitos (Finnish Institute of Occupational Health), 2001. Preface available online at www.occuphealth.fi/Internet/partner/tthosicoh/Publications/Book_People+and+work+Research+Reports+45.htm (viewed 19 April 2007).
5. Bjørnstad O. *Bedriftshelsetjenesten og helsearbeid i virksomheter – et fokus på tjenester til bedriftene innen områdene ernæring, fysisk aktivitet, røyking, alkohol* (Occupational health services and health work in enterprises: a focus on services to workers in the fields of nutrition, physical activity, smoking and alcohol) Report 2005:2. Oslo: Statens Arbeidsmiljøinstitutt, 2005. Available online at www.stami.no/Forsiden/filestore/05nr.2.pdf (viewed 19 April 2007).
6. Lie A, Gudding I H, Bjørnstad O & Aasnæss S. 'Inclusive Working Life' in Norway – a challenge to the occupational health services. *Book of abstracts, ICOH Conference 2004 in Modena.* Rome: International Commission on Occupational Health, 2004: page 38.
7. Lie A, Jacobsen K, Aasnæss S, Ingebrigtsen A & Bakken B. *Inkluderende arbeidsliv: hva karakteriserer de gode virksomhetene?* (Inclusive working life: what characterises

successful enterprises?) Report 2005:7. Oslo: Statens Arbeidsmiljøinstitutt, 2005. Available online at www.stami.no/Forsiden/filestore/05nr.7.pdf (viewed 19 April 2007).

8. Lie T, Karlsen J E & Tharaldsen J E. *Evaluering av verne- og helsepersonale i virksomhetene*. Report 1999/007. Stavanger: Rogalandsforskning, 1999.

9. Lie A, Bjørnstad O & Jacobsen K. *Good occupational health service: workbook with audit matrix*. Version 5. Oslo: Statens Arbeidsmiljøinstitutt, 2000. Available online at www.stami.no/filestore/01nr.2eng.pdf (viewed 20 April 2007).

10. Bjørnstad O. *Landskonferansen for bedriftshelsetjenesten 2004*. Lillestrøm: Statens Arbeidsmiljøinstitutt, 2004.

11. Arbeidstilsynet. *Forskrift om hvilke virksomheter som skal ha knyttet til seg verne- og helsepersonale (bedriftshelsetjeneste)* (Provision on which enterprises must have an occupational health service). Forskrift 914/1989. Oslo: Arbeidstilsynet, 1989. Available online at www.lovdata.no/cgi-wift/ldles?doc=/sf/sf/sf-19890608-0914.html (viewed 20 April 2007).

12. Olesen K. *Evaluation of occupational health services in small enterprises*. Taastrup: Teknologisk Institut, Arbejdsliv, 2001 (in Danish).

13. For more information on the Cochrane Collaboration, see www.cochrane.org/index.htm (viewed 14 May 2007).

14. Verbeek J H, Dijk F J van, Malmivaara A, Hulshof C T, Rasanen K, Kankaanpaa E E *et al*. Evidence-based medicine for occupational health. *Scandinavian Journal of Work and Environmental Health* 2002; 28 (3): 197–204.

15. Norsk Arbeidsmedisinsk Forening. *Arbeidsmedisinske veiledninger*. Available online at www.nhi.no/amv (viewed 20 April 2007).

16. Westerholm P, Øvretveit J & Nilstun T. *Practical ethics in occupational health*. Oxford: Radcliffe Medical Press, 2004.

Occupational health services in Sweden

Lars Bohlin and Lars Hjalmarson, Swedish Association of Occupational Safety and Health, Stockholm, and Peter Westerholm, University of Uppsala

Structure of services, distribution and coverage

Occupational health services in Sweden – developments since 1992

The establishment of occupational health (OH) services in Sweden took place between the 1960s and the 1980s. It was based on national collective agreements between the social partners in the labour market. These agreements included provisions for health and safety at work and for commissioning OH expertise on work environment matters and occupational care. On this basis, OH services were developed into a set of non-public health service units operating through collective agreements between employers and trade unions. The OH service unit or department was commonly subordinated to a bipartite body at local level (representing employers and trade unions), which dealt with matters of occupational safety and health. From early on, a significant part of service output was the curative care provided by occupational physicians, occupational nurses and physiotherapists. OH services received funding subsidies of 20–25 per cent of their annual budget from the public social insurance system. The formal motive for this arrangement was to provide financial compensation to OH service organisations for curative services provided under the Swedish public health service.

In 1992 and 1993, important changes took place with significant consequences for the conditions of existence of OH service organisations. The collective work environment agreement between the social partners – ie Svenska Arbetsgivareföreningen (the Swedish employers' confederation, SAF), Landsorganisationen i Sverige (the Swedish trade union confederation, LO), and Privattjänstemannakartellen (the federation of salaried employees in industry and services, PTK) – was terminated, and the government withdrew all state economic subsidies. The deregulation compelled OH service units to assume the role of free agents in the health service market. In parallel, there was a structural development, involving increasing numbers of mergers of OH service units into fewer but larger organisations. The ownership picture changed accordingly. The number of health professionals in the OH sector decreased rapidly (by approximately one-third).

Number of OH service organisations

There is at the present time no reliable information on the number of active OH service units and enterprises on the market, or on the number of OH professionals employed. Nor are there any obligations to notify or record activities, to undertake quality certification, or to register as a provider of health services. What constitutes an OH service is not legally defined, and the concept of the OH service does not therefore have any formal legal protection. The term 'OH service' may refer to anything from a quality-certified comprehensive service to the provision of the services of a single physiotherapist.

Föreningen Svensk Företagshälsovård (the Swedish Association of Occupational Safety and Health, FSF) estimates the current number of OH service organisations at just over 700. Some of these, roughly 150 units, are very small, consisting of only one health professional. In February 2004, the number of legal OH service entities – ie companies or undertakings – was estimated in a joint report by Arbetsmiljöverket (the Swedish Work Environment Authority,

SWEA) and Arbetslivsinstitutet (the National Institute for Working Life, NIWL) as approximately 250, many of which have numerous subsidiaries. There is an ongoing structural rationalisation, implying mergers of OH service undertakings. The two largest companies, Previa and FeelGood, jointly own roughly 130 units.

OH service staff and competences

The staffing of OH service organisations in Sweden is not standardised. Commonly, there are occupational physicians, occupational nurses, physiotherapists, ergonomists, work environment engineers and psychologists on most OH service teams. Presently, there are roughly 800 occupational physicians, 1,500 occupational nurses, 600–700 physiotherapists and ergonomists, 300 work environment or safety engineers, and 250–300 psychologists. In addition, there is a heterogeneous category of 200 other professionals, including health promoters, health educationalists, occupational therapists and social workers, as well as staff with managerial and administrative tasks.

For many years, the training of OH professionals has been organised at the NIWL, or at universities by contract with the NIWL. Following a decision by the government formed after the 2006 elections, the NIWL will be closed down and all staff disbanded on 01 July 2007. It has not yet been decided how the training of OH professionals will be organised after that date.

Occupational physicians currently go through a diploma course of nine weeks, with a curriculum stretching over one and a half academic years (NIWL, Stockholm) or one academic year (University of Göteborg), plus a tutored field project to be carried out by and presented at a final examination. The course is rated as equivalent to 15 university credits (20 credits equal roughly half a year of university studies). From July 2007, a new specialism for physicians will be introduced, carrying the title 'occupational and environmental medicine', which implies significant changes to the present training. This new specialism will be available as a specialised option that students can take immediately after receiving their MD degree. It is predicted that this will lead to the recruitment and specialist training of younger occupational physicians than at present. It is not possible at this stage to predict the systematic impact on OH services of the introduction of the new specialism, which has already been decided on and outlined by Socialstyrelsen (the National Board of Health and Welfare).

OH nurses are trained on a 40-credit training programme stretching over one academic year, which includes a 13-week course at the NIWL in Stockholm or at the Universities of Lund or Örebro. A tutored field project is required, just as for occupational physicians. Occupational physiotherapists and ergonomists go through a 20-credit training programme stretching over one academic year, with a six-week curriculum at the NIWL and Karolinska Institutet in Stockholm, or at the University of Lund. A tutored field project is required.

Occupational psychologists attend a five-and-a-half-week course stretching over one academic year. Completion of a field project with an accompanying report is required. Until now, work environment engineers have been trained at the NIWL in Umeå on a half-time study programme of two years. The programme gives 40 university credits.

One immediate consequence of the closure of the NIWL is that training programmes for OH professionals need to be transferred immediately to universities. At the time of writing (December 2006), it is not known how this will be carried out. It is very likely that there will be revisions of vocational training curricula at the same time.

OH service coverage

In a report published in 2001,[1] based on a questionnaire survey of private companies and public administration, Statskontoret (the Swedish Agency for Public Management) estimated that the number of employees covered by OH services in any form is approximately 2.6 million. This estimate implies that around 1 million employees in Sweden have no organised OH care. The great majority of these – about 750,000 – work in small enterprises. The number of employees in the public sector with access to OH care was estimated at 1.2 million, and the corresponding number of private employees at 1.4 million. On this calculation, the proportion of employees covered by OH services was estimated at 72 per cent.

Legal basis for OH services

The Swedish Work Environment Act (Arbetsmiljölagen, AML) defines an OH service as:

> ... an independent expert resource within the areas of work environment and rehabilitation. In particular, an OH service is to take action aimed at the prevention and elimination of health hazards at work and to be competent in identifying and describing the relationships between work environment, organisation, productivity and health (Section 3d §2b).[2]

The role of OH services is defined as advisory. The task is clearly of significant scope. There are, however, no official criteria for what counts as an 'expert' or 'competent' resource. Without such criteria or norms, the legal requirements quickly lose their meaning.

Legal regulation: interaction with client undertakings

A cornerstone of the AML is that employers are responsible by law for work conditions and the health and safety of employees at work. In situations where employers find themselves unable to fulfil their duties, they are obliged to consult external expertise, such as an OH service. The rules concerning OH care are linked to the employer's obligation, under Section 3 §2a of the AML, to pursue 'systematic work environment management' ('systematiskt arbetsmiljöarbete', or SAM) and to ensure that there are suitably organised programmes for work adaptation and vocational rehabilitation. It should be noted that the requirement to consult with OH services is directly connected to rules on systematic work environment activities, both in the AML and in regulations issued by the SWEA.

Section 3 §2b of the AML stipulates that employers must take responsibility to ensure that the OH care necessitated by work conditions is at their disposal. It is important to note that this does not entail a demand on employers actually to use OH services. The duty of employers stretches only to ensuring that they have access to a particular service and that the OH service consulted is judged to possess the necessary competences to deal with the existing work conditions.

In 2001 it was made explicit in regulatory texts issued by the SWEA[3] that the employer's duty to obtain external help applies when his or her own operational competences are not sufficient for SAM. For adaptation of work tasks and the work environment or vocational rehabilitation, employers need to seek expertise or equivalent competent advice from outside. It is at the employer's discretion to judge whether this is needed. In this regard, the regulation is very broadly framed:

> When OH services or equivalent expert help is commissioned, it must be sufficient in scope, and possess adequate competence and resources, for the work in question.

There are no underlying criteria or norms to help interpret the regulation. The general assumption and rationale is that the assistance of OH services, or of another external expert, is necessary to compensate for insufficient competence on the part of the employer.

The ILO Convention

In 1985, the International Labour Organization (ILO) adopted Convention 161[4] on occupational healthcare. Under the articles of the Convention, requirements are specified for the organisation of OH services in the member states of the ILO. These include guidelines for national OH service policies and more detailed specifications of responsibilities, tasks and organisational aspects. Countries ratifying the Convention, including Sweden, assume a legal commitment to take steps to organise OH services so that they are accessible to the entire labour force.

Sweden's compliance with the legal requirements of Convention 161 can be summarily described. There has been no direct transposition of the ideas and intentions of the Convention into Swedish legislation.

The EU Framework Directive[5]

The European Union (EU) Framework Directive has had a major influence on Swedish law and provision of OH services. The Directive aims:

> ... especially in the working environment, to guarantee a better level of protection of the safety and health of workers so as to secure a higher level of protection for employees.

It lays down 'minimum requirements':

- Article 7(1) addresses protective and preventive services. It states that 'the employer shall designate one or more workers to carry out activities related to the protection and prevention of occupational risks for the undertaking and/or establishment'.
- Article 7(3) regulates the use of expert help. 'If such protective and preventive measures cannot be organised for lack of competent personnel in the undertaking and/or establishment, the employer shall enlist competent external services or persons.'

In Sweden, the reference to 'competent external services' has commonly been interpreted to mean OH services. This is no coincidence. In consequence, the rules on 'competent external services or persons' have been transposed into Swedish regulations through the parts of SAM that involve OH services.[3]

The European Social Charter

In 1954, the Council of Europe embarked on the preparation of a European Social Charter as a complement to the European Convention. The Charter was made available for ratification in 1961, and was ratified by Sweden the following year. Some specific articles, however, were not ratified. The Charter came into force in 1965.

The Charter lists a series of principles and obligations to be pursued by ratifying countries. The first part of the list includes the statement that 'all workers have the right to safe and healthy working conditions'. The second part (Articles 1–19) lays down the rights which the signatories have committed to guarantee, including a commitment 'to formulate, implement and periodically review a coherent national policy on occupational safety, occupational health and the working environment'.

This Social Charter was revised in 1996. In 1998, Sweden ratified the revised Charter, with the exception of Article 3.4,[6] which carries an obligation 'to promote the progressive development of occupational health services for all workers with essentially preventive and advisory functions'. Sweden refrained from ratifying Article 3.4 while awaiting the outcome of a then-ongoing government inquiry into OH services. The report of the public inquiry was presented in December 2004. A decision by the government is still pending in December 2006.

Relationship to the national public health services

Current legislation does not envisage that OH services will be given tasks in the public healthcare system. To the extent, however, that there are client demands on OH services to deliver curative treatment, individual agreements on such arrangements may be negotiated by OH service organisations and concluded with local authorities (according to regulations in the Healthcare Act). This has met resistance in many local authorities.

Main focus of programmes

Range of services supplied by OH providers

OH service organisations have a task agenda deriving from official occupational safety and health regulations. There are, in addition, other tasks arising from the role of OH services as a player in a health market supplying services demanded by clients. These include voluntary health examinations, keep-fit activities, curative medical care, and activities assigned to the generic category of health promotion.

In a report based on a questionnaire survey concerning the scope of services provided by OH service undertakings in 2001, Statskontoret gave the information on OH service organisations' performance shown in Table 1. It is based on the services' own assessment of consumption of professional time in serving client companies.

The validity and precision of these assessments are questionable. In particular, on the basis of a questionnaire survey, there is a certain degree of arbitrariness in allocating activities to statutory and non-statutory categories. Also, the response rate to the questionnaire was only around 50 per cent. It may well be that some of the activities specified as being beyond employers' obligations are in fact statutory. Reservations have been voiced about the survey method and also the interpretation of results. The important point, however, is that a substantial proportion of the activities of OH services do not seem to derive from the definition of those tasks in prevailing legislation. The breadth of scope of activities is considerable. Significant resources are taken up by rehabilitation (both examination and treatment), which accounts for about 20 per cent of activities. It is also noteworthy that the areas that might be expected to show large proportions – employers' compliance with SAM, technical services, and organisational development – are rated as jointly forming only a small part of service performance.

The Work Environment Survey of 2003, carried out by Statistiska Centralbyrån (Statistics Sweden),[7] contained a number of questions about OH services that had not been previously asked, which means that it is difficult to compare with previous surveys. While it should be noted that 67 per cent of respondents reported having access to an OH service, not all of these may have been aware of the activities OH services actually undertake. Of respondents with access to an OH service, 28 per cent (women 25.9 per cent, men 31.1 per cent) reported that they had received a visit from an OH service unit in their workplace during the preceding year. When asked whether an OH service had made an assessment of their work situation as an individual, 29.5 per cent (women 27.2 per cent, men 31.1 per cent) answered yes.

Table 1
Time distribution
of activities
undertaken by
OH services

Activity	% of total activity
Statutory health examinations	5.5
Systematic work-environment tasks (SAM)	7.6
Training in first aid, crisis management	3.0
Basic training in the work environment	3.0
Investigation of rehabilitation needs	11.8
Rehabilitation treatment	8.3
Training in rehabilitation methods	1.7
Education/training of risk groups for rehabilitation purposes	2.8
Subtotal for activities related to employers' mandatory/statutory obligations	*43.2*
Work-related healthcare (curative)	9.6
Other healthcare	4.3
Education/training (not rehabilitation)	3.6
Supervision of and support for managers	2.3
Keep-fit activities, including health profiling	4.5
Health examinations (not statutory)	6.5
Conflict/crisis management	2.7
Alcohol and drugs	1.9
Organisational development	1.9
Work injuries (examinations, assessments)	2.0
Technical services	4.3
Other activities	1.9
Skills development (OH service personnel)	2.1
In-house development	2.1
Administrative tasks	7.2
Subtotal for other activities	*56.8*
Total for all activities	**100**

Target of intervention	Men %	Women %	Both sexes %
Work postures, work movements or heavy workload	27.5	23.6	25.7
High work-related strain or stress	17.3	13.6	15.6
Co-operation or relations in the workplace	8.9	7.5	8.2
Adaptation of work tasks or rehabilitation	8.6	6.0	7.4
Technical equipment (machinery, lighting, noise and so on)	21.1	13.7	17.6
Sickness absence	7.4	5.6	6.5
Alcohol/drug abuse	4.2	1.6	3.0
Other	10.4	7.6	9.1

Table 2
Distribution of targets of OH services' interventions

Accordingly, a supplementary question was posed to respondents who had received some form of intervention from OH services to ascertain what each intervention was about. This gave an opportunity to broaden the picture of the work of the services. The affirmative responses were distributed as shown in Table 2.

The work of OH services was assessed as 'very good' or 'quite good' by 66.9 per cent of respondents (women 67.9 per cent, men 66.4 per cent). On the other hand, in a nationwide field questionnaire survey of OH services, Westerholm & Bostedt[8] observed in 2004 that company managers' and trade union representatives' appraisals of OH services' competences varied according to the problem area. Competence in ergonomics and the provision of medical services was consistently rated as 'good' or 'high', whereas competence in stress-related health disorders and work organisation were given much lower ratings.

Tasks and orientation of OH services

As emphasised above, the work done by OH services is advisory. It is stated in the AML that OH services 'shall work especially towards the prevention and elimination of health hazards in workplaces'. The looseness of this definition of the task becomes even more obvious when the necessary competences of OH services are described. The services must be able 'to identify and describe the relationships between work environment, organisation, productivity and health'. It should be observed that this general provision in the Act reflects an ambition to influence, in general terms, the direction of OH services' activities without providing instruments of control in the form of incentives or legal sanctions. OH service organisations are players in a free market, and may in principle engage themselves in whatever they like as long as they have clients to pay for it. In practice, this implies seeking to comply with customer demands. Since the phrase 'occupational health service' is not patented, practically any organisation active in the work environment arena can describe itself as a provider of OH care.

A reasonable conclusion is that, given the market dependence of OH service organisations, the direction of OH services cannot be governed by the rules in current Swedish legislation that indicate what the organisations should do. The Act may specify the services requiring external competence that employers should purchase, but can hardly compel a player on the market to supply them. If the range of services is to be pushed in a certain direction, it must correspond to client demand. No-one can seriously demand that OH service undertakings – operating in a free market – must maintain a stock of services for which there is no demand. Accordingly, the provision in the AML concerning what services 'shall work with especially' comes across as superfluous rhetoric. In any case, it can be regarded as having only a minimal impact.

Quality and its development

When the state subsidy to OH services was abolished in 1992, the quality control that consisted in examining whether an OH service unit met the terms and conditions specified in collective agreements between employers and trade unions also disappeared. Accordingly, in 1993, the government commissioned the Swedish Work Environment Fund to support the development of a system for establishing norms for assessing the quality of OH service organisations. A project was set up with representatives of the agencies concerned, the parties to the labour market (trade unions and employers' associations) and OH services themselves. The project resulted in 1995 in a draft quality manual for Swedish OH services, which introduced a system for quality assurance based on a combination of ISO 9001 and selected parts of the Swedish Quality Award standard (Utmärkelsen Svensk Kvalitet, USK). Responsibility for administering and revising the document was placed on the OH services' umbrella organisation, the FSF. The quality manual was eventually approved by the Swedish Board for Accreditation and Conformity (SWEDAC), the state agency responsible.

Following adoption, the standard quality assurance system has been used by OH service organisations for voluntary certification via an auditing process. The auditing and certification are handled by organisations or bodies accredited by SWEDAC following a statutory procedure. There are at present (December 2006) five accredited certification bodies for Swedish OH service organisations.

The original quality manual, renamed *Requirement specifications for Swedish occupational health services*, has undergone major revision. It now entirely follows the new SS-EN ISO 9001:2000 quality standard, with – as previously – specific supplementary requirements for OH services. The National Board of Health and Welfare's regulations concerning quality assurance and quality development, and also the SWEA's prescriptions regarding systematic work-environment activities,[3] have been integrated into the manual. It is envisaged that revisions will take place in consultation with a broad range of stakeholders, including public agencies, client systems and labour market organisations. The current position of state stakeholders on quality issues in OH services has been clarified by the SWEA,[9,10] but the OH service quality system has not been assessed independently in published reports, either as a consumer evaluation or as a third-party evaluation.

There is no central register of third-party certified OH service units. According to the SWEA/NIWL report mentioned above, there were 48 certified OH service undertakings in August 2002. The certified OH service units had 2,200 employees, which corresponds to approximately 43 per cent of all employees in the sector (according to Statskontoret's estimate). The client companies of these undertakings have around 1,235,000 employees, representing 34 per cent of the Swedish labour force.

Size of organisation	Mean expenditure per employee per year on OH services, €	
	Private sector	Public sector
<10 employees	126	113
10–49 employees	120	98
50–199 employees	194	96
>200 employees	145	93
Unweighted mean	146	100

Table 3
Annual cost of OH care per employee by size of company and sector

To these figures should be added the in-company OH service units of large enterprises and corporations. These are generally encompassed by the parent company's organisation and quality management system. Thus, the numbers and proportions of people in employment covered by quality-certified OH services given above are underestimates.

Financing structure

In its report of 2001, Statskontoret reported the average annual cost per client and employee for contracted occupational healthcare by size of company.

The average values shown in Table 3 reflect major differences with regard to the opportunities for OH services to take action in different workplaces. Inspection of the raw data from 2002 (not shown) makes these differences even clearer. There were companies that invested more than €316 per employee per year on OH, but there was one municipality showing an annual cost of only €14.

It should be observed that the average cost per contract is not likely to give a full picture of economic relationships, since there is a significant variation in the nature of the business relations between client companies and OH service undertakings. No official statistics exist on the service content of basic OH services (sometimes called 'standard packages') or on supplementary services that are customised and charged per item. There is, however, an observable tendency for client enterprises, in particular smaller companies, primarily to seek person-oriented, curative services.

In the Swedish public sector there is a procurement procedure for OH services which entails the assessment of quality and cost. Experience shows that perceptions of quality vary significantly. Price therefore often turns out to be the decisive factor in signing service contracts.

Public surveillance

The National Board of Health and Welfare supervises the registered medical personnel of OH services. The SWEA has the task of 'monitoring and promoting' occupational healthcare, but does not exercise any direct surveillance.

Strengths and weaknesses: the need for development and change

One important strength of Swedish OH services lies in its extensive coverage, both geographically and quantitatively, of the Swedish labour force. Also, in terms of competence, the professional skills of the staff of Swedish OH services are generally recognised by clients as reasonably satisfactory. Most existing OH service organisations can present a multidisciplinary set of competences, involving occupational physicians and nurses, physiotherapists and ergonomists, work-environment engineers, and psychologists.

As mentioned above, Sweden has a purely demand-governed market for OH services, which gives rise to several problems. Firstly, the demands of clients may not match the needs of the populations served. There may be unaddressed needs that are not raised, or even unknown to the client. Client enterprises operate in an increasingly short-termist economic reality, characterised by quarterly financial reporting and immediate decision-making. In a market where OH service organisations compete for contracts, client companies may regard a low cost of OH provision to be a more important and competitive characteristic than perceived service quality. Under such circumstances, long-term preventive programmes and comprehensive risk/cost assessments become less attractive and, consequently, less in demand. They are perceived as time-consuming and fraught with practical and educational problems. It should also be added that, in Sweden, a large proportion of the cost of long-term sickness absence is borne by the national social insurance system, ie the taxpayer. This means that there are no strong incentives for employers to assume an active role in dealing with long-term sickness absence and vocational rehabilitation.

The second problem is largely professional and ethical by nature, and is related to the multiple loyalties of the professionals involved. OH service personnel have been groomed in professional ethical conduct, and are also subject to their own professional association's rules. Among other things, this entails giving priority to what can be called the 'work line' – that is, the goal of keeping people in work or enabling their return to work. This imposes the professional responsibility of taking into account the perspectives of individual employees, the employer and society at large, not just those aspects that the client company deems important.

These two perspectives in the market for OH services highlight another area concerned with competence within the sector. Given a health market with competition as a prominent characteristic, what are the priorities for the development of professional and managerial skills? Here, it has to be remembered that development is to be paid for by the clients.

Firstly, there is the challenge of developing the competence and ability to take on the dominant OH challenges of a changing world. A consequential question is whether such skills and competences can be achieved by OH services as they are presently organised.

Secondly, OH services must strike a balance between developing health professionals' skills and competence within areas such as marketing and communications. The latter are essential to survival in a market where competition is the most obvious determining feature.

Thirdly, there is the issue of how, by adopting a long-term, holistic and sustainable perspective, good occupational healthcare can be provided. In the authors' experience, given the realities of Swedish working life, the practical implementation of 'multidisciplinarity' in OH services is no easy task.

Traditionally, OH services in Sweden have benefited from meeting the vitally important long-term conditions for efficient collaboration between employers and employees and their organisations. For several reasons, this spirit of collaboration and mutual trust was eroded in key respects during the second half of the 1990s. However, there are signs that the relationship is now recovering. Sweden has still some way to go to achieve the consensual spirit that provided the precondition for collective agreements on OH, including consultations with external bodies such as OH services. On the other hand, there are indicators of increasing awareness, on the part of both employers and trade unions, of workplace health and life quality issues, and of a healthy environment, as vitally important assets in terms of company productivity and survival on the market. From this perspective, the cost of long-term sickness absence is a real problem. In 2005, the government imposed a legal obligation on employers to contribute 15 per cent of the long-term sickness costs that were previously borne entirely by taxpayers. The implications of this regulation, with ensuing expectations regarding the performance of OH service organisations, remain to be seen. In any case, this new awareness presents a major challenge to Swedish OH services.

OH service development – the current societal climate

Generally speaking, business prospects can be regarded as very good for OH service undertakings operating in a commercial health market. The issues involved are increasingly attracting strategic interest on the part of companies, since there is growing awareness of their links to productivity.

At a political level, however, there is some uncertainty. The new Swedish government, primarily through the Ministry of Finance, seems bent on retaining the full market dependence of OH service organisations. In the parliamentary elections of September 2006, the Social Democrats were defeated and replaced in government by a four-party Conservative, Liberal, Centre and Christian Democratic alliance. It is thought unlikely that the new government will intervene and commit itself to significant economic investments to subsidise or otherwise support OH service organisations on the Swedish labour market. A policy intended to retain full market dependence of OH services will mean that the OH agenda is determined primarily by customer/client demands and the services for which the customer is willing to pay. The state, by implication, will downgrade the importance of OH as a domain in the broader arena of public health. The current quandary of the Swedish government is one of balancing the pressures for short-term cost containment against the medium- and long-term benefits and profits to be obtained from OH investments that serve public health objectives. Clearly, the requirements arising from the ratification of ILO Convention 161 on OH services are demanding. A political commitment to guarantee access to OH services to everyone in the Swedish labour force will probably incur costs for Swedish taxpayers. This is likely to be an important disincentive for the new government.

Reflecting on this dilemma, the authors consider that it is important to take into account the significant costs of sickness absence and the high rates of early retirements and exits from the Swedish labour market. Some fundamental issues concerning the role and financing of Swedish OH services were examined in the recent public inquiry (mentioned above). The position of the government on these issues is not known at present.

Conclusions

The current and likely future state of OH services in Sweden can be summarised in the following points:

- OH services in Sweden are most likely to remain dependent for survival on income from a market consisting of client enterprises and organisations, in both the public and private sectors, that make purchases primarily for the prevention of health hazards at work and vocational rehabilitation

- one of the durable features of the OH market is competition for contracts between service providers, which challenges professional quality and ethics
- it remains to be seen whether OH service organisations offering prevention and occupational rehabilitation without any curative element have a sustainable future in the Swedish health market
- the state is unlikely to withdraw from its present commitment to provide specialist education to OH service professionals via the funding of training programmes
- the need for ongoing competence development of OH professionals following specialist training is to be met by the professionals themselves, in interaction with their markets
- there is a considerable challenge in confronting the essential need to strengthen and recast the competence profile of OH service organisations
- the present voluntary quality-assurance system of Swedish OH services, which leads to accredited certification, still needs to be evaluated with regard to its impact on OH and its relevance to public health
- employers are responsible for occupational safety and health at work, including the prevention of health hazards. OH service organisations and professionals assume advisory roles in this regard. Vocational rehabilitation is a responsibility shared between employers and public health bodies, primarily social insurance agencies. OH service professionals assume an advisory role in this area as well
- the curative healthcare tasks of OH services and the integration of these tasks into the functions of the public health service are currently an unresolved problem.

References

1. Statskontoret. *Utnyttja företagshälsovården bättre* (Better use of occupational health services). Report 2001:29. Stockholm: Statskontoret, 2001. Available online at www.statskontoret.se/upload/Publikationer/2001/200129.pdf (viewed 23 April 2007).
2. Arbetsmiljölagen 1977:1160 (Work Environment Act). English version, as amended in July 2005, available online at www.av.se/inenglish/lawandjustice/workact (viewed 23 April 2007).
3. Arbetsmiljöverket. *Systematiskt arbetsmiljöarbete*. AFS 2001:1. Stockholm: Arbetsmiljöverket, 2001.
4. International Labour Organization. Occupational Health Services Convention. C161. Geneva: ILO, 1985. Available online at www.ilo.org/ilolex/cgi-lex/convde.pl?C161 (viewed 23 April 2007).
5. Council Directive 89/391/EEC of 12 June 1989 on the introduction of measures to encourage improvements in the safety and health of workers at work (the Framework Directive). *Official Journal* L183; 29 June 1989: 1–8.
6. Government Bill 1997/98: 82, pages 19ff. Report 1997/98 AU12, Circular Letter 1997/98: 187.
7. Statistiska Centralbyrån & Arbetsmiljöverket. *Arbetsmiljön 2003* (The work environment 2003). Report AM 68 SM 0401. Stockholm: Statistiska Centralbyrån, 2003.
8. Westerholm P & Bostedt G. Företagshälsovården i förändring (Occupational health services in change). In: Johansson B, Frick K & Johansson J (eds). *Framtidens arbetsmiljö- och tillsynsarbete* (Future work environment and law enforcement). Lund: Studentlitteratur, 2004.
9. Arbetsmiljöverket. *Kompetens, kvalitet och kundnytta* (Competence, quality and benefits to customers). Stockholm: Arbetsmiljöverket, 2004.

10.   Statens Offentliga Utredningar. *Utveckling av god företagshälsovård – ny lagstiftning och andra åtgärder. 2003 års Företagshälsovårdsutredning.* Report SOU 2004:113. Available online at www.regeringen.se/sb/d/264/a/34689 (viewed 23 April 2007).

The future for occupational health in the United Kingdom*

Lawrence Waterman, Sypol Ltd and London 2012 Olympics Delivery Authority

Introduction

The United Kingdom (UK) does not have, as this chapter will show, a single, coherent approach to the provision of occupational health (OH) services or access to those which do exist. OH is a patchwork quilt of public and private providers, with some limited encouragement for their utilisation from statutory requirements for health surveillance. Since the 1970s, the UK has had a health and safety strategy that has driven down the rate of accidents, injuries and deaths at work, but the realisation of the huge cost burden and personal suffering associated with health issues has lagged far behind. This has led to a number of 'calls to arms' at a national level, as new initiatives have been launched and have tested some of the emerging ideas from this effort in pilot studies exploring new ways of bringing employers, especially small and medium-sized enterprises (SMEs), into contact with good, practical advice. This chapter seeks to outline both the national debate, the models that have emerged and how they have been or are being tested. Above all, this chapter argues that this process represents the mainstreaming of occupational health in the UK system for health and safety, and in the process encourages a workplace, management-centred approach rather than an occupational physician-led strategy.

Background

The UK does not have a statutory OH service. When this matter is raised, the response historically has been to point out that the UK has a National Health Service (NHS) which provides medical care free at the point of delivery (with minor exceptions such as prescription and dental charges, but even these apply only to a proportion of people of working age), and that this can encompass the personal needs of workers arising from their employment. As a result, the OH services available have been provided in three unco-ordinated ways.

State provision

It has become a commonplace that the NHS doesn't 'do prevention', only treatment, so there was never a place for health surveillance and initiatives to reduce workers' exposure to health risks. In theory the NHS should be available for routine matters such as audiology but in practice the resources are not there. The NHS is primarily a treatment service: individual workers who have developed an illness through exposure to health risks at work can be treated, but the link back to the workplace to prevent harm to work colleagues is absent. Rehabilitation support for injured workers declined during the 1980s, as the government did not require the managers and funders of healthcare, the regional health authorities, to provide rehabilitation services. At the same time, there was great pressure to reduce expenditure in real terms. This resulted in the closure of established units which had helped returning injured and disabled war veterans.

Employer provision

The practice of directly employing a small team of occupational physicians, nurses and support staff has always been restricted to the largest of companies, public bodies such as

---

* This paper is dedicated to the memory of George Brumwell (1939–2005), former general secretary of the construction trades union UCATT, and architect of and inspiration to Constructing Better Health.

local government, and often those with a statutory obligation to conduct health checks, for example airlines obliged to evaluate the health of pilots. These directly employed teams suffered huge reductions in the 1980s and early 1990s as part of the general business dynamic described as 'downsizing and business re-engineering'. Many such services were cut because they had been run by people who assumed that what they did was self-evidently beneficial and as a result there were no business justifications which could win over boards wielding the financial axe. Similarly, the few group schemes, such as those set up by the Nuffield charitable trust, for numbers of companies in a particular area, found it very hard to maintain their subscriptions and survive.

Private provision
This is paid for by contracting service users – ie employers – but run outside the organisation with a restricted menu on offer. The quality of this provision varies wildly. On one hand, there are highly professional private services, where the difference between in-house support and the external supplier is simply in the payment arrangements – an invoice rather than a payroll number. On the other hand, the sector also includes wholly inappropriate health checks, with blood cholesterol testing for executives high on the list, alongside a failure to engage with the worker–workplace–task interface. With horror stories such as the well-documented 15 years of lung surveillance demonstrating the level of silicosis among stonemasons[1] but no linkage to workplace controls on dust exposure, it is important to recognise that debates about the numbers of OH physicians available if the UK really begins to take up OH miss the point. More may not be better!

This state of affairs, with only 8 per cent of private sector companies using some form of OH support[2] and by 2005 over 2.5 million people on incapacity benefit,* has finally been identified as undesirable. Government analysis suggests that there are four outcomes to having such a large group excluded from the workforce:

- the people themselves are impoverished, for however generous the benefits may be, they fall short of the income of those on the UK's minimum wage
- the exclusion from the workplace has other consequences in social interaction, resulting in many in this group being more generally socially excluded
- the workplace is denied the labour that the workers could provide, and labour shortages have been an issue for certain sectors of UK industry during a period of strong growth relative to other economies in the late 1990s and early 21st century
- there is a national financial cost if people are receiving benefits rather than being in employment, where they pay income taxes and make national insurance contributions. This has formed a business case for 'UK plc' to address OH more seriously than it has in the past.

One of the strengths in the current position is provided by the professional bodies for the range of OH disciplines. The Faculty of Occupational Medicine has been particularly far-seeing, developing guidelines deliberately designed to empower people with or at risk from work-related ill health. The guidelines on back pain, one of the major causes of ill health absence from work, were drawn up after the careful evaluation of outcomes from different interventions, providing very clear evidence-based advice.[3,4] This was a partnership between

---

* Incapacity benefit is paid to people of working age who have been certified by medical practitioners as unable to work because of ill health. The largest categories are those incapacitated by mental ill health (most commonly depression) and through musculoskeletal disorders – these two account for approximately two-thirds of the total.

the Faculty and the British Occupational Health Research Foundation. It provides a comprehensive guide to the ways in which OH practitioners can reduce the scale of this major problem. There are 14 professional bodies for practitioners of aspects of OH and together they form a collective grouping to facilitate discussion on strategic matters, called Professional Organisations in Occupational Safety and Health. This group, co-ordinated since its inception by the Institution of Occupational Safety and Health and now administered by the Faculty of Occupational Medicine, is currently working on a guide to help employers and workers who are seeking professional advice and need to be guided to competent persons in the various fields such as occupational hygiene and ergonomics. One example of a collective approach was marked by the publication of *Professionals in partnership*,[5] which called for greater involvement of all practitioners and an increase in teamwork – a publication designed to make a contribution to the ambition of the Health and Safety Executive's strategy, *Securing health together*,[6] to encourage technical experts in occupational safety and health to work together more co-operatively.

Development of UK government policy and strategies

Recent pronouncements from the UK government (both the Department for Work and Pensions (DWP) and the Department of Health (DoH)) and from the regulator, the Health and Safety Commission (HSC) and Executive (HSE), have all emphasised the importance of OH. It is common ground that work-related ill health represents a huge economic and human cost. Thus, of the 40 million working days lost in the UK to absence associated with work-related injury and ill health, only 10 million are associated with accidents. In any event, for some years bodies such as the World Health Organization (WHO) have, not unreasonably, treated accidents as a health issue so that the relevance of workplace health and safety to the well-being of workers becomes even clearer. Once a government decides that OH is of significance, it becomes necessary to establish how it is to be addressed and improved. In the UK there have been some major developments in theory, which are beginning to be translated into practice through pilots and programmes. These are being evaluated and their evidence published as a key element in the HSC's strategy for improving the health and safety system and its performance. The focus has shifted from OH services to OH support.

The traditional approach to OH is to position it as a category of medicine – and characterise the nature of the provision in terms of numbers of OH physicians and nurses. This is not helped by the obscurity of some of the professional designations – the term 'occupational hygiene' (or its US equivalent 'industrial hygiene') is not self-explanatory. Nevertheless, the claims for more resources to be put into OH in order to reduce work-related ill health often founder on the reality that traditional practice has not been hugely effective. There really has not been a 'golden age' to which we should endeavour to return. If one wishes to address the appalling health toll from cigarette smoking, the sensible approach is to invest in strategies to reduce smoking rather than simply to improve medical services for people with smoking-related illnesses. In the same way, for work-related ill health the bulk of the effort needed has clearly got to be focused on reducing workers' exposure to health risks. To address prevention, classical occupational hygiene and safety management – in the workplace rather than as treatment-led services – require a sea change in perception, and this is being led by some far-sighted people across the spectrum, particularly by the HSE and OH professionals both individually and through their professional bodies.[3]

One major initiative, NHS Plus, a network of OH services based in NHS hospitals, was launched in 2000. The network provides an OH service to NHS staff and also sells professional services to the private sector, working to agreed quality standards. As an employer, the NHS provides an OH service to its own staff. Some of the NHS OH departments are large, and the wealth of experience they have gained makes them an obvious source of advice and help for companies who are looking for an OH service. They charge for the services that they provide to non-NHS employers, so in one sense add to the availability of such services provided commercially. There are currently over 90 NHS Plus providers, although they vary a great deal in size. Overall, while this has added to the capacity for OH in the UK, the amount of resource most NHS Trust OH departments have to make available to local companies is limited. What is surprising, given the repeated calls for evidence-based practice, is that while the DoH as recently as October 2006 announced the creation of a £10 million capital fund to improve NHS OH services – both for support to NHS staff and also NHS Plus – there has been no evaluation of the effectiveness of NHS Plus beyond the usual internal clinical reviews of service provision within each provider.

In 2000 the HSC published two documents designed, through the setting of targets, to reinvigorate the health and safety system of the UK as a whole and begin to move OH forward. *Revitalising health and safety*[7] was a serious attempt to address the twin problems of poor OH and a plateau in what had been the declining graph of accidents, including fatalities at work, which illustrated the improvements since the 1974 Health and Safety at Work etc Act.[8] The strategy, with its specific targets (reductions in accidents and work-related ill health) and action points (44 of them), addressed OH but only briefly. It represents the overarching programme of action that was reported at the half-way stage against the battery of targets.[9] Expanding on the OH component of the *Revitalising* programme and operating within it, a focused document was published one month later which addressed the issue of 'healthy work, healthy at work, healthy for life' – *Securing health together*.[6] The commitment to a reduction in the incidence of work-related ill health (20 per cent by 2010) among workers and members of the public affected by work, and of days lost to work-related ill health (30 per cent by 2010) represented a real challenge when there was uncertainty as to both the starting point (there is some baseline data but it is not wholly precise or reliable) and the mechanisms. *Securing health together* sought to define some overarching aims reflecting the *Revitalising* targets, and to act as a motivator encouraging trade unions, employers, public bodies, the NHS and OH practitioners to join together in developing specific strategies to achieve those aims.

This ambitious programme was accompanied by an analysis of the needs of small businesses for advice and assistance to tackle OH problems, with evidence that only 5 per cent of small firms had access to occupational health services.[2] From the beginning, there was careful use of language to shape the model for OH support:[6]

> … occupational health can embrace:
> a the effect of work on health, whether through sudden injury or through long term exposure to agents with latent effects on health, and the prevention of occupational disease through techniques which include health surveillance, ergonomics, and effective human resource management systems;
> b the effect of health on work, bearing in mind that good occupational health practice should address the fitness of the task for the worker, not the fitness of the worker for the task alone;
> c rehabilitation and recovery programmes;
> d helping the disabled to secure and retain work;
> e managing work related aspects of illness with potentially multifactorial causes (e.g. musculo-skeletal disorders, coronary heart disease) and helping workers to make informed choices regarding lifestyle issues.

The OH Services Working Group* includes the term 'occupational health services' in its title but it soon became clear that this was too narrow a description of the kind of help that employers needed to fulfil in order to protect the health of their employees. Although there is no generally accepted definition of what constitutes an OH service and no clear single form of practice, such services are traditionally understood to be medically based and led by doctors or nurses. Many existing providers of OH services, particularly in the private sector, are now able to field multidisciplinary teams including occupational hygienists, ergonomists, psychologists, health and safety specialists, counsellors and so on, but such teams are still likely to be led by a doctor or nurse. However, what many SMEs need in practice is simple, sector-specific guidance on practical measures to reduce exposure to hazardous agents and advice on enabling workers with health problems to continue working, together with information they can pass to their employees about ways of keeping healthy. Such advice may be obtainable from engineers and other technicians, trade associations, suppliers of material and equipment, and safety representatives. Many workers in small businesses are likely to remain reliant on primary care, trade unions and safety representatives for advice. Therefore this report uses the expression 'OH support' throughout to indicate the full range of advice that SMEs and workers may need to tap into.[10]

Thus in 2000 the arguments for a broad-based, multi-skilled team approach to addressing OH issues were matched by a focus on supporting those who were to be encouraged to make the appropriate decisions. This would mean supporting the legal duty holders for health and safety compliance – directors, managers, the 'officers' of an organisation, and the organisation itself as an employing body. Further research was undertaken to explore the extent to which occupational health support was accessed by companies.[11]

A new paradigm – the occupational health support model

The time seemed to be right to try again to raise the profile of OH. While *Revitalising* argued that accident rates had been reduced since 1974 and the problem was a plateau rather than deterioration, for health the story was not one of such success. It has been estimated that 32.9 million working days were lost through illness caused or made worse by work in 2001/02.[12] This high cost in human and economic terms of occupational ill health and the rising burden of incapacity benefit formed the context for *Securing health together*, which, unusually, was launched by ministerial representatives of a number of government departments, notably the DoH and the DWP, the sponsoring department for the HSE. (There was a notable absentee: at this time the Department of Trade and Industry (DTI) was still not engaged with occupational safety and health. Despite years of effort by the HSE to convince the business community that 'good health and safety is good business', the government department for business remained on the sidelines.) After its launch, the initiative was taken forward by the establishment of five Programme Action Groups (PAGs). The Support PAG developed a model for OH support which drew on OHAC's work.[13] The model is summarised in Figure 1.

The Support PAG was arguably the most significant of the groups established by the *Securing health together* initiative, and from the beginning had a composition which almost guaranteed that it would approach the challenge to define support in a radical way. With practitioners

---

* The working group with a mandate to investigate and advise on the development of OH services was a subset of the Occupational Health Advisory Committee (OHAC), which was set up to advise the HSC on systems for managing health at work. OHAC has now evolved into the Occupational Health Reference Group, with a remit that reflects the priority that is now placed on OH and meeting the *Revitalising* health targets.

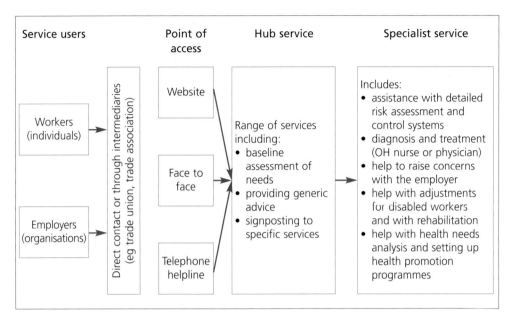

Figure 1
The Support PAG
model for OH
support

from a variety of disciplines – medicine, occupational hygiene, nursing, and also local government activists and trade unionists – the discussions concentrated on what employers and workers needed to help them manage work-related health issues. There was a ready consensus that what was needed was assistance to:

- identify health issues for recruited workers – fitness for work
- assess workplace risks to health and define how to reduce exposure – traditional occupational hygiene
- enable workers with ill health (whether originally work-related or not) either to retain their jobs or to return to employment after absence – retention and rehabilitation.

The minutes of the Support PAG reveal that from the first meeting (11 April 2001)[14] there was agreement as to the scope of the exercise:

1. Scope of the Support Programme Action Group
1.1 The group discussed the scope of the matters covered by the programme action group. They decided that they will use 'occupational health support' in its broadest sense to cover a diverse group of disciplines.
1.2 They gave examples of the range of advice, expertise, skills and providers of services that are already available. They wanted to establish what they already know of so they can identify the gaps.
1.3 They recognised that ill health caused by work, rehabilitation and support in the workplace for people with disabilities have traditionally been dealt with separately. They considered that all are within their scope. They concluded that the type and quality of service delivered would be valid issues for them to consider.

Defined in these terms, the group was clear that the key people to deal with these issues were the directors, managers and workers in each organisation and what they needed was help, while leaving them in their key positions as decision-formers and decision-makers. The new way of discussing these matters as defined by the OHAC Report was adopted.

It is worth emphasising this aspect of the new approach, for not only does it underpin the current initiatives under way in the UK, but it also represents the fundamental divide in the debate in Europe and worldwide. Essentially, the argument is between those who see OH professionals as supporting the key relationship between workers and employers, and those who see the practitioners providing a service which stands outside the normal day-to-day management of enterprises. The conversations about this were informed by an awareness of the growth of small businesses and the lack of enthusiasm for the 'big government' solution of a national, mandatory OH scheme (in countries such as Sweden and Denmark, where such schemes had been pioneered, they have been closed or are in the process of being dismantled). To develop the ideas expressed in *Securing health together*, a number of action groups were established to propose new ways of working, and one of them looked specifically at fleshing out the ideas of OH *support* rather than always thinking in terms of OH *services*. As noted above, the Support PAG, without any substantial disagreement among its members, endorsed and defined the challenge as one of getting all employers and workers to take responsibility for work-related health standards, rather than rebuilding a professional team which would try to take this on from outside the workplace. The debate was deemed 'over and won' when one of the 'early deliverables' identified by the HSC in its 10-year strategy was 'Proposals for support based on models for occupational health and safety support'.[15]

The support model envisages an individual employer or worker making contact with the support team in a variety of ways, such as responding to an advertisement, being recommended to do so by a trade association or trade union, meeting a representative at an event such as a trade fair or local community gathering, and – once the programme is established – by meeting people who are already taking advantage of the support available. Once engaged with the support team, the worker or employer's representative is then able to gain practical assistance in evaluating the risks to health that characterise their workplace, establishing what the control priorities should be. The final stage of the support available, having raised general awareness and specifically drafted an action plan for tackling significant health risks, is signposting to other organisations – commercial and public – with the competence to provide longer-term support. This latter group of support bodies can include training, occupational hygiene, medical and other services which can be purchased in a targeted fashion, tailored to the previously identified needs. This has been described as a 'hub and spoke' model, whereby the core initial support which assesses current and future needs is provided by the hub support service, and the other organisations which can help later are represented by the spokes radiating outwards from the hub (see Figure 2, where some of the possible spokes are indicated).

In Scotland, Safe and Healthy Working[16] was already under way, reflecting the urgency of getting to grips with a very poor public health situation. It was no accident that one of the programme's architects, Ewan Macdonald, was invited to chair the Support PAG and took responsibility for drafting its final report and recommendations. There grew up, in a fairly short time, coherence between the parties driving this forward. Based on the support model, a new pilot was established in early 2005 at Kirklees in Yorkshire, largely hosted by the local authority, and plans were developed for a major set of pathfinder projects in five regions in England and Wales to be launched early in 2006 as Workplace Health Connect. In the event, the first project set up to test this model in England was one focusing on construction, on the not unreasonable basis that if it worked in such a particular and challenging industry it was

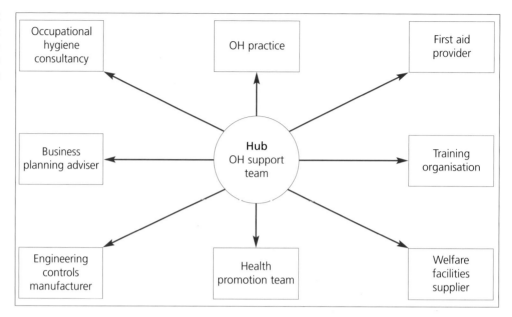

likely to have general applicability. Reviewing that project will assist in developing a picture of how OH support can work in practice. Essentially the questions were straightforward; they looked at whether an emphasis on workplace management and the control of exposure to health risks can achieve what many years of encouraging employers to make use of doctor-led OH services had failed to do. In particular, they investigated whether the workplace management approach could make a real difference in small firms, by testing the arguments in the construction industry, which is populated largely by workers in SMEs.

Testing the model in the construction sector

While the generic approach to OH moved towards a preventive approach employing a multi-skilled team, the construction sector was trying to grapple with its own evidence of the health harms arising within the industry. Accurate data are unavailable for the prevalence or incidence of ill health among UK building workers, but results of a self-reported work-related illness survey published in 2003 indicate significant levels of dermatitis, respiratory disease and, in particular, asbestos-related disease.[17] In addition, insurance claims history suggests significant levels of noise-induced hearing loss and hand–arm vibration syndrome. In 2000 the UK's first conference on health in construction – 'Tackling health risks in construction' – was held in London under the auspices of the Working Well Together (WWT) campaign. WWT was developed by the HSC's Construction Industry Advisory Committee (CONIAC) to raise health and safety standards in the industry. Its original manifesto when launched in 1999 itemised several areas in which the construction industry needed to improve:

The construction industry's current health and safety record is, in the words of the deputy prime minister, John Prescott, 'unacceptable'; these statistics show why:

- workers in the construction industry represent just over 6 per cent of the working population, but account for more than 30 per cent of the fatal accidents and over 14 per cent of the major accidents

- workers in the construction industry are almost five times more likely to be killed than the average for all industries
- they are more than twice as likely to sustain a major injury than the average for all industries
- almost a quarter of all inspections carried out by HSE are of construction activities
- the overall risk of ill health in construction is nearly twice the average for all occupations
- it is estimated that about 1 in 20 workers, currently or recently working in construction, have suffered a work-related musculoskeletal disorder
- there are about 600 deaths annually from asbestos-related disease among workers in construction trades.[18]

A workshop discussed OH support and at the final plenary session there was unanimity in calling for exploration of the development of a national scheme. Two studies were commissioned by the HSE to outline such a scheme for the industry.[19,20] In the first, the particular needs and specificities of the construction industry were explored.

Workforce mobility

The construction workforce is transient in the sense that, for most workers in the sector, employment with a particular employer is temporary. Contracts and projects or phases of projects come to an end, and the particular skills offered by an employee are no longer required, and may never be needed again – or not for a considerable period – by that employer. According to DTI figures, approximately one-third of workers in the sector are self-employed, and other studies suggest that many thousands move employer every month. This transience and mobility is likely to have an adverse impact on workers' access to conventional NHS services. For example, workers living in the north of England who travel weekly to work on the construction of Terminal 5 at Heathrow Airport (currently the UK's largest single-site construction project*) may simply not have time to visit their family doctor at home. Employers are often not in a position to conduct health surveillance, which presumes continual employment and periodic checks on aspects of health, as the workers concerned move on to new employment.

Small and 'micro' firms

According to available data, employment in the industry is highly fractured – over 93 per cent of employees work for firms employing fewer than eight people, and 83 per cent for firms employing three or fewer. There is great difficulty in accessing 'micro' firms to gather information or supply it – something frequently reflected in HSE documents and strategies:

> Our consultations show that some businesses, particularly small businesses, say they want to comply with health and safety standards but are fearful of approaching HSE or local authorities for advice.[15]

Contractual complexity

Many large projects are led by a very small directly employed team from a major contractor, working to a design developed for the client by an independent design team. The work on site

---

* The holder of this title changes frequently; it will soon transfer to the work for the 2012 Olympic Games and the associated development at Stratford in east London. Currently, the Channel Tunnel Rail Link project is larger than Terminal 5, but is operating on a long and non-contiguous work site.

is then carried out by a supply chain of smaller contractors, some of whom make use of labour-only suppliers (and this is one of many operational structures) all controlled through contractual relationships. The freedom to make decisions which could reduce exposure to health risks is thus heavily constrained. Legislation (largely through the Construction (Design and Management) Regulations, first introduced in the mid-1990s[21]) and guidance for the industry has emphasised the potential role of designers in selecting less hazardous materials and processes, but a recent HSE survey indicated that about a third of designers were unaware of their duties.[22] In fact, almost nothing is done on a construction site that is not connected with the design, so that in a sense exposures to health risks are designed in (and similarly many of them could be designed out).

The description above of a flexible labour market and a sector dominated by small firms reflects the direction that a lot of employment has taken in recent years, with the growth of part-time working, portfolio and self-employed freelance work and the reduction in pensioned, job-for-life work. There was a growing acceptance that if the support model could work in the challenging environment presented by the modern construction industry, there would be a strong case to argue for its usefulness across much of modern, flexible, small business-dominated employment. The two debates – OH support in the UK that is suited to the modern world of work, and the specific needs of the construction industry – converged with the creation in 2003 of an Action Forum under the auspices of CONIAC, comprising many of the major organisations in the industry (including the HSE, the Construction Industry Training Board, the Construction Confederation, the Federation of Master Builders, the National Federation of Builders, the Union of Construction, Allied Trades and Technicians, the DTI and others). This body developed a specification for a pilot scheme. Following a public competitive tender, a supplier was appointed and a company established to oversee and fund the work. The pilot, called Constructing Better Health, was launched in October 2004 in Leicestershire to run for two years, and represented another initiative – in this case within an industrial sector – that could be seen as a spin-off from the national debate fostered by *Securing health together*, and designed to test a practical approach in the building sector to meeting the *Revitalising* targets for the reduction of work-related ill health.

The pilot was unusual in that it involved the formation of a limited company, Constructing Better Health Ltd, whose four board members were drawn from the trade unions and employers' bodies. The company was set up by the financial services organisation B&CE,* which acts as company secretary. The funding for the project is unique, with provision made by the DWP, the DTI and the HSE, but with further monies coming from B&CE, industry bodies, the trade unions, the Association of British Insurers and other interested parties as charitable donations. A steering group was established to advise the board and oversee the technical work of the pilot.

As mentioned above, the pilot was designed to test the *Securing health together* model and accordingly offered support, advice and assistance to both employers and employees – small construction firms based or operating in the target area of Leicestershire. They had a number of points of access to the core services, including a website, which remains operational, at www.fitbuilder.com, a telephone advice line widely advertised across Leicestershire, and through face-to-face contact with members of the pilot team. Access was also encouraged and

---

* B&CE provides a complete range of employee benefits, pensions and personal insurance for everyone in the construction industry. It is a registered charity run by the industry (ie employers' organisations and trade unions).

facilitated by the many organisations, locally and nationally, which became partners to Constructing Better Health. These included the Leicester Regeneration Company – an important player in the area, as Leicester is embarking on a very ambitious construction-led programme to regenerate the city. Indeed, this programme formed part of the evaluation data which resulted in Leicester being selected as the site of the pilot.

Once a contractor made contact with the pilot staff, they received immediate advice on the topic in question, followed by a site visit. These visits were designed to carry out a speedy baseline review of how the site and/or individual contractors were addressing OH issues. The visiting team used a pro forma to shape the checks and assist reproducibility, both from site to site and over time as revisits were used to evaluate progress. Based on research into health hazards and risks in construction,[23] the priorities in the health evaluations for the pilot were:

- musculoskeletal disorders
- skin disorders
- respiratory disease
- noise-induced hearing loss
- hand–arm vibration syndrome.

In addition, the reviews considered working at height and the risk of falls, and workplace transport and the risk of collisions with people (the two largest groups of fatal accident causes in the UK construction industry and among the HSE's current priorities) when it was apparent during a visit that there was a significant risk of a serious accident.

The site visit team offered advice on practical ways in which exposure to risk could be reduced by simple management interventions in each of the priority areas. The opportunity was taken to encourage and demonstrate the methodology for risk assessment. Briefings, toolbox talks in the topic areas and other ways of raising awareness and competence to manage were also employed. The small firms were encouraged to embed the better practice in their policies and procedures. In sum, the pilot sought to act as a free and confidential external source of the type of straightforward, practical OH risk management advice that larger firms are able to buy through consultancy or the direct employment of competent people. The support services were all provided free at the point of delivery, funded by a range of supporters from government and industry. This economic element will shape the provision of the national service, as there is a limit to the Treasury's appetite for paying employers to do what they should do anyway both in their own economic interests and also to comply with their statutory obligations.

Once a site visit had been conducted, and the key risks and practical control options identified, the small employers were encouraged to book a visit from the pilot's mobile OH facility. In many cases, this was such an attractive prospect that site managers requested that the OH unit form part of the first visit by the Constructing Better Health team. An OH nurse offered a confidential health check to individual building workers who accepted the invitation; there was no compulsion in any aspect of participating in the pilot. The check focused on evaluating workers' health status in connection with the significant risk exposures identified for the type of work they did, with an emphasis on the five areas listed above. In addition, more general health factors were considered, in an attempt to counter the institutional lack of engagement between building workers and their general practitioners caused by the peripatetic nature of the job. Thus height, weight, blood pressure and so on were assessed to see whether there were any significant health problems which could be readily identified. Finally, the consultation between the nurse and the worker also created a brief opportunity to discuss health protection issues that typically form part of health promotion programmes.

If the health check revealed OH problems, this information was used to guide the advice offered to the employer to help reduce exposures to health risks. If the checks revealed a health problem which is, in general terms, not work-related, then the person concerned was encouraged to seek further help from their general practitioner. Finally, if a health problem was identified that could prejudice the continued employment of the worker, the OH team took on a case management role, seeking to help the person manage the condition and retain his or her job. In all the situations, confidentiality was carefully protected – construction is a highly casualised industry and any hint of a health problem in an individual could result, with some employers, in dismissal rather than the offer of consideration and support. If confidentiality were breached, the pilot would lose the trust of the Leicestershire workforce and co-operation would evaporate.

The pilot sought to encourage contractor employers, site workers, designers and clients to reduce exposures to health risks and encourage proactive rehabilitation. The vision of those involved remains that construction workers' health should not be adversely affected by their work, and that those with existing illness should be helped back into work in as short a time as possible. The team considered that managing health should be regarded as similar to managing safety – that is, it should be based on a sequence including risk assessment, risk control, site planning, information, instruction and training. The team that was assembled to reach out to small building firms and their employees reflected this philosophy. While part of the team was formed by OH nurses and a physician from a commercial OH practice, the team was led by occupational safety and health professionals. The work carried out on site, the methodology for dealing with telephone enquiries and all other aspects of the work of the pilot team was shaped by the use of pro formas and the structure of the database used to record activities and the engagement of contractors and construction workers. This was carefully designed to facilitate analysis of the progress of the pilot – of obstacles and successes – so that the independent evaluators, the Institute of Employment Studies, could gather the evidence they needed to inform the future approach, not only to OH in construction but also to the national pilots of Workplace Health Connect.

The ambition of Constructing Better Health was to provide the evidence for designing a national scheme which has a cost-effective and positive impact on the health of construction workers and on the efficiency of construction firms. The vision of a national approach was articulated in the final report of the *Securing health together* Support PAG:

> ... a minimum level of integrated occupational health, safety, rehabilitation and job retention service established for all. The objective of such a service is to maximise the functional capacity of individuals, the organisations in which they work and the wider economy.[13]

This is why, in addition to facilitating and partially funding the pilot, the HSE appointed an independent evaluation team to ensure that the lessons of this project were fully absorbed into the future plans.

Constructing Better Health was not the only cutting-edge OH project testing the support model. The Kirklees OH support pilot was established through Kirklees Metropolitan

Authority teaming up with Huddersfield's three primary care trusts, Jobcentre Plus and the HSE to form a partnership targeting support at SMEs in their area. This pilot was fully operational in January 2005, and again independent evaluation is being provided by the Institute of Employment Studies. Meanwhile, established projects such as Workwell in the West Midlands (which forms the nucleus of the OH support pathfinder project in the West Midlands), and others in Liverpool, Sheffield and elsewhere continue to develop the methodology for OH support. The previous emphasis on services continually foundered on two rocks: supply, given the shortage of OH physicians and nurses, and usage, given the financial obstacle for small businesses to accessing professional OH services. Now the debate has shifted, through the recognition that managing exposure to health risks – essentially a health and safety issue – is the route to making a significant difference. Supply and cost remain real problems, particularly in connection with rehabilitation, but the support model may provide the mechanism for reducing the next generation of work-damaged workers by putting health on the management agenda instead of seeing it primarily as a medical problem.

The future for OH support appears secure. Workplace Health Connect is described by the HSE in a manner wholly recognisable by a 'customer' of Constructing Better Health as:

- a confidential service designed to give free, practical advice on workplace health, safety and return to work issues to smaller businesses (with 5 to 250 workers) in England and Wales
- an Adviceline and a supporting website – giving tailored practical advice to callers, both managers and workers – on workplace health, safety and return to work issues
- a service that aims to transfer knowledge and skills direct to managers and workers, enabling them to tackle and solve any future workplace health issues themselves
- set up in partnership with the HSE and based around an Adviceline/website and problem-solving services available locally.

Workplace Health Connect will operate as a national marketing effort to encourage workers and employers to take health at work seriously, while the 'hubs' initially established in London, the West Midlands, South Wales, the North West and the North East will provide initial advice and guidance to small firms and workers in their regions. Difficulties with funding will mean that the health checks that formed a central part of the construction pilot will not be available. More information on these pathfinder projects is available at www.hse.gov.uk/workplacehealth, but it must be remembered that the ambitions expressed five years earlier to reduce work-related ill health were mainly going to be realised by existing institutions, bodies and professionals working together more effectively – and this failed to have any significant impact on the many millions of workers employed by SMEs. Like Constructing Better Health for a single sector, Workplace Health Connect is a programme aimed at reaching those small firms and providing practical advice and encouragement to begin to reduce exposures to health hazards at work and improve diagnosis, treatment and rehabilitation for those already affected. The government paper on work-related ill health published in late 2005, *Health, work and wellbeing*,[24] broke new ground in bringing together the DoH and DWP and included a vision of the future of the UK world of work in which:

... health is not adversely affected by work, and good quality advice and support is available to, and accessible by, all.

The key challenge remains winning hearts and minds – the UK has recognised that although formal enforcement is needed for legal compliance, the thousands upon thousands of small firms which employ an increasing proportion of UK workers demand a powerful marketing strategy to communicate the benefits of looking after health and managing exposures to health risks. One of the lessons of the construction pilot appears to be the extent to which the programme required a huge 'sales' effort to get small firms to agree to participate. Even though the service offered was free, there was apparent suspicion and reluctance. The OH support strategy in the UK is being developed as the new face of OH for the 21st century. Only time and epidemiology will tell whether, against the background of declining industrial accidents, it is really getting to grips with the high level of work-related ill health and disability that the UK currently experiences.

These developments are not being made without continuing debate. There remains a strong argument with a large constituency calling for a more formal approach, the creation of a proper national OH service available across the UK to all workers and employers. There are companies that continue to operate or contract in physician-led OH programmes that deal with individual cases of work-related ill health but rarely impinge on the way in which workplaces are managed. However, as the scale of the ill health problems has become clear, all stakeholders have been forced to acknowledge that the few thousand physicians and nurses currently available cannot make enough of a difference unless they are employed to bring about a real change in workplaces, and for that to happen it is essential that those within those workplaces take on OH issues themselves. To achieve this will require a lot of support to workers, managers and directors, and the pilots have provided useful information as to how that support may be marketed, sold and delivered.

The key messages to come out of all this effort can be summarised as follows:

- OH is too important to leave to doctors! So many people are adversely affected that only by engaging with managers and workers is it possible to reduce the burden of work-related ill health. Support rather than service leaves the responsibility where it belongs, in the workplace itself
- health is not divisible, and the absence of mobile teams providing free health checks for workers is leaving significant numbers (particular older working men) without real access to professional healthcare. The ambition of Workplace Health Connect needs to be raised to make it a portal to healthcare generally, not just for work-related issues
- so far, the initiatives have concentrated on preventing harm, but wellbeing is also vital. Good work is good for us; it leads to higher levels of fitness, higher incomes (poverty and ill health are inseparable twins), and longer, higher-quality lives. To achieve this, there is still some way to go in developing a holistic approach that addresses psycho-social as well as physical health risks, and OH support teams are essential.

References

1. See for example Creely K S, Van Tongeren M, While D, Soutar A J, Tickner J, Agostini M, De Vocht F, Kromhout H, Graham M, Bolton A, Cowie H & Cherrie J W. *Trends in inhalation exposure: mid 1980s till present.* Research Report 460/2006. Sudbury: HSE Books, 2006. Available online at www.hse.gov.uk/research/rrpdf/rr460.pdf (viewed 11 May 2007).
2. Health and Safety Executive. *Survey of occupational health provision at work 1993.* Cited in: Pilkington A, Graham M K, Cowie H A, Mulholland R E, Dempsey S, Melrose A S & Hutchinson P A. *Survey of use of occupational health support.* Contract Research Report 445/2002. Sudbury: HSE Books, 2002; pages 1–2. Available online at www.hse.gov.uk/research/crr_pdf/2002/crr02445.pdf (viewed 23 April 2007).

3. Waddell G & Burton K. *Occupational health guidelines for the management of low back pain: evidence review and recommendations.* Faculty of Occupational Medicine, 2000. Available online in three parts at www.facoccmed.ac.uk/library/docs/backs1.pdf, www.facoccmed.ac.uk/library/docs/backs2.pdf and www.facoccmed.ac.uk/library/docs/backs3.pdf (viewed 23 April 2007).

4. British Occupational Health Research Foundation. *Back pain at work: a guide for people at work and their employers.* BOHRF, 2004.

5. Institution of Occupational Safety and Health. *Professionals in partnership.* Wigston: IOSH, 2003. Available online at www.iosh.co.uk/files/technical/Professionals%2D prtnrshp%2Epdf (viewed 23 April 2007).

6. Health and Safety Executive. *Securing health together.* Sudbury: HSE Books, 2000. Strategy document and supporting materials available online at www.hse.gov.uk/sh2/index.htm (viewed 23 April 2007).

7. Health and Safety Commission. *Revitalising health and safety: strategy statement.* Sudbury: HSE Books, 2000. Available online at www.hse.gov.uk/revitalising/strategy.pdf (viewed 23 April 2007).

8. Health and Safety at Work etc Act 1974 (ch. 37). London: HMSO, 1974. Available online at www.healthandsafety.co.uk/haswa.htm (viewed 23 April 2007).

9. Health and Safety Executive. *Achieving the Revitalising health and safety targets: statistical progress report, November 2006.* HSE, 2006. Available online at www.hse.gov.uk/statistics/pdf/prog2006.pdf (viewed 23 April 2007).

10. Occupational Health Advisory Committee. *Report and recommendations on improving access to occupational health support: section 3.* HSE, 2000. Available online at www.hse.gov.uk/aboutus/hsc/iacs/ohac/access.htm (viewed 23 April 2007).

11. Pilkington A, Graham M K, Cowie H A, Mulholland R E, Dempsey S, Melrose A S & Hutchinson P A. *Survey of use of occupational health support.* Contract Research Report 445/2002. Sudbury: HSE Books, 2002. Available online at www.hse.gov.uk/research/crr_pdf/2002/crr02445.pdf (viewed 23 April 2007).

12. Epidemiology and Medical Statistics Unit, Health and Safety Executive. *Occupational health statistics bulletin 2002/03.* Office for National Statistics/HSE, 2003. Available online at www.hse.gov.uk/statistics/overall/ohsb0203.pdf (viewed 23 April 2007).

13. Support Programme Action Group. *A vision for health, safety and rehabilitation support in work for Great Britain.* HSC, 2003.

14. Support Programme Action Group. Minutes of the first meeting, 11 April 2001.

15. Health and Safety Commission. *A strategy for workplace health and safety in Great Britain to 2010 and beyond.* Sudbury: HSE Books, 2004. Available online at www.hse.gov.uk/aboutus/hsc/strategy2010.pdf (viewed 23 April 2007).

16. National Health Service and Health Scotland. Safe and healthy working website at www.sahw.co.uk/top-section/contact-us/adviceline.cfm (viewed 23 April 2007). See also Macdonald E & Docherty G. Healthy working lives: the Scottish strategy for improving health in the workplace, on page 141 of this book.

17. Jones J R, Huxtable C S, Hodgson J T & Price M J. *Self-reported work-related illness in 2001/02: results from a household survey.* Office for National Statistics/HSE, 2003. Available online at www.hse.gov.uk/statistics/causdis/swi0102.pdf (viewed 23 April 2007).

18. Working Well Together: Construction Industry Awareness website, wwt.uk.com/articleserve.asp?HPID=1&SHPID=1 (viewed 11 May 2007).

19. Waterman L. *Proposal and scoping: specification for a feasibility study for a comprehensive occupational health scheme for all construction workers.* Sypol/HSE, 2001.

20. Amey Vectra. *National occupational health support scheme for the construction industry: an initial feasibility study.* HSE, 2001.

21. The current version of these regulations is the Construction (Design and Management) Regulations 2007, SI 2007/0320. London: HMSO, 2007. Available online at www.opsi.gov.uk/si/si2007/uksi_20070320_en.pdf (viewed 24 April 2007).

22. Rigby N. *Designer initiative: final report 17 March 2003.* HSE: Scotland and North of England Unit, Construction Division, 2003. Available online at www.hse.gov.uk/construction/pdf/designinit.pdf (viewed 24 April 2007).

23. Pilkington A, Donaldson J, Groat S & Cowie H A. *Mapping health hazards and risks across aspects of the construction process.* Contract Research Report 447/2002. Sudbury: HSE Books, 2002. Available online at www.hse.gov.uk/RESEARCH/crr_pdf/2002/crr02447.pdf (viewed 24 April 2007).

24. Department for Work and Pensions, Department of Health and Health and Safety Executive. *Health, work and wellbeing – caring for our future. A strategy for the health and wellbeing of working age people.* London: HM Government, 2005. Available online at www.dwp.gov.uk/publications/dwp/2005/health_and_wellbeing.pdf (viewed 24 April 2007).

Healthy working lives: the Scottish strategy for improving health in the workplace

Ewan B Macdonald, Healthy Working Lives Research Group, University of Glasgow, and Gabe Docherty, Health Promotion Manager, NHS Lanarkshire

Introduction

Scotland has a long history of independence in its administration and philosophy. When the union took place between Scotland and England in 1707, Scotland retained its own legal, education and health administrations. In 1998, partial devolution of Scotland from the rest of the United Kingdom (UK) was agreed and a new Scottish parliament sat from 1999. Some powers remain reserved to the UK government, and these include health and safety legislation and the powers of the UK enforcing body, the Health and Safety Executive (HSE). The HSE currently forms part of the UK Department for Work and Pensions, which is responsible for all social security, including industrial injury benefits. There is therefore a common legislative basis for occupational safety and health across the UK. However, many of the changes in the delivery of occupational safety and health in Scotland have originated in the public sector, through the Scottish health department, and indeed these developments have often influenced the UK agenda. This chapter describes the Scottish situation and its response to UK legislation, with emphasis on Scottish developments and innovation.

Legislative requirements

In the UK, the Health and Safety at Work etc Act 1974[1] requires all employers with more than five people to undertake risk assessments and institute control measures for workplace health hazards. In relation to the provision of health and safety services, the legislation merely requires employers to seek 'competent' advice, without defining competence or specifying the extent of the advice to be obtained. Thus there has been no state provision of occupational safety and health services to workplaces, and the responsibility has rested with the employer to determine the level of resource required. While this pragmatic approach to provision can be criticised, it is nevertheless true that, according to accident statistics, the UK has some of the safest workplaces in Europe.[2] Within the UK, Scotland has slightly higher rates of workplace accidents compared to England and Wales.

UK national strategy

In 2000, the UK government published a national strategy for occupational health (OH), *Securing health together*.[3] This committed the Scottish Executive and other government bodies to work towards the following targets by 2010:

- a 20 per cent reduction in the incidence of work-related ill health
- a 20 per cent reduction in ill health to members of the public caused by work activity
- a 30 per cent reduction in the number of days lost to work-related ill health
- greater awareness of rehabilitation opportunities for those off work due to ill health or disability
- that everyone not currently in employment due to ill health or disability should, where necessary and appropriate, be made aware of and offered opportunities to prepare for work, and be helped to find it.

The importance of the health of working age people across the UK was reinforced by the publication in 2005 of a government strategy entitled *Work, health and wellbeing – caring for our future*.[4] This strategy pulls together all the different strands of work under way in this area within government in order to improve the prevention of work-related illness and accidents, and to ensure that injured or sick workers get fast treatment and can access OH when it is needed. It explicitly recognises that people in work are healthier than those out of work, and that work can improve mental and physical health, reduce health inequalities and improve life chances for workers and their families. It therefore identifies the prevention of work-related ill health, effective rehabilitation and provision of occupational safety and health as cornerstones in the drive to improve and maintain general public health, by reducing the significant health inequalities which exist between the employed and unemployed populations. It stresses the importance of effective rehabilitation by the National Health Service (NHS), appropriate vocational rehabilitation thereafter, and improved support to enable people with disabilities to stay in employment. Its focus is not simply the employed population, but everyone of working age. Therefore, the scope of OH professionals is being widened beyond the traditional workplace setting to include and recognise their role in improving the health of the general public.

As part of these developments, a national director for OH has been appointed, with a remit to implement the *Work, health and wellbeing* strategy, raise awareness of work and its relationship to health and wellbeing, and develop specific outcome measures to monitor the strategy's progress and success.

OH provision

The ability of the OH community to respond to these challenges is currently limited and new models of service delivery are being developed. Historically, occupational safety and health provision in the UK was developed by large enterprises. In more recent times, there has been a growth in private OH companies, together with more subcontracting of OH services by large enterprises rather at the expense of traditional internal resources.

However, there has been poor OH coverage of small and medium-sized enterprises (SMEs) (under 250 employees), micro-enterprises, the self-employed and home workers. One international survey in 2001 reported that only 34 per cent of all UK workers had access to OH services.[5]

A survey undertaken on behalf of the HSE confirmed that only 3 per cent of companies had fully comprehensive occupational safety and health services. In 2003 it was estimated that in Scotland 51 per cent of the workforce was employed by 243,000 SMEs, and that more than 60 per cent of these workers had little or no access to OH provision.

As part of *Securing health together*, a multidisciplinary Support Programme Action Group developed the strategy for the provision of OH support across the UK.[6] This was modelled on a system of regional occupational safety and health advisers supported by a free telephone advice line, both of which had been developed in Scotland.[7,8]

The Scottish profile

Demographics

Scotland has an ageing population with a low birth rate and lower levels of immigration than the rest the UK.[9] Without substantial immigration, the population is expected to reduce from 5.2 million to under 5 million over the next 20 years, and the number of people of working age will fall by 8 per cent from 3.15 million in 2002 to 2.88 million in 2027. The number of people of pensionable age will increase by 45 per cent by 2027 and the number of Scots aged between 16 and 29 will reduce by 9 per cent.[10] These projections have serious implications for the staffing of public services and private industry and enterprise, and for the socio-economic development of the country. As in many developed countries, a smaller proportion of the population will be responsible for producing the economic wealth to sustain an increasing non-working population.

Health

These changes are occurring against a background of relatively poor health and high levels of health inequality between socio-economic groups.[11] The health of working-age people is a cause for concern, with higher rates of smoking,[12] problem drinking[13] and obesity than the rest of the UK. In Scotland, at least 2.2 million working days are lost each year through ill health[14] and among men and women aged between 15 and 74, Scotland has one of the worst records in Europe for both overall mortality and specific conditions such as lung cancer, oesophageal cancer and ischaemic heart disease.[15]

Long-term disability

Around 335,000 Scots claim sickness and/or disability benefits, of whom 285,000 claim long-term incapacity benefits. Of these claimants, 45 per cent have been on incapacity benefits for five years or more and the highest concentrations of these claimants are to be found in the most disadvantaged communities.[16] Older men have lower levels of employment in Scotland than elsewhere in the UK, and there are lower rates of employment for disabled people.[17]

Employment

Despite these relatively low levels of employment among certain social groups, Scotland has relatively full employment and there are numerous job vacancies which remain unfilled. There is therefore the paradox of a high level of economically inactive people alongside the existence of job vacancies. In the city of Glasgow there are 22,000 job vacancies, while at least 100,000 people of working age are economically inactive.[18]

Work-related ill health

The UK situation in relation to work-related ill health is less certain. Surveys have found that 6 per cent of the working-age population report a health problem caused or made worse by work. This is confirmed in repeated Labour Force Surveys.[17] Other studies have shown that work-related ill health and accidents can account for up to 24 per cent of Scottish family doctor consultations by working-age people[17] and up to 16 per cent of emergency attendances at hospital.[19]

Developments in provision in Scotland

In Scotland, the NHS, which has 150,000 workers, has developed its own comprehensive OH provisions during the past 20 years and some aspects of this coverage have been used to provide contract services to industry and public-sector organisations. The NHS in Scotland has also recognised the impact of work-related ill health and supported the development of free advisory services to smaller industrial enterprises.

One of the NHS services, the Lanarkshire occupational safety and health service (Salus), based in central Scotland, has been at the forefront of innovations in the provision of services to SMEs in the UK. In 1996 an initiative was developed between the OH and workplace health promotion departments of the NHS to provide a free advisory service to SMEs in part of central Scotland. This service offered a free workplace visit, which combined a confidential health and safety risk assessment, a workplace health promotion needs assessment and a report and proposed action plan with follow-up advice.[7]

A further development arose from the piloting of a free occupational safety and health telephone advice line in central Scotland.[8] This service was extended nationally throughout Scotland in 2003 with the launch of the Safe and Healthy Working service, which provides a free telephone advisory service and access to a network of health and safety and OH advisers across Scotland, aimed at the SME sector.[8]

This provision is organised in three regional hubs to cover the country. These hubs are based in NHS OH organisations. In the first three years of this service, it received 7,765 telephone enquiries, undertook 1,536 workplace visits and assessments, and responded to 510 email enquiries from enterprises.[20]

Workplace health promotion has a longer history. It began with the launch of the Scotland's Health at Work (SHAW) scheme in 1996, which encouraged employers to engage in workplace health promotion programmes and meet the bronze, silver and gold standards of the scheme. This programme has been successful and reached over 40 per cent of Scottish employees by 2006, with an estimated 810,000 workers participating. The SHAW programme was set up as a health promotion initiative, focusing on traditional health promotion areas such as diet, exercise, non-smoking and lifestyle. But recently it has become involved in the delivery of programmes focused more on work-related health issues, such as guidance on the prevention and appropriate management of back pain and stress at work.[21] Given the historically low coverage of enterprises by OH services, the SHAW scheme has been very valuable in raising awareness of general health issues among employers and employees in Scotland and preparing the way for further initiatives.

The Scottish strategy for health improvement
In 2002, the Scottish Executive published its strategy for health improvement, *Improving health in Scotland – the challenge*. In this document it identified the workplace as one of the key settings for future health improvement initiatives.[22]

A multidisciplinary working group, including social partners, was established to develop the workplace strategy, taking into account the goals of *Securing health together*, existing Scottish services such as Safe and Healthy Working, the SHAW scheme, and NHS-based OH services, and overall population needs. As a result, the Healthy Working Lives (HWL) action plan was published in 2005.[9]

Healthy Working Lives
This plan recognises that being in work brings physical, mental, spiritual and financial benefits and can promote confidence, independence and social inclusion.[23] Conversely, it accepts that being out of work for any length of time is detrimental to health and wellbeing.[24]

It defines a healthy working life as:

> ... one that continuously provides working-age people with the opportunity, ability, support and encouragement to work in ways and in an environment which allows them to sustain and improve their health and wellbeing. It means that individuals are empowered and enabled to do as much as possible, for as long as possible, or as long as they want, in both their working and non working lives.

HWL is thus a plan for the whole population, whether employed or unemployed, in whatever setting and for all age groups. A fundamental principle of the HWL action plan is that, in order to maximise the functional capacity of the population and that of each individual at various times in their life, they will need the following:

- health improvement, eg through health promotion
- health protection, eg through OH and a healthy and safe living environment
- effective treatment and rehabilitation following illness and injury, including vocational rehabilitation and employability advice
- lifelong learning and employability advice.

The competences of OH professionals are seen as important to the delivery of many of these requirements.

To a greater or lesser extent, all of the services needed to meet these requirements already exist, though access to all of them could be better co-ordinated. A challenge for Scotland is how to deliver these services at the right time, in the right place and in a way that suits the individual who needs them.

The developing model for the delivery of HWL

Three existing publicly funded programmes providing free advice to Scottish workers and employers – the Safe and Healthy Working service, the SHAW award scheme and Scotland Against Drugs – have been brought together in a new organisation called the Scottish Centre for Healthy Working Lives.[9] This centre is based within and funded by the NHS.

The new centre is not an enforcement agency and will seek to engage all sectors and providers in its programmes. So far, the centre and HWL implementation are in their infancy and much work has to be done to create the necessary infrastructure and facilitate improved networking and synergy of existing agencies, including those involved in rehabilitation and employability.

The strategy is to build on the existing services now based within the centre, which include a free telephone advisory service and a network of advisers based in three hubs across Scotland. The model was first described in the Support Programme Action Group report,[6] which was published in 2003 and based on pilot projects in Scotland.[7,8]

The operational framework (Figure 1) identifies clients as being in three groups: employers, employees and those wishing to return to or start work. These individuals will be able to be referred or to refer themselves to an integrated menu of services. An important aspect of the framework will be to provide access to a holistic range of services, including one that can identify the needs of the client according to HWL and ensure that these needs are addressed by pointing the client towards the appropriate agencies. Some of the services will be based within the NHS, but many others will be supplied by other providers, such as the educational sector, occupational safety and health services, health promotion services, and employability and vocational counselling services which are part of local multidisciplinary teams, supported by the regional hub and co-ordinated nationally by the centre.

The Scottish HWL strategy – implications for OH

This strategy goes beyond the traditional boundaries of occupational safety and health provision in that it aims to:

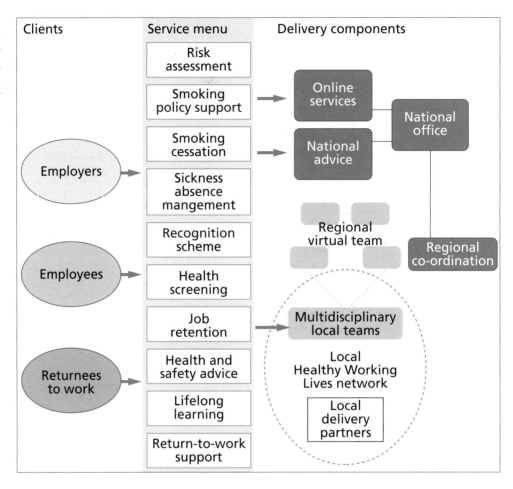

Figure 1 Operational framework for Scotland's Healthy Working Lives strategy

- provide access to advice to both the employed and the unemployed
- recognise the benefits of being in work and facilitate access to safe employment
- harness and co-ordinate existing services rather than create new ones
- recognise the importance of effective occupational safety and health provision in maximising the functional capacity of the workforce, which is the overall goal
- extend the paradigm of what has traditionally been considered as the goal of the OH professional.

Evaluation of this strategy in Scotland will be essential and will require a parallel research programme.

These developments provide opportunities for OH professionals to broaden their scope and the settings in which they can work, for the following reasons:
- the target population may include the unemployed as well as people in work, who have been the traditional target of OH services
- the potential role of OH professionals in improving the general health of the community is at last being recognised

- there is greater emphasis on rehabilitation and return to work
- they may have to work more closely with the many other disciplines which have a role in the HWL agenda
- they may be working in the general community rather than in enterprises.

As well as opportunities, these developments in Scotland pose challenges to which OH professionals must respond. These include:

- the need to develop their roles and competences to meet the needs of society
- other players being involved in areas they traditionally regard as their own
- the need to get a much broader understanding of population and community health issues and understand how they can contribute to addressing them
- being active in driving the agenda forward, rather than being driven
- especially for those working in a community setting, the need to develop models of service delivery which are appropriate and which will be different from the traditional company-based service.

Implications of training OH professionals for the new agenda in Scotland

The implementation of the HWL strategy in Scotland will require new ways of working by the expanded multidisciplinary team that will deliver it to working-age people. New models of service delivery will mean changes to the training of all the professional groups involved. These include not only those involved in health and safety, but also occupational hygiene, ergonomics, psychology, physiotherapy, occupational therapy, vocational rehabilitation, case management, social work, employability advice, health promotion, education, healthcare and occupational medicine. There is a particular need for all these groups to have a better understanding of the role of other members of the team, and become more effective in the delivery of the holistic care required by the population.

In Scotland there has been a research focus on the competences required by occupational physicians.[25-31] The competence domains of occupational physicians were agreed by a modified Delphi study and conference workshop[30] in 1997. These were:

- hazards
- fitness
- communication
- exposure
- promotion
- research
- management
- law.

More recently, these were tested again in a survey of UK employers, employees, and their representatives to identify the priorities of the customers of occupational physicians.[31] This survey confirmed that while all the established competence areas for occupational physicians were regarded as important by their potential customers, the three most important areas were law, hazards and fitness. These were different from the priorities of physicians.

There is thus a need to review continually the competences required of all the disciplines involved in delivering HWL. Similarly, workplace-based training programmes need to take account of these developing models of OH provision, particularly as it becomes more integrated with general population health strategies, as is the aim in Scotland.

References

1. Her Majesty's Stationery Office. The Health and Safety at Work etc Act 1974 (Ch. 37). London: HMSO, 1974. Available online at www.healthandsafety.co.uk/haswa.htm (viewed 20 April 2007).
2. Health and Safety Laboratory. *Literature review on the reporting of workplace injury trends*. Report HSL/2005/36. Buxton: HSL, 2005. Available online at www.hse.gov.uk/research/hsl_pdf/2005/hsl0536.pdf (viewed 20 April 2007).
3. Health and Safety Commission. *Securing health together: a long-term occupational health strategy for England, Scotland and Wales*. Sudbury: HSE Books, 2000; see also the SH2 webpages, www.hse.gov.uk/sh2/index.htm (viewed 20 April 2007).
4. Department for Work and Pensions, Department of Health & Health and Safety Executive. *Work, health and wellbeing – caring for our future*. London: HM Government, 2005. Available online at www.dwp.gov.uk/publications/dwp/2005/health_and_wellbeing.pdf (viewed 20 April 2007).
5. Hämäläinen R M, Husman K, Räsänen K, Westerholm P & Rantanen J. *Survey of the quality and effectiveness of occupational health services in the European Union, Norway and Switzerland*. Research Report 45. Helsinki: Työterveyslaitos (Finnish Institute of Occupational Health), 2001. Preface available online at www.occuphealth.fi/Internet/partner/tthosicoh/Publications/Book_People+and+work+Research+Reports+45.htm (viewed 19 April 2007).
6. Health and Safety Commission. Support Programme Action Group. More information available online at www.hse.gov.uk/sh2/pags/support.htm (viewed 20 April 2007).
7. Houston K M, Atkinson R G, Macdonald E B & O'Connor M E. A multi-disciplinary approach to assessing health promotion, occupational health and health and safety in the workplace. *International Journal of Health Promotion and Education* 1999; 37 (3): 101–109.
8. Smith M. *Safe and healthy working: an occupational health and safety service for SMEs in Scotland*. London: HSC, 2003. Available online at www.hse.gov.uk/aboutus/hsc/meetings/2003/141003/c141.pdf (viewed 20 April 2007).
9. Scottish Executive. *Healthy working lives – a plan for action*. Edinburgh: Scottish Executive, 2004. Available online at www.scotland.gov.uk/Resource/Doc/924/0034156.pdf (viewed 20 April 2007).
10. General Register Office for Scotland. *Projected population of Scotland (2002-based)*. Edinburgh: GROS, 2003. Available online at www.gro-scotland.gov.uk/statistics/publications-and-data/popproj/02population-projections/index.html (viewed 20 April 2007).
11. Scottish Executive. *Inequalities in health – report of the Measuring Inequalities in Health Working Group*. Edinburgh: Scottish Executive, 2003. Available online at www.scotland.gov.uk/Resource/Doc/47171/0013513.pdf (viewed 20 April 2007).
12. Shaw A, McMunn A & Field J (eds). *The Scottish health survey 1998. A survey carried out on behalf of the Scottish Executive Department of Health*. London: Joint Health Surveys Unit, University College London, 2000. Available online at www.sehd.scot.nhs.uk/scottishhealthsurvey/sh8-00.html (viewed 20 April 2007).
13. Office for National Statistics. *General household survey*. Available online at www.statistics.gov.uk/ssd/surveys/general_household_survey.asp (viewed 20 April 2007).
14. Health and Safety Commission. *Statistics of occupational safety, ill health and enforcement action 2003/04 – Scotland*. London: HSC, 2004.

15. Leon D A, Morton S, Cannegieter S & McKee M. *Understanding the health of the Scottish population in an international context. Report commissioned and funded by the Public Health Institute of Scotland.* London: London School of Hygiene and Tropical Medicine, 2003. Available online at www.healthscotland.com/uploads/documents/ UnderstandingHealthofScotlandP2.pdf (viewed 20 April 2007).

16. Scottish Executive. *Intelligence report: Welfare to Work Task Force Disabled/Inactive Benefits Working Group.* Edinburgh: Scottish Executive, 2002.

17. Office for National Statistics. *Labour force survey five-quarter longitudinal dataset, June 2003–August 2004.* Report SN 5045, second edition. Economic and Social Data Service, 2005. Abstract available online at www.esds.ac.uk/findingData/snDescription.asp? sn=5045 (viewed 20 April 2007).

18. Glasgow Community Planning Partnership. *Regeneration outcome agreement 2006– 2008.* Glasgow: GCPP, 2005. Available online at www.communitiesscotland.gov.uk/ stellent/groups/public/documents/webpages/otcs_011399.pdf; see also www.glasgowcommunityplanningpartnership.org.uk (viewed 20 April 2007).

19. Harker C, Matheson A B, Ross J A S & Seaton A. Occupational accidents presenting to the accident and emergency department. *Archives of Emergency Medicine* 1992; 9: 185–189.

20. Healthy Working Lives National Advisory Group. Minutes of meeting held on 19 August 2005. Available online at www.healthscotland.org.uk/hwl/documents/ 050819%20HWL%20Advisory%20Minutes.doc (viewed 20 April 2007).

21. Scottish Executive. Scotland's Health at Work website, www.shaw.uk.com (viewed 20 April 2007).

22. Scottish Executive. *Improving health in Scotland – the challenge.* Scottish Executive, 2003. Available online at www.scotland.gov.uk/Publications/2003/03/16747/19929 (viewed 20 April 2007).

23. Acheson D. *Independent inquiry into inequalities in health report.* London: The Stationery Office, 1998. Available online at www.archive.official-documents.co.uk/ document/doh/ih/contents.htm (viewed 20 April 2007).

24. Brenner M H. *Unemployment and public health. Interim report to the European Commission.* DG EMPL/A/1 VC/2000/0022. Brussels: Directorate General of Employment, Industrial Relations and Social Affairs, 2000. Available online at ec.europa.eu/ employment_social/news/2002/may/ConfRepBruss_Part_4.pdf (viewed 20 April 2007).

25. World Health Organization. *Global strategy on occupational health for all. Recommendation of the second meeting of the WHO Collaborating Centres in Occupational Health.* Geneva: WHO, 1995.

26. Royal College of Physicians. *Occupational medicine training record.* London: Faculty of Occupational Medicine of the Royal College of Physicians, 1995.

27. International Labour Organization. Occupational Health Services Convention. C161. Geneva: ILO, 1985. Available online at www.ilo.org/ilolex/cgi-lex/convde.pl?C161 (viewed 23 April 2007).

28. International Labour Organization. Recommendation concerning occupational health services. R171. Geneva: ILO, 1985. Available online at www.ilo.org/ilolex/ cgi-lex/convde.pl?R171 (viewed 24 April 2007).

29. International Commission on Occupational Health. *International code of ethics for occupational health professionals.* Rome: ICOH, 2002. Available online at www.ilo.org/ encyclopaedia/?print&nd=857400068 (viewed 24 April 2007).

30. Macdonald E, Elder A & Ide C. *Competencies of occupational physicians: requirements of occupational medicine training in Europe.* Glasgow: University of Glasgow Press, 1998.

31. Reetoo K N, Harrington J M & Macdonald E B. Required competencies of occupational physicians: a Delphi survey of UK customers. *Occupational and Environmental Medicine* 2005; 62: 406–413.

Preventive services in Europe: expanding amid a crisis of confidence

Laurent Vogel, European Trade Union Confederation, Brussels

Introduction

Coverage of preventive services is still patchy across the European Union (EU). Legal frameworks and professional practices vary widely. Unprecedented resources have been put into services which cannot be said to be delivering the goods. It would not be overstating the case to talk of a crisis of confidence – and perhaps even a crisis of legitimacy – in the preventive services.

This paper seeks to bring out the common problems beyond the strictly country-specific aspects. Setting the development of the preventive services within the more general context of the different components of a health and safety at work strategy[1] is beyond the scope of this paper; likewise, the picture in the countries which joined the EU in 2004 and 2007 has particular traits that will not be addressed here.

Anything but universal coverage

With the occasional exception, self-employed workers are not covered by preventive services anywhere in Europe. Among employed workers, EU legislation excludes domestic staff (overwhelmingly women), who therefore as a general rule have no access to preventive services. Coverage of other employed workers is very patchy from country to country. Estimates made in 2000[2] suggested that 50 per cent of employed workers were likely to have access to preventive services in the EU.

The very sketchy figures on the coverage of workers by preventive services in most EU countries are surprising. They vary greatly depending on the data source. This alone is a disturbing indicator that preventive services are seen more as a mere in-house support function than as a key component of a public system of health and safety at work. Systematic surveys are needed of existing preventive provision in the EU and workers' access to it.* This could be a task for the Risk Observatory set up by the Bilbao-based European Agency for Safety and Health at Work.

Some countries come close to universal coverage of employed workers by requiring firms that lack a company preventive service with sufficient aptitudes to sign up to an external service. The Netherlands, Luxembourg and Belgium are cases in point. France has universal coverage, but only by occupational medicine services.

Austria, too, has universal coverage in principle, but again, estimates vary widely depending on the data source. Coverage may possibly be up to just over 70 per cent of all workers in 2003, but it is still fairly notional because the minimum service times of occupational health

---

* The report on the practical implementation of the Framework Directive adopted by the European Commission in February 2004[3] is short on data and unable to provide an overall view, while the description of some national situations lacks credibility. The estimate that 85 per cent of British firms have preventive services, for instance, seems highly unlikely.

(OH) doctors and safety engineers are so low (1.2 and 1.5 hours respectively) that many firms with under 50 workers simply use the preventive service set up by the industrial accident insurance system (AUVA). Barring health checks, there are few organised preventive activities. This explains the much more downbeat assessments that only around 10 to 15 per cent of all workers really have access to preventive services (see 'Occupational health services in Austria', on page 05 of this book).

Preventive service coverage of workers has expanded quite rapidly in Spain. National working conditions survey data show that in 1999, only 24 per cent of firms were entirely without preventive service provision.[4] That proportion had fallen to about 9 per cent by 2003.[5] The downside of this picture is the widespread outsourcing of prevention activity. Most firms with fewer than 500 workers rely on an external preventive service, which has little impact on prevention in the workplace. Even among firms with 500 and more workers, which are obliged to set up an in-house preventive service, over a quarter do not do so.

With their work environment reforms of the 1970s, the Scandinavian countries set the pace in implementing a national preventive strategy in which the preventive services played a pivotal role.[6] Thirty years on, the situation stands out for different reasons. Criticism of the old model has not produced coherent system-wide reform. Existing provision is being watered down but no new and ambitious approaches are being explored. The free market reform backlash has undermined national preventive strategies, especially in Sweden and Denmark, the changes seemingly driven by cost-cutting and attempts to roll back the extent of workers' oversight over business. Assessments for Finland vary depending on the source consulted. While there is full coverage for employed workers in large and medium-sized firms, the situation of self-employed workers and employees of very small firms (fewer than 10 workers) still gives cause for concern. According to an estimate in 2005 by Suomen Ammattiliittojen Keskusjärjestö (the Central Organisation of Finnish Trade Unions, SAK), real coverage of employed workers is now no higher than 80 per cent owing to fragmentation of firms, and that of self-employed workers is below 20 per cent.* Sweden's coverage has retreated drastically since the 1980s, when up to 80 per cent of workers were generally thought to have access to preventive services. Now, it could be closer to 60 per cent, with currently available data putting the figure between just over 50 per cent[7] and 72 per cent[8] of workers. This broad estimate reflects the lack of organisation of services and linkages into a national prevention policy. Coverage in Denmark is judged to be between 35 and 40 per cent of workers, and the future of preventive services is beset by deep uncertainty (see 'Occupational health services in Denmark – the rise and fall of a multidisciplinary and preventive approach', page 25 in this book). About half of Norway's workers are thought to have access to a preventive service (see 'Occupational health services in Norway – legislative framework, trends, developments and future perspectives', page 103 in this book).

The number of workers with access to a preventive service in the United Kingdom has fallen dramatically.[9] The expansion of the small firm base and the privatisation of public services have been major factors in this. The British Trades Union Congress (TUC) reports a fall in the number of workers with access to health and safety professionals from 12 million in 1992 to 7.5 million in 2002. This equates to a fall in coverage from 50 per cent to 30 per cent of the national workforce. A survey of selected functions, missions and tasks – rather than organisational

---

* 'The Finnish occupational health system – challenges and approaches' (see page 39 of this book) gives similar figures: 85 per cent of employed workers and 20 per cent of self-employed workers.

procedures – carried out by the Institute of Occupational Medicine claims that barely a seventh of workers (employed in 3 per cent of all firms) are covered by OH activities, which are relatively narrowly defined as including training, job engineering, risk factor measurement, and health monitoring. A total of 7.5 million workers (in 15 per cent of firms) have access only to a sort of bare-bones service that consists of risk factor identification, risk management and information. Specialised health and safety staff are found in about half of firms that have organised prevention activities. The three most frequently cited professions are health and safety officers (in 45 per cent of cases), general practitioners (29 per cent) and OH nurses (29 per cent). The Health and Safety Executive's strategy for giving a new impetus to prevention in the United Kingdom does not have the development of preventive services as a priority.

There is virtually no gender-specific data on preventive services. Two inferences can be made from what little information is available.[10] Female workers on average have less access to preventive services than their male counterparts; and when they do have such access, they have less of an individual and collective voice in specifying prevention priorities and activities. Some of the reasons for this include:

- female workers' segregation into what are wrongly stereotyped as low-risk sectors and occupations
- the higher concentration of women in small and medium-sized enterprises (SMEs) in the private sector, and in public services where the organisation of prevention is deeply deficient
- the growing contingency of female employment, and the scale of part-time work, which is disproportionately carried out by women.

Professional skills in preventive services

The different national prevention cultures have been dominated by a handful of professional disciplines. Occupational medicine has taken a central place in most of the Mediterranean countries, but has also featured prominently in the Netherlands and Finland. It is the only discipline for which training requirements have been harmonised across the EU. The development of OH nursing has been largely overshadowed by occupational medicine, although it has carved out a relatively autonomous role in some countries such as the United Kingdom, or in association with therapeutic practices in the Nordic countries (in particular in connection with physiotherapy). Occupational hygiene skills are widespread in the United Kingdom, but have developed much later in most continental countries. Safety-related disciplines have always been in evidence, but their preventive services role has varied widely. Ergonomics, psychology and other disciplines related to work organisation and psychosocial factors developed belatedly as prevention disciplines. Ergonomics and occupational psychology were for a long time an adjunct of production organisation objectives, and in the latter case, even employee selection.[11,12]

The 1989 EU Framework Directive[13] does not specify what aptitudes preventive services must have. It leaves that responsibility to the member states. Given how widely the scope of prevention is defined, the necessary aptitudes should logically relate to the main disciplines involved in prevention. This is how the Directive has been carried over into law in some countries (Belgium, the Netherlands and Spain). In these jurisdictions, there is a common core of five disciplines covering occupational medicine, safety, occupational hygiene, ergonomics and psychology.

The Spanish regulations refer to a range of disciplines, but allow employers to choose just two to make up a preventive service. There is evidence of growing multidisciplinarity in the company preventive services of large firms with at least 250 workers, 60.9 per cent of which included three or four different specialist disciplines in 2003 (against 43.8 per cent in 1999). Just 3 per cent of services now rely on a single specialism (against 20.3 per cent in 1999). Workplace safety awareness has become very widespread, ergonomics and psychology are expanding rapidly, occupational hygiene is slowly gaining ground, while occupational medicine has declined sharply, being found in only 46 per cent of company services in 2003, compared to 55.6 per cent in 1999.

The only required professionals in Austrian and Portuguese preventive services are OH doctors and safety engineers. This narrow approach to multidisciplinary working has prevented other professionals such as ergonomists, psychologists and industrial hygienists from attaining a specific status.

The only aptitude specified in any detail by all states is occupational medicine, even though health surveillance is not always carried out by OH doctors. In Germany, for example, OH doctors (in the strict sense of doctors qualified in occupational medicine) make up less than a third of all doctors involved in workplace prevention. The same problem exists in Finland, where many doctors who work in preventive services are not specialised in occupational medicine,* but are often general practitioners who have undergone a fairly cursory seven weeks' additional training. In Italy since a 2001 reform, the doctors who provide workplace health surveillance do not have to be specialised in occupational medicine.[15] In many Western European countries, the number of occupational doctors added to the system by training each year does not even offset retirement losses.

OH provision in many countries is far from being organised into services that offer universal coverage. EU Directives require surveillance in certain cases (eg exposure to hazardous chemicals, work on display screen equipment, manual handling of heavy loads), with the proviso that all workers should also be able to receive health surveillance when they feel it necessary. The reality in many countries falls short of these aims. Arguably, the requirement for surveillance, especially of workers in insecure or contingent jobs and in SMEs, is widely flouted in countries where there is no universal coverage by preventive services that include occupational medicine. On-demand access to health surveillance for workers is rarely assured in firms that do not have to provide compulsory surveillance. A lose–lose situation is to be found everywhere in Europe: either workers have no access to any form of health surveillance by specialists qualified in occupational medicine, or health surveillance is provided but does not make best use of what occupational medicine can contribute to collective prevention. One especially significant problem lies in the tenuous link between individual medical check-ups and a prevention policy whose key focus is to engineer change in collective working conditions.

Some countries have not specified the precise aptitudes that preventive services should have, which has given employers a free choice of how to make up their services, or even to draft in expert 'hired guns', with no joined-up working within or between services. Ireland, the United Kingdom and Sweden are cases in point. Regrettably, the judgments of the European Court of Justice (ECJ) have adhered strictly to the letter of the law on this, tending to lose sight of the aim of the Framework Directive. While an ECJ judgment in 2001 found Italy at fault for

---

* A 2003 survey found that two-thirds of doctors working full-time in preventive services in Finland were not specialists in occupational medicine.[14]

failing to specify any aptitudes at all,[16] a judgment in 2006[17] held that the Swedish regulations' vague and general pseudo-definition did not violate the Framework Directive.

The failings of the United Kingdom's public authorities are partially offset by the system of accreditation and registration of health and safety professionals set up by private agencies.[18] The main professional body for this is the Institution of Occupational Safety and Health (IOSH), which groups together some 30,000 practitioners divided into three groups according to their level of training and professional experience. IOSH has grown considerably over the past 10 years. Other bodies also act as training certifiers. But none of this intervention by private agencies is enough to regulate the prevention market because employers are always free to employ prevention staff who do not meet the standards set by them. There is no guarantee that prevention operators are independent.

The freedom that Italian employers have to appoint the head and personnel of the preventive service has created a situation where most of these officials play only a backseat role because of their lack of authority, means and sometimes capabilities. A national survey on the status of prevention describes the situation in these terms:

> Preventive service heads feel deeply short-changed by what they do. They cite the limitations and difficulty of being front-line players in workplace prevention when they lack the power to take big decisions that have practical effects.... Few heads talk openly about the organization of workplace protective and preventive services; their role is essentially administrative and technical, and their single overriding concern is whether the employer is keeping within the law.[19]

One failing of the Italian preventive services is the lack of training. As a result of the ECJ's judgment against Italy in 2001, the Berlusconi government passed an executive order on 23 June 2003 specifying the skills required by service heads and personnel. The order laid down fairly vague, lowest-common-denominator criteria, and in practice resulted in widely varying levels and qualities of training provision. On 26 January 2006, the new Italian government reached an agreement with regional and provincial authorities to improve the training of preventive service heads and personnel. The progress represented by this agreement, however, does not necessarily mean more multidisciplinary working between specialists from different backgrounds. The training itself consists of a basic introduction to different disciplines. Just four hours is given over to training in ergonomic risks, for example, while total training for a head of preventive services can vary from 64 to 120 hours, according to sector. The same problem can be seen in Spain. A report by a member of the President of Spain's Consejo Económico y Social (Economic and Social Council), F Durán, claims that the training of hygiene, safety, ergonomics and psychosociology specialists is nothing short of shambolic.[20] Progress to date has been unimpressive.

Multidisciplinary or two-track working?
Most recent reforms have focused on multidisciplinarity in preventive services. But this is not the case in all countries. In Germany, in particular, the existing system was kept largely unchanged. Most firms must have safety engineers, and must have health surveillance done by OH doctors. And while linkages are to be found between the two forms of intervention, by and large preventive activity is not often run along multidisciplinary lines.

Any preventive service set up in Austria must include both occupational doctors and safety engineers. But employers can have a two-track arrangement by enlisting the services of a safety engineer and an OH doctor separately. This has not really helped to create multidisciplinary working. Most OH doctors still provide their services as independent contractors rather than as part of a preventive service. Neither ergonomists nor psychologists have official standing under the rules, and so are not found to any great extent in preventive services.

Greece has also kept a two-tier arrangement. All employers must appoint a safety officer, regardless of company size. In firms regarded as lower risk, the employer can act as the safety officer providing he or she undergoes a fairly cursory 10 hours' training. Also, firms employing at least 50 workers (with lower thresholds for special risk firms) must provide health surveillance by contracting an OH doctor. A service need not be set up for either specialism. The organisational arrangements can vary from appointing an employee to enlisting outside expertise. Signing up to an external preventive service, which will necessarily have both safety and occupational medicine aptitudes, is just one possible way of organising preventive services.

France has had a long-running debate on overhauling its occupational medicine services,[21] which have now been renamed 'occupational health services' since they now include personnel who are not OH doctors. Most prevention professionals who are not OH doctors operate without regulation and multidisciplinary working is at a minimal level. The personnel whose skills are not spelled out in detail are mainly ancillaries to OH doctors. The situation in France is being held back by powerful employers' lobbies pursuing an agenda which does not include assessing prevention needs. They want cost-neutral reform, and see multidisciplinarity only in terms of least-cost subcontracting of some OH doctor duties. The employers do not intend to be dispossessed of their absolute dominion over company prevention specialists, who tend to be sidelined from health and safety committee activities.

Italy has developed a hybrid multidisciplinary/two-track system through a statutory differentiation between the preventive service and the protective service – which does not in practice have to be a service and whose personnel have no clearly defined skills – and the 'competent doctor', who does not have to be, and usually is not, part of a preventive service. Relations between the competent doctor and the preventive service are usually confined to an annual meeting (called the periodic prevention meeting) held with workers' representatives in firms with more than 15 workers.

Case-specific, unco-ordinated activities

The Framework Directive requires a coherent overall prevention policy to be developed. This entails giving a meaningful definition to the concept of service(s) used in the heading of Article 7 of the Directive. Two points must be made here:

- the main focus must be on setting up a company service. External services are to be enlisted only for functions that a company service cannot perform itself*
- the need for (in-house and external) expertise should be determined by the requirement to have a prevention policy. That means that external expertise should not just be drafted in on an *ad hoc* basis, but that links should be established between the different sources of expertise, as well as between the activities of company and external services. Having publicly approved external services overseen by joint employer–employee watchdogs is to

---

* The European Commission stresses that the first priority must be to set up a company service, an interpretation endorsed by ECJ case law.[22]

be preferred to the piecemeal provision of expertise and consultancy services by individuals or profit-making companies.

Many countries have set size criteria to determine whether in-house services are required. The thresholds vary widely from 20 workers in Belgium to 500 in Spain (but 250 workers for high-risk industries). In Portugal, it is 400 workers (30 workers for a list of high-risk sectors). In Italy, it differs by sector from 10 workers in farm businesses to 30 workers in craft and light industrial firms, up to 200 workers in other firms. If no service is set up, the employer performs the duties of the company service, but is not always properly trained to do so.* In France, a company OH service must be set up by firms with at least 2,200 employees. Luxembourg sets the bar highest: a company OH service is only compulsory for firms employing at least 5,000 workers (or 3,000 if 100 of them are subject to health surveillance due to working in safety-critical jobs or exposure to the risk of an occupational disease).

The relationships between company and external services also differ widely from one country to another. There is a clear emphasis on company services in Belgium and Germany (but only as regards safety). Under the Belgian regulations, all firms employing at least 20 workers must set up a company service, and any firm whose company service cannot fulfil all the responsibilities and tasks laid down in regulations must also enlist assistance from external services. The clearly established principle is that of a single system for company and external services alike, to ensure an integrated and permanent approach. The Nordic countries focus more on external services, although their activities must be integrated into a comprehensive employer's policy to ensure health and safety (see, for example, Sweden's and Norway's rules on 'internal control'). The Netherlands, Spain and France have favoured external services (essentially limited to occupational medicine in France†). The lack of a specific regulatory framework in the United Kingdom means that most prevention professionals are not part of organised services. Unlike other countries, even external prevention provision is mostly confined to large firms.

In many countries, a fairly unstructured and unregulated market in all kinds of expertise has developed. External expertise is not necessarily pooled in preventive services in Italy, France (apart from OH doctors), Germany (including OH doctors), the United Kingdom, Ireland or Spain. Even in countries where external provision is organised in a permanent form, the procedures for approving and policing it fall short of the mark.

Independence and workers' confidence

Preventive services must have full professional independence in how they do their job. That means that health protection must override all other criteria that the employer might seek to impose (profitability, health-based recruitment, absence controls and so on). Independence does not mean taking a neutral stance halfway between employers and workers, because it is workers' lives and health that may be at risk. Also, workers' insights into their own jobs are key to identifying the risks and putting effective prevention strategies in place. As far as

---

* There is no training requirement in Belgium, and only very cursory training in Italy.

† However, the executive order of 24 June 2003 provides that 'occupational risk prevention personnel' must be appointed from among company employees who possess the necessary skills, including in firms that enlist the services of an external occupational health provider.

professional ethics go, workers have no choice but to use these services, so they must have confidence in them. A Dutch trade union publication asks the pointed question: should you be absolutely open with your OH doctor?

Independence means that there must be effective protection for prevention personnel against any pressure from employers. Few countries have specific rules to protect against dismissal, suspension or retaliatory action by the employer.* In Belgium, all prevention personnel in company and external services alike have similar statutory protection (under an Act of December 2002) to that already enjoyed by OH doctors. The grounds for dismissal must not infringe the independence of prevention specialists, and allegations of incompetence must be substantiated. Control is exercised at several levels: a compulsory prior agreement by the workers' representatives, mediation by the labour inspectorate if need be, and finally a judicial review. An employer who fails to fulfil the substantive and procedural requirements will be liable to pay compensation to the dismissed prevention professional.

In France, prevention specialists other than OH doctors lack any guarantee of independence in the performance of their duties. A distinction has to be made between 'workplace risk prevention operators' and other prevention professionals on the company payroll (including almost all safety engineers). Both are in the same position of subordination to their employer as any other unprotected worker. 'Operators' simply have accreditation. The only form of check on independence is through an unsworn affirmation by the operator. The perilous situation of unprotected prevention professionals was illustrated by the dismissal in April 2003 of a safety engineer who had the temerity to attend a company health and safety committee meeting. Her reinstatement was ordered by the Paris Court of Appeal on 25 March 2004. The ruling found that prevention professionals other than occupational doctors lacked any specific protection, and so ordered her reinstatement on the basis of the general right that all employed workers have to give their opinion on their working conditions (article L 461-1 of the Labour Code).

Participation by workers and trade unions

Workers' participation and representation, and the activity of preventive services, have been extensively explored as separate issues. But that approach offers no understanding of the role played by preventive services in the social dynamics of the firm and society.

While there are few systematic studies of workers' participation in health and safety at work,[23] the available data point to a positive link between the level of workers' collective participation and the implementation of systematic, collective prevention activities.

Participation by workers and trade unions in the activities of preventive services centres on three elements:

- external oversight
- direct input as a source of knowledge
- direct intervention in setting priorities and identifying preventive solutions and putting them into effect.

---

* Staff of external preventive services must be doubly independent – from their own employer and from the employers in firms using their services. Experience shows that pressure from business employers can undermine the employment status of the most proactive and honest prevention specialists in external services.

Clearly, these three levels all affect one another. External oversight is the most common form of interaction. Most national laws require workers' representatives to be regularly consulted on the activities of preventive services. For external services, some countries have set up statutory joint supervisory bodies to give unions some say over these activities. In other countries, workers' representatives have real joint decision-making powers – their approval is required to set up a company service or a contract with an external service (as, in varying ways, is the case in the Netherlands, Belgium, and Germany*). In Belgium, workers' representatives who feel that an external service prevention adviser lacks the necessary skills or has lost the confidence of the workforce can have him or her removed. They effectively wield a veto – their unanimous decision must be accepted by the employer, and the prevention adviser must be replaced. There is no doubting the value of such forms of external oversight in partly helping to prevent the tasks and priorities of preventive services being unilaterally prescribed by employers. But they nevertheless remain limited. For one thing, many workers lack representation in health and safety at work (commonly in SMEs, among temporary agency staff and so on). Also, external oversight is likely to be exercised only in extreme situations unless augmented by direct intervention by workers and trade unions.

Direct input may be mainly passive, as a source of knowledge, or much more active when concerned with priority setting, task definition and implementation. Halfway-house situations – where worker intervention, while not wholly passive, does not go as far as having a decisive say in all aspects of preventive activity – are quite common. All across Europe, the debates surrounding risk assessment have brought resistance to workers' intervention into sharp focus. The very incomplete data available in some countries show that participation by workers and workers' representatives in risk assessment remains patchy. There has even been controversy in Italy over whether employers have to disclose a copy of their risk assessment document to workers' representatives or whether they can treat it as confidential! A specific Ministry of Labour circular was needed to set the record straight on such a 'no-brainer'.[24]

The quality of multidisciplinary work is directly related to worker participation. Workers' intervention, and employers' recognition of the importance of their experience as a source of knowledge and as a criterion for validating preventive activities, are a big help in avoiding futile conflicts between the different 'expert' disciplines. So, if workers' experience is not used to inform work equipment design, effective interworking between the disciplines of safety and ergonomics is unlikely to happen.[25,26] Using workers' experience makes it considerably easier to pull the different expert disciplines together into a holistic approach to prevention that is more than purely technical and embraces work organisation as a whole. This is what emerges from a survey on collective risk perception by male and female ceramics industry workers in Spain:

> Rather than using the pigeonholing jargon words usual to prevention techniques, workers tend to voice their spontaneous, collective perception of work-related risks as an interconnected whole where, for example, health and safety hazards are connected with specific forms of work organisation and perceived through the practical health damage they cause.... In focus groups where a less mediated collective perception of risks comes out,

---

* In Belgium, co-decision is found only in firms with a Workplace Prevention and Protection Committee (50 workers upwards) or a shop stewards' committee set up under an industry collective agreement which may lay down a workforce size criterion. In the Netherlands, co-decision is found only in firms with a works council (35 workers upwards). In Germany, the threshold for setting up a works council is five workers.

workers voice problems and priorities distinct from those identified by technicians. More specifically, workers place importance on work organisation-related health problems compared to technicians' almost exclusive focus on safety issues and work accidents.[27]

Antonio Grieco, the long-serving director of the Istituto di Medicina del Lavoro (Institute of Occupational Medicine) in Milan, argues that two different cultures are to be found: that of prevention technicians and that of workers. They are:

> ... original, discrete cultures ... with completely different experiences, instruments, categories of thought, and methods of assessment, which exist alongside one another in the real world and must do so even where they clash, and must work together. Only testing practical inputs against each other – each with its own specific experience and means – will really deliver in terms of solutions.[27]

Do preventive services serve prevention?

Preventive services in the Netherlands have experienced spectacular growth over the last 10 years.[28] In 2000, 98 per cent of workers were covered by their activities. Between 1994 and 2002, preventive service headcounts nearly doubled from just over 5,000 to nearly 10,000. There are 93 health and safety at work specialists employed by preventive services per 100,000 workers (figures for 2000). The average spend per worker per year on preventive services rose from €92 in 1995 to €127 in 2001.

The picture could not look rosier. And yet there is growing disquiet among prevention professionals and workers alike about whether these are truly preventive services and whether they are really improving collective working conditions. For the past 15 years or so, a debate has been under way in the Netherlands on the very large numbers of employees off work due to long-term incapacity or invalided out of the labour market entirely.[29] The main thrust of government policies on OH has been to ease the cost pressures it places on the social security system. But this has taken its toll on preventive provision. Workers' confidence in preventive services has been undermined by the medical checks carried out on workers who are on sick leave. Individual measures to get sick and injured workers promptly back to work take precedence over improvements to collective working conditions. This diversion of the system has been made worse by the failure to set specific regulatory criteria for the activities and control of preventive services. Activities are largely specified by employers themselves on the basis of their contract with a preventive service. Quality control of services is privatised and based on certification procedures in which neither trade unions nor the labour inspectorate have a say. Quality certification systems work at cross-purposes. While certification can have a positive impact on some aspects, like vetting skills or work procedures, it falls down by taking customer satisfaction as the key criterion. The 'customer' is not an appropriate concept for preventive services. A set of contradictory and often conflicting demands are in play: the employer's demands driven by his or her short-term goals; workers' and their unions' demands; and a more diffuse social demand about the priorities of workplace health policies. Certification procedures are driven by employers' demands. The finding of Dutch researchers is that:

> The delicate balance between client (mostly employers') demands and professional responsibility is disturbed by the unconditional dominant role of the clients in some quality assurance systems. In our opinion, the [OH service]–client relationship should be terminated when a persistent substantial difference in visions comes in serious conflict with professional integrity.[30]

The under-reporting of occupational diseases illustrates the system diversion that puts the 'customer's' (ie firm's) interests above those of workers' health. In 2000, just under half of preventive service doctors had reported at least one occupational disease. A survey of preventive service doctors was undertaken in 2000 to identify the reasons for not reporting occupational diseases.[31] Just under half (43.3 per cent) of responding doctors said it was too time-consuming; 41 per cent claimed a lack of data on causality; while 22.9 per cent said it was to prevent workers taking the employer to court.* Around a fifth (22.9 per cent) of replies claimed unfamiliarity with the reporting criteria or that the preventive service in which the doctor worked tended not to report occupational diseases (19.9 per cent; note that the Arbodiensten have been obliged to report occupational diseases since November 1999, while they could use their discretion between 1997 and 1999). The under-reporting of diseases tends to conceal workplace health problems. It says much that to assess the scale of work-related skin diseases, a surveillance system had to be set up based on reporting by dermatologists, who find a higher prevalence than preventive service doctors.[32]

The public authorities' withdrawal from responsibility is made worse in the Netherlands by the oligopolistic characteristics of the markets created. Five external services provide for nearly 90 per cent of firms. The control market is dominated by two certification companies (Lloyd's and Det Norske Veritas). The growth of a flourishing market does not square with growing dissatisfaction among those who actually use the system. The Netherlands, indeed, is the only European country to have set up a complaints office to which workers can take their grievances against preventive services. The conclusion drawn by the Dutch research is disturbing:

> In practice, the Dutch Arbodiensten hardly contribute to prevention at all, but are medical centres specialized in individual care and control. Over 90 per cent of the contracts concluded with the OH services consist either entirely or for their major part of sickness absenteeism guidance. The medical problems of individual workers are hardly ever converted into a preventive approach, aiming to improve working conditions in the workplace. The added value of the OH services as compared to general practitioners is deemed to be very limited.[33]

There are serious issues about how much prevention is carried out by services in Spain, where most firms have signed up to external preventive services set up by *mutuas*, the insurance companies that run the work-related risk compensation schemes, resulting in large-scale outsourcing of preventive activities. The privatisation of certain social security activities has also led, since 1994, to the *mutuas* playing a greater role in the management of incapacity for work due to non-occupational diseases or accidents.† The *mutuas*' preventive health and safety role and their role in absence controls are mutually inconsistent.

Preventive services focus more on the individual than on collective working conditions. Health checks are widespread (done in up to 70 per cent of firms in 2003), as increasingly are training and information for workers. In 2003, there was a sharp rise in the share of workplaces performing initial risk assessments (61 per cent, against 30.2 per cent in 1999 and 24.1 per

---

* More than one answer could be given, hence the total of more than 100 per cent.

† The workforce covered by the *mutuas* for the management of 'ordinary' incapacity was estimated at 8.1 million in 2002, against 1.1 million in 1996, and 5.4 million in 1999.

cent in 1997). But these risk assessments are often of dubious quality and arguably designed more as tick-box exercises to 'do things by the book'.

The Spanish trade unions sum up the situation broadly as follows:

- The outsourcing of prevention activity has led to prevention being seen as a product and an activity disconnected from the company, requiring no commitment or involvement from the employer;
- poor quality, officialistic prevention activity. Little urge to find out in order to act properly and make the changes required to working conditions... That is reflected in particular by purely safety-focused risk assessments that disregard psychosocial, toxic or ergonomic risks; health surveillance that is unconnected with evaluation or prevention planning and limited to general health checks which do not cover occasional but regular activities connected to the main job; prescriptive, unvarying training that is not adapted to the specific job; general preventive recommendations to avoid conflict with the employer;
- little worker participation and involvement. Information supplied by workers is not used as an input to, or to evaluate the results of, prevention activities and prevention management. Workers are not recognized as able to come up with ideas, and they are not given training.

> There are two issues of responsibility. For employers, it is about democracy and preserving their power in the firm. For technicians, the problem is a technocratic approach to prevention.[34]

What Spain and the Netherlands share is having combined a market-driven approach with an insurance approach in which prevention is focused on the items with the highest short-term cost. In Spain, this insurance approach is managed by the *mutuas*, which have set up most of the external preventive services and are now looking to capture new markets through making inroads into the public health system.[35] In financial terms, workplace prevention is little more than a marginal part of mutual insurance organisations' business (barely over 2 per cent of their total spending for 2002). In the Netherlands, the insurance approach has been given impetus by government policies in which cutting absence rates tops the workplace health reform agenda. In both cases, employers' direct demands clearly take precedence over a long-term prevention policy. But there is one difference. In the Netherlands, strong pressure from the employers to cut absence rates (which represent a high direct cost for them) has led to health-based recruitment and action focused on getting individuals fit for and back into work which never enquires into the root causes of ill health. In Spain, employers are more concerned to stave off checks and prosecutions: every effort is made to give the impression of a working prevention policy, while in practice, preventive services are confined to those areas that least affect actual work organisation: individual health checks, boiler-plate risk assessments that have no bearing on reality, or prevention plans that are never put into effect.

The crisis of confidence in preventive services in the Netherlands and Spain is but the distilled expression of pan-EU trends. Sweden presents certain similarities and one big difference – the crisis of confidence there is linked to a rollback in services. The origins of the problem can be traced back to the late 1980s.[36] In 1992, the Swedish employers' confederation ripped up the collective agreements on compulsory membership of preventive services by firms in many sectors. In 1993, the state withdrew funding for preventive services, which must now operate with no specific regulatory framework and are at the mercy of the market – in other words, direct employer demand – for their funding. And employers are free to switch preventive services at will or dispense with them completely. The preventive services have been severely downsized, shrinking from some 10,000 to 7,000 personnel. But above all, the essential purpose of preventive service activity has been comprehensively thrown open to question. Profitability of services has become the abiding concern. Many have changed the way they charge for their services. From a flat-rate charge per worker, they have moved to a 'basic package' of services with bolt-on options in response to employer preferences for short-term contract services and a reluctance to enter into long-term relations with a preventive service. In the words of Remaeus & Westerholm, 'occupational health services have become free agents in a deregulated health market'.[37]

The importance of collectivising experiences

The most basic level of collectivisation is having a preventive service at all. This is a long way off what happens in countries where employers enlist individual specialists, consultants and experts for what may be ongoing or just one-off assignments. But over and above prevention activities organised into services, the most important levels of collectivisation lie on a bigger scale at industry, area, national and EU level.

Collectivisation of prevention activities allows several aims to be delivered.

- By sharing experiences of problems and solutions, prevention experts get access to hands-on expertise that is not readily available within a single workplace or preventive service. The experience of networks of prevention specialists on replacing hazardous products with less dangerous ones is a good example.
- Collectively framed 'good professional practice' is vital for withstanding pressure from employers. Such rules combine scientific and technical validation criteria with political and ethical criteria that allow professionals to do their core job – preserving workers' health. The quality of preventive services is the focus of much current debate. In many cases, quality is dictated by internal rules and procedures as well as a blinkered, short-term results approach (eg cutting absence or reported accident rates). In other cases, the criteria may be even more questionable when dictated by 'customer satisfaction'. The collective framing of good practice should not be a pigeonhole exercise for each specialisation. Specific practice must be laid down for each profession (occupational medicine, OH nursing, ergonomics, industrial hygiene and so on) but set within a framework of best practice which is common to the different prevention specialists that also incorporates the insights and priorities of the people that OH is all about: the workers.
- Collectivisation of the activities of 'frontline' prevention experts is an immense resource for OH research. Networking the information generated by preventive service activities provides the necessary critical mass that the activity of one service alone will find it hard to develop. It is often only through this that properly designed scientific work can be done. The SUMER survey[38] on OH in France answered by 2,000 OH doctors is a good example. In most EU countries, there is still too wide a divide between institutional OH research and prevention specialists.
- Collectivising the experiences of prevention specialists informs public policy-making and performance assessment in health protection. Some issues cannot be addressed through prevention activities alone – they need policy decisions. Be it banning asbestos or child labour, or imposing restrictions and controls on agency work and subcontracting, prevention is locked into a political and legal framework that sets the ground rules. The inability to feed back their experience in order to call the public authorities to account is often a major frustration for OH professionals.

During the 1970s and 1980s, the collectivisation of prevention activities delivered excellent results in the Nordic countries and Italy. In Italy, the first moves were made by the trade unions and led to locally organised public preventive services being set up. The 'Centro ricerche e documentazione sui rischi e danni da lavoro' (CRD) played a key role in collectivising the workplace experiences of workers and prevention professionals alike. It was set up by the three Italian trade union confederations in 1974 and ran until 1985.[39] Collectivisation of experiences in the Nordic countries was supported by the creation of work environment funds run on a tripartite basis. These schemes are now flagging but have not entirely run out of steam. The different guides published by the Conferenza delle Regioni (Conference of the Regions) in Italy are an object lesson in the collectivisation of good prevention practice. The recent decision of the new right-wing Swedish government to dismantle Arbetslivsinstitutet, the National Institute for Working Life, is an unprecedented setback in Europe.

Elsewhere, prevention specialists themselves have felt the need to band together in professional organisations in order to have a collective voice. Some focus more on framing common policy positions or demands, others on scientific research and exchanging professional experiences. Some initiatives have managed to bridge this divide by combining strands of thought from both camps. Some of these are trade union initiatives, like the forums on health surveillance and quality in prevention set up in Spain by the Instituto Sindical de Trabajo, Ambiente y Salud (trade union institute for work, environment and health).[40]

A question of legitimacy: private workplace operators or public health players?

Changing patterns of work and the new approaches to prevention are to some extent undermining preventive services from the outside. The 1989 Framework Directive rightly makes the employer's responsibility central. It sets a very wide scope for preventive activities: work equipment, chemical substances, work organisation, labour relations, eliminating monotonous and repetitive work and so on. It stresses the importance of participation by workers and trade unions in preventive activities. All these factors dramatically change the traditional role of preventive services. They entail a shift from individual risk-based technical or medical responses to an overall socio-technical approach which embraces all the constituents of work organisation and how they interact. It holds out new prospects for prevention specialists, but at the same time puts question marks over the traditional foundations of their legitimacy towards employers. Employers' readiness to admit the legitimacy of purely technical or medical expertise for specific risks is matched by their rejection of any critical analysis of their management in general.

Changes in the world of work are also helping to undermine preventive services. The growth of contingent employment and widespread subcontracting, and the creation of interworker rivalries that fragment workforces, are all imperative reasons for moving away from a technical approach in order to tackle corporate strategies. Against all this, employers are trying to downgrade the preventive service function to a sort of damage-limitation social support, focused on improved induction and training, co-ordinating certain preventive activities and so on. But that support function cannot affect the deregulation of work that this onslaught on the work sphere by unbridled commercial competition represents. Where an activity is outsourced for the lowest cost, an induction meeting on health and safety can easily be nothing more than disingenuous lip-service in which the prevention specialist is asked to help tighten the grip on subcontracted workers by specifying requirements that they cannot possibly meet.

Since they first emerged over a century ago, preventive services have been under pressures pulling in opposite directions: while being generally paid for by their employers, they operate within a framework in which public rules place limits on employers' dominion. Differing demands have developed in OH and in other disciplines, such as safety, psychology and ergonomics. Employers' priorities have tended to focus on direct costs and benefits, such as cutting health damage that incurred a cost to the business or boosting productivity. But the employers' purely financial priorities are only one of many contributing factors, such as pressure from official sources (in particular, the need for demonstrable compliance with the rules) and from the workers themselves. In the specific field of OH services, there is also an added factor: the OH doctor's patients are not the ostensible 'purchaser' of the service (the employer fills this role) and, in most cases, their health problems are caused by the latter's profit-seeking. The defining features of an OH service do not square with the standard setting for medical decision-making ('informed consent'). For other disciplines, the blurring of lines between contributing to the employer's productivity and profits on one hand, and health protection on the other, produces questionable professional practices.

Employers' control of preventive services was fundamentally thrown into question in the 1970s, most radically by the reform of the Italian health system, which transferred responsibility for health checks from company doctors to the public health service. Regulations were introduced to put in place minimum levels of workers' control (through consultation of health and safety committees) and public control (through the labour inspection system).

The current crisis in the preventive services comes from the failings of these control mechanisms. Left broadly under the employers' sway, preventive services have split loyalties. Attempts have been made to paper over this identity crisis with glib soundbites that the job of OH services is to see that workers stay healthy to keep business healthy, whereas in fact, employers' profits are inconsistent with workers' health in many instances. Recognition that a conflict of interests exists is key to implementing effective prevention. A considerable body of research points to a link between unhealthy working conditions and high productivity and profit levels. This is particularly so for long-term health problems which are near cost-neutral to business, but may also be true to a lesser extent for work accidents. Flexibility, quality management systems and multiskilling have all been linked to higher work accident rates.[41,42] Where musculoskeletal disorders and stress are concerned, there is a clear link between damage to health and work intensification.

One answer might be to strengthen the role of preventive services as public health providers. There are good arguments for taking this approach. Rising social inequalities in health in Europe are partly due to working conditions. Work hazards create health problems outside the factory wall. They go beyond the time boundaries of working life when they develop or have consequences that continue well after the employment relationship has ended. So much is shown by studies on ageing and work as well as data on work-related cancers. They also go beyond the factory gate if taken in terms of the many health impacts of insecurity and other psychosocial factors. Contributing to a public health policy aimed at tackling social inequalities in health can give new legitimacy to preventive services. It stands in opposition to blinkered approaches to workplace health promotion that focus on so-called 'lifestyle' factors (smoking, drinking, drug-taking, diet). It is not the job of preventive services to do the work of other public health providers in addressing these factors. Their role is to act more effectively on working conditions as factors that shape health. But to fulfil that brief also demands a significant improvement of the mechanisms of collectivising health and safety at work.

References

1. See in particular Walters D (ed.). *Regulating health and safety management in the European Union. A study of the dynamics of change.* Brussels: PIE – Peter Lang, 2002.

2. Hämäläinen R-M *et al. Survey of the quality and effectiveness of occupational health services in the European Union, Norway and Switzerland.* Helsinki: Työterveyslaitos (Finnish Institute of Occupational Health), 2001.

3. European Commission. Communication from the Commission to the European Parliament, the Council, the European Economic and Social Committee and the Committee of Regions on the practical implementation of the provisions of the Health and Safety at Work Directives 89/391 (Framework), 89/654 (Workplaces), 89/655 (Work Equipment), 89/656 (Personal Protective Equipment), 90/269 (Manual Handling of Loads) and 90/270 (Display Screen Equipment). COM/2004/0062 final. 05 February 2004. Available online at europa.eu.int/eur-lex/en/com/cnc/2004/com2004_0062en01.pdf (viewed 05 April 2007).

4. Instituto Nacional de Seguridad e Higiene en el Trabajo. *IV Encuesta Nacional de Condiciones de Trabajo* (Fourth National Working Conditions Survey), 1999. Available online at internet.mtas.es/Insht/statistics/4enct_orga.htm (viewed 04 April 2007).

5. Instituto Nacional de Seguridad e Higiene en el Trabajo. *V Encuesta Nacional de Condiciones de Trabajo* (Fifth National Working Conditions Survey), 2003. Available online at www.mtas.es/insht/statistics/enct_5.htm (viewed 04 April 2007).

6. Vogel L. *Prevention at the workplace. The impact of Community Directives on preventive systems in Sweden, Finland, Norway, Austria and Switzerland.* Brussels: TUTB, 1998.

7. Marklund S (ed.). *Worklife and health in Sweden 2000.* Stockholm: Arbetslivsinstitutet (National Institute for Working Life), 2001 (page 65).

8. Arbetarskyddsstyrelsen (Swedish Occupational Safety and Health Administration). Fact sheet on Sweden, March 2002 (pages 2–3).

9. Ponting L. The sad case of occupational health provision in Britain. *Health and Safety Bulletin* August–September 2002; 311: 11–14.

10. Vogel L. *The gender workplace health gap in Europe.* Brussels: TUTB, 2003.

11. Billiard I. *Santé mentale et travail : l'émergence de la psychopathologie du travail.* Paris: La Dispute, 2001.

12. Omnès C & Bruno A S. *Les mains inutiles. Inaptitude au travail et emploi en Europe.* Paris: Belin, 2004.

13. Council Directive 89/391/EEC of 12 June 1989 on the introduction of measures to encourage improvements in the safety and health of workers at work (the Framework Directive). *Official Journal* L183; 29 June 1989: 1–8.

14. Manninen P & Piirainen H. Evaluation of the qualification of occupational health professionals provides clues on how to develop their training. *Työterveiset Journal* 2005; Special issue 2: 12–14. Available online at www.ttl.fi/Internet/English/Information/ Electronic+journals/Tyoterveiset+journal/2005-02+Special+Issue/Evaluation+of+the+ qualification+of+occupational+health+professionals+provides+clues+on+how.htm (viewed 04 April 2007).

15. Italian government. Dispozioni urgenti in materia di personale sanitario. Decreto-legge 12 novembre 2001 n. 402. Available online at legacy.aosp.bo.it/rad2/Rad/Leggi/ dl_402.htm (viewed 04 April 2007).

16. European Court of Justice. Judgment of 15 November 2001, European Commission *v* Italy. C-49/00, ECR p. I-8575.

17. European Court of Justice. Judgment of 16 June 2006, European Commission *v* Sweden. C-459/04.

18. Dyer C. Getting the ticket. *Health and Safety Bulletin* November 2002; 313: 15–20.
19. Birindelli L, Montanari E & Sordini M. Da soli si fa male. Il sistema partecipato di prevenzione e sicurezza sul lavoro. *Quaderni Rassegna Sindacale* October–December 2001; 4: 153.
20. Durán F. *Informe sobre los riesgos laborales y su prevención*, Madrid: Presidencia del Gobierno, 2001.
21. Dedessus-le-Moustier N. La pluridisciplinarité en santé au travail : analyse juridique, *Travail et emploi* 2005; 103: 65–78.
22. European Court of Justice. Judgment of 22 May 2003, European Commission *v* Netherlands. Case C-441/01.
23. Walters D, Nichols T, Connor J, Tasiran A C & Cam S. *The role and effectiveness of safety representatives in influencing workplace health and safety*. RR363. Sudbury: HSE Books, 2005. Available online at www.hse.gov.uk/RESEARCH/rrpdf/rr363.pdf (viewed 04 April 2007).
24. Ministerio del Lavoro (Italian Ministry of Labour). Circolare n. 40/2000 del 16 giugno 2000.
25. See the collection of case studies in Morris W, Wilson J & Koukoulaki T. *Developing a participatory approach to the design of work equipment. Assimilating lessons from workers' experience.* Brussels: TUTB, 2004.
26. Ringelberg J A & Koukoulaki T. *Risk estimation for musculoskeletal disorders in machinery design – integrating a user perspective.* Brussels: TUTB, 2002.
27. Boix P, García A M, Llorens C & Torada R. *Percepciones y experiencia. La prevención de los riesgos laborales desde la óptica de los trabajadores.* Valencia: Instituto Sindical de Trabajo, Ambiente y Salud, 2001.
28. Sociaal-Economische Raad. *Arbodienstverlening.* Advies 04/03. 20 February 2004. Available online at www.ser.nl/publicaties/default.asp?desc=b22455 (viewed 05 April 2007).
29. Geurts S, Kompier M & Gründemann R. The Dutch disease? Sickness absence and work disability in the Netherlands. *International Social Security Review* 2000; 53 (4): 79–103.
30. Van Dijk F J H, Hulshof C T J & Verbeek J H A M. Good occupational health practice: concepts and criteria. In: *Proceedings of the international symposium on good occupational health practice and evaluation of occupational health services, Espoo, Finland, 1999.* Helsinki: Työterveyslaitos (Finnish Institute of Occupational Health), 1999 (pages 22–23).
31. Nederlands Centrum voor Beroepsziekten. *Signaleringsrapport Beroepsziekten 2001.* Amsterdam: NCvB, 2001. Available online at www.arbobondgenoten.nl/arbothem/aansprk/NCBsignalering2001.pdf (viewed 05 April 2007).
32. Nederlands Centrum voor Beroepsziekten. *Signaleringsrapport Beroepsziekten 2002.* Amsterdam: NCvB, 2002. Available online at docs.szw.nl/pdf/35/2002/35_2002_3_2994.pdf (viewed 05 April 2007).
33. Popma J, Schaapman M & Wilthagen T. The Netherlands: implementation within wider regulation reform. In: Walters D (ed.). *Regulating health and safety management in the European Union. A study of the dynamics of change.* Brussels: PIE – Peter Lang, 2002 (page 204).
34. García Jiménez J. *Report presented to a conference organised by the Greek central labour confederation and the TUTB.* Piraeus: April 2003 (slightly abridged translation).
35. Rodrigo Cencillo F. Presente y futuro de las Mutuas de accidentes de trabajo y enfermedades profesionales de la Seguridad Social. *Cuadernos de Relaciones Laborales* 1999; 4: 69–97.

36. For an overview, see: Frick K. Sweden: occupational health and safety management strategies from 1970 to 2001. In: Walters D (ed.). *Regulating health and safety management in the European Union. A study of the dynamics of change.* Brussels: PIE – Peter Lang, 2002 (pages 211–234).

37. Remaeus B & Westerholm P. Official supervision and the occupational health service. In: Marklund S (ed.). *Worklife and health in Sweden 2000.* Stockholm: Arbetslivsinstitutet (National Institute for Working Life), 2001 (pages 51–70).

38. Ministère de l'emploi, de la cohésion sociale et du logement (French Ministry of Labour). Surveillance médicale des risques (SUMER) website at www.travail.gouv.fr/ etudes-recherche-statistiques/statistiques/sante-au-travail/enquetes/sumer-2013.html (viewed 05 April 2007).

39. Grieco A & Bertazzi P A (eds). *Per una storiografia italiana della prevenzione occupazionale ed ambientale.* Milan: Franco Angeli, 1997.

40. Instituto Sindical de Trabajo, Ambiente y Salud website, www.istas.ccoo.cs (viewed 05 April 2007).

41. Askenazy P. *The consequences of new workplace practices in the United States.* Paris, CEE-CEPREMAP, 2000.

42. Askenazy P & Caroli E. Pratiques 'innovantes', accidents du travail et charge mentale : résultats de l'enquête française 'Conditions de travail 1998'. *Pistes* 2003; 5 (1): 20–25.

Status and future challenges of Japanese occupational health services

Takashi Muto, Department of Public Health, Dokkyo Medical University School of Medicine

Status of Japanese occupational health services

Legislative basis of existence

The laws and ordinances regarding occupational health (OH) services* in Japan are shown in Table 1. The principal law regarding OH is the Industrial Safety and Health Act (ISH Act) of 1972.[1]

The purposes of the ISH Act are to ensure the health and safety of workers in workplaces and to facilitate the establishment of a comfortable work environment by promoting comprehensive and systematic countermeasures to prevent industrial accidents and occupational diseases.[1] Employers are required to take measures to improve the work environment in workplaces where there is exposure to the harmful conditions listed in the ordinances attached to the ISH Act, and to provide workers exposed to hazardous jobs with health examinations twice a year. They are also required to provide workers engaged in non-hazardous jobs with annual health examinations.

Structure of OH services

The ISH Act stipulates that companies employing 50 or more workers must establish a health committee (also safety committee in the case of workplaces involving hazardous jobs), appoint an occupational physician, and appoint at least one health officer from among their employees. Large companies, with more than 1,000 employees (500 employees in hazardous workplaces), must appoint at least one full-time occupational physician. A health committee meeting is held every month by the attending occupational physician to discuss OH issues in the workplace, and to propose measures to the company. The health officers are in charge of implementing the measures proposed by the health committee, with advice from occupational physicians.

The Ordinance on Industrial Safety and Health stipulates seven duties of occupational physicians, all of which are preventive by nature, as shown in Table 2. Curative medical services are not included as duties of occupational physicians or OH service providers, although such services are voluntarily provided by some large companies or factories for the convenience or benefit of employees. The maintenance and control of the work environment and work are primarily the duties of employers, but occupational physicians make the necessary recommendations to employers where it is deemed necessary to maintain the health of employees. When an employer receives a recommendation from an occupational physician, he or she is bound to respect it.

---

* The term 'occupational health services' is often used in two ways, depending on context: one is a concrete programme or functions provided by OH service providers; the other is such a provider itself. In order to avoid misunderstanding, the phrase 'occupational health services' is used in this chapter to mean concrete programmes or functions that employers or employees obtain from providers or organisations. Such providers or organisations are referred to here as OH service providers.

Names of acts and ordinances	Year
Workmen's Accident Compensation Insurance Act	1947
Industrial Safety and Health Act	1972
Pneumoconiosis Act	1960
Industrial Accident Prevention Organization Act	1964
Work Environment Measurement Act	1975
Ordinance on Industrial Safety and Health	1972
Ordinance on Prevention of Organic Solvent Poisoning	1972
Ordinance on Prevention of Lead Poisoning	1972
Ordinance on Prevention of Tetra-alkyl Lead Poisoning	1972
Ordinance on Prevention of Hazards Due to Specified Chemical Substances	1972
Ordinance on Safety and Health of Work under High Pressure	1972
Ordinance on Prevention of Ionizing Radiation Hazards	1972
Ordinance on Prevention of Anoxia, etc	1972
Ordinance on Prevention of Hazards Due to Dust	1972
Ordinance on Health Standards in the Office	1972
Ordinance on Prevention of Hazards Due to Asbestos	2005

The ISH Act does not make any specific demands regarding the functions, premises and facilities of OH service providers. Large companies with more than 1,000 employees usually organise their own in-house OH by employing occupational physicians and nurses, and these professionals conduct health examinations. Companies with 300 to 1,000 employees mostly employ nurses (full time or part time), and sometimes part-time occupational physicians depending on the needs of the company. In such companies, and also in some larger companies, health examinations are conducted by external OH service providers. It is difficult for most companies with fewer than 300 employees to employ nurses because of financial constraints, so for these enterprises external OH service organisations provide the necessary coverage, including health examinations.

There are 347 Labour Standard Inspection Offices located all over Japan, which periodically inspect the degree to which OH service providers are performing their duties. There is no formal requirement for evaluation and surveillance of the quality of OH service providers by customers/clients or public health agencies, but OH professionals usually evaluate the quality of services provided from a practical point of view.

Coverage of OH services

The proportion of workers covered by OH services is considered to be an important indicator in the evaluation of national OH service levels, but the definition of the term 'coverage' varies

		Table 2
1	Matters relating to the implementation of the medical examination of workers and implementation of a healthcare programme for workers based on the result of medical examinations	The seven areas of a Japanese occupational physician's duty as stipulated in the Ordinance on Industrial Safety and Health
2	Matters relating to the maintenance and control of the work environment	
3	Matters relating to the control of work	
4	Matters relating to the healthcare of workers in addition to matters set forth in the above three items	
5	Matters relating to health counselling and other measures for the maintenance and promotion of workers' health	
6	Matters relating to health education	
7	Matters relating to the investigation of the causes of impairments to health and preventive measures for workers	

from author to author.[2] In terms of legislation, the ISH Act covers all employed workers. Workplaces with fewer than 50 employees are not required to appoint an occupational physician, organise a health committee, or submit reports on health examinations to the Labour Standards Office. Considering the key roles that the occupational physician and the health committee play in OH activities, it is difficult for these workplaces to be covered by appropriate and effective OH service providers unless they go beyond the legally required minimum. These small organisations comprise 97 per cent of all workplaces, and 60 per cent of the employed workforce.[3] The average implementation rate of the annual general health examination, which is required by the ISH Act, is 87 per cent of all workplaces; this can be broken down to 84.1 per cent in workplaces with 10–29 employees, 93.3 per cent in organisations with 30–49 employees, 96.2 per cent for those with 50–99 employees, 99.4 per cent for those with 100–299 employees and 100 per cent for large organisations with over 300 employees. These figures come from the latest survey of the Ministry of Health, Labour and Welfare (the Ministry), which is conducted every five years.[4] The ISH Act does not apply to the self-employed, including farmers and fishermen, or to workers in the public sector.

Relationships between occupational healthcare and public health services and primary or hospital care

In Japan, public health centres or community health centres do not provide OH services. Most hospitals do not have a section or department that provides OH services, although some physicians employed by public or private hospitals and some general practitioners work part time as occupational physicians. Some in-house OH providers offer employees curative medical services, but most other providers do not give such services.

In 1993, the Ministry adopted a new policy of providing OH services to small workplaces with fewer than 50 employees. The establishment of 347 Regional Occupational Health Centres (ROHCs) was completed in 1998, and 47 Occupational Health Promotion Centres (OHPCs) were opened by 2003. The ROHCs were established by the government, and their management was entrusted to regional medical associations. ROHCs provide health guidance for employers or employees, workplace visits to give advice on the improvement of the work environment and work procedures, and information on OH services. The OHPCs were established by the Labour Welfare Corporation, which is closely affiliated to the Ministry, and is responsible for supporting the OHPCs financially. The OHPCs have five functions:

- supporting the ROHCs
- providing technical consultations for OH personnel
- collecting and providing information on OH
- training OH personnel
- managing public relations concerning OH.

The services available to client workplaces are supplied by ROHCs and OHPCs without any cost to the clients.

Staffing and competence

Occupational physicians must have sufficient knowledge, meeting the requirements laid down by the Ministry, to provide occupational healthcare for workers. To be an occupational physician, medical doctors have to have one of the following four qualifications:

- a completed basic OH course provided by the University of Occupational and Environmental Health, which lasts nearly two months
- a qualification from the Japan Medical Association, which started an accreditation system for qualified occupational physicians in 1990 – becoming qualified entails at least 50 hours of fundamental education and training in OH. By 2006, there were around 70,000 qualified occupational physicians in Japan
- a national licence to practise as an OH consultant
- a professorship or associate professorship at a university that offers – or has offered in the past – courses on OH.

In order for occupational physicians to get up-to-date knowledge on OH that reflects global changes and development, they are required to undertake at least 20 hours of education and training over five years if they want to maintain their qualification.

The Japan Society for Occupational Health started board certification for occupational physicians in 1993.[5] Applicants must fulfil all of the following five conditions:

- they must have had two years' training in clinical medicine
- they must have been members of the Japan Society of Occupational Health for at least five years
- they must have completed basic OH training
- they must have done three years' practical training on OH under the guidance of senior certified occupational physicians
- they must have presented a paper on OH research at an annual conference of the Japan Society of Occupational Health, or have published a research paper in the *Journal of Occupational Health*.

Certification is given to physicians who pass the two-day certification examination, which includes a knowledge test, individual and group interviews, and a test of presentation skills. The number of certified occupational physicians was 357 in 2005. A problem that still needs to be resolved is that certified occupational physicians are not acknowledged by the Ministry as occupational physicians, despite their high level of OH expertise.

There are no legal requirements for working as a nurse in OH settings; it is only necessary to be a qualified nurse of some kind. There is no certification system for 'occupational nurses'. There are about 1,500 health nurses and several thousand other nurses working in OH settings.[6] In the revised ISH Act, the functions of health nurses have been specified for the first time. Health nurses are to engage in guidance for employees requiring assistance to maintain their health.

Nothing is stipulated in the ISH Act concerning ergonomists, industrial hygienists or psychologists. However, the functions of OH consultants and work environment measurement experts are stipulated in both the ISH Act and the Work Environment Measurement Act. OH consultants, mostly experienced occupational physicians, health officers or health nurses who hold a licence issued by the Ministry, can consult on the health of a workplace at the request of an employer. The ISH Act stipulates that workers who handle acid should be examined by a dentist.

Under the ISH Act, workplaces employing 1,000 or more workers (100 or more in forestry, mining, construction and transport; 300 or more in the case of other hazardous workplaces, such as manufacturing) are obliged to appoint a general health and safety manager. This individual, who is usually a factory or branch manager, exercises general control over the health of the workplace.

Regarding safety, workplaces in which 50 or more workers are employed and which belong to outdoor industries and manufacturing industries must appoint a safety officer from among those employees who hold the qualifications required by the Ministry of Health's Labour and Welfare Ordinance. Within the overall remit of the general health and safety manager, the safety officer must take charge of technical matters related to safety.

Workplaces employing 50 or more people must appoint health officers from among their employees. Health officers, who are licensed by the director-general of the Prefectural Labour Bureau, take charge of the technical matters related to health in the workplace. All workplaces employing between 10 and 49 workers are obliged to appoint a health promoter, whose responsibilities are almost the same as those of health officers. Their main responsibility regarding OH is the planning and implementation of OH activities in the workplace. They are also expected to play an active role as co-ordinators between employers and occupational physicians.

The revised ISH Act of 1988 requires employers to make continuous and systematic efforts to maintain and promote workers' health by taking appropriate measures, such as providing health education, health counselling and other services. It also requires the Minister to announce guidelines on measures to be taken by the employer for the maintenance and promotion of workers' health, so that their implementation can be enforced appropriately and effectively.

Guidance on the Total Health Promotion Plan, which is an administrative measure based on the Labour and Welfare Ordinance, refers to concrete aspects of workplace health promotion. The objective of workplace health promotion is the prevention of lifestyle-related diseases, such as hypertension, diabetes, hyperlipidaemia and obesity. Thus, the target is workers' lifestyles: management of nutrition, physical activity, smoking, alcohol and stress. Personnel involved in health promotion programmes therefore include health educators, mental health advisers, dieticians and healthcare trainers. These are new professions, created to implement health promotion programmes in the workplace.

Main orientations or focus of programmes

Prevention of *karoshi*

In Japan, *karoshi* (death brought on by overwork or job-related exhaustion) has become a serious problem in recent years. In 1996, the Ministry issued guidelines to prevent *karoshi*, which requested employers to take appropriate measures on the basis of the opinions of occupational physicians, including reducing working hours, changing the location or nature of work, and reducing the frequency of night shifts. In 2001, the Ministry changed the authorisation standard for *karoshi*, and workers who die from cardiovascular diseases are now more likely to be considered cases of *karoshi* if it is shown that they were affected by overwork. In 2002, the Ministry issued a list of comprehensive measures to prevent ill health due to overwork. Employers were required to reduce overtime working, and to provide health guidance by occupational physicians to workers who engaged in more than 100 hours of overtime per month, or more than 80 hours per month during the previous 2–6 months. In 2005, the ISH Act was amended to reflect the 2002 notification to require employers to refer overworked employees for interviews with occupational physicians and to ask for recommendations and health advice from them.

Prevention of mental health disorders

The number of workers who are absent from work because of mental disorders is increasing, and the word *karo-jisatsu* (suicide brought on by overwork or job-related exhaustion) has recently been introduced. In 2000, the Ministry issued guidelines on mental health promotion in the workplace to promote early detection, treatment, and return to work of people with depression.[7] Employers are required to develop a mental health promotion plan with special reference to the system, its implementation, staffing and a privacy policy. They are also required to implement the plan through four routes:

- self-care by employees
- care through line management, carried out by managers and supervisors
- care provided by the company's healthcare staff
- care provided by external healthcare staff.

In view of the increase in the number of suicides among workers – from 6,200 in 1997 to 8,700 in 2000 – the Ministry started a comprehensive project to reduce the problem in 2001. Although there are no guidance documents specifically addressing the roles of OH service providers in this scheme, OH professionals are expected to play a key role in the prevention of mental health disorders.

Prevention of hazards due to asbestos

Mesothelioma caused by exposure to asbestos has become a widespread social and political problem in Japan since June 2005, when an asbestos-related company disclosed the number of its employees and ex-employees who have died of the disease. Japan has a relatively long history of asbestos regulation. In 1971, the Ordinance on the Prevention of Hazards Due to Specified Chemical Substances was promulgated; asbestos was named as one of the hazardous chemicals, and its handling was regulated. In 1975, employers were required to provide special health examinations for workers who handled asbestos. In 1995, the production, import and use of amosite and crocidolite were prohibited. In 2004, production, import and use of asbestos-containing products used as building material were prohibited. In 2005, the Ordinance on the Prevention of Hazards Due to Asbestos was promulgated. Employers now expect OH service providers to engage in the elimination of asbestos hazards more than ever

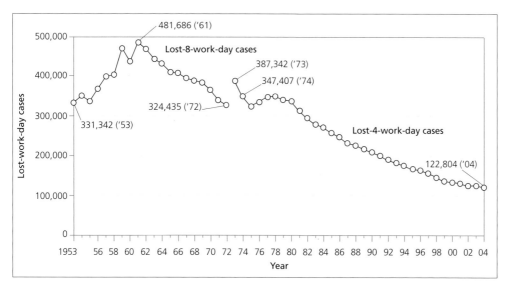

Figure 1
Number of lost-work-day cases of workplace injury and disease in Japan, 1953–2004

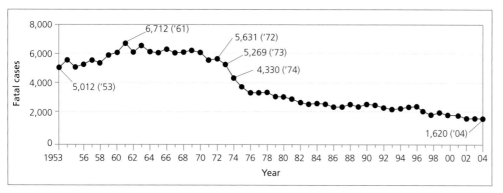

Figure 2
Number of deaths as a result of workplace injury and disease in Japan, 1953–2004

before. Since the disclosure of June 2005, the Ministry has been trying to impose a total ban on asbestos through using asbestos substitutes.

Smoking policy
In 1996, the Ministry issued guidelines on smoking measures in the workplace to protect non-smokers from tobacco smoke and to create comfortable work environments. Although the number of workplaces grappling with smoking issues in the workplace has increased, additional efforts have been needed because of the great interest in the adverse effects of passive smoking and WHO initiatives on a framework treaty on smoking policies. The guidelines were modified in 2000 to include an outline of an educational programme for promoting smoking reduction measures in the workplace. In 2003, the Ministry issued further guidelines which reflected the provisions of the Health Promotion Act, which came into force in 2003 and obliged employers to take appropriate measures to protect non-smokers from smoke in their working environment.

Quality and its development
Figure 1 shows the trend in the number of occupational injuries requiring four or more days of absence from work.[8] The number of injuries decreased from more than 300,000 in the late

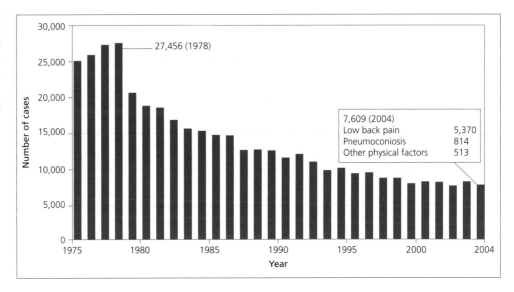

Figure 3
Number of new cases of occupational diseases per year in Japan, 1975–2004

1970s to about 130,000 in 2003. Figure 2 shows the trend in number of workers' deaths caused by occupational accidents. The number of deaths decreased from more than 3,000 in the late 1970s to fewer than 2,000 in 2003. Figure 3 shows the trend in the number of occupational diseases. The number of occupational diseases also shows a decreasing tendency. Although these official figures may not be the best basis on which to estimate the true incidence of occupational and work-related diseases, it is nevertheless true that the criteria for including incidents of occupational ill health have not changed over the time covered by Figure 3. OH services are likely to have played a positive role in this reduction.

In 1999, the Ministry issued guidelines for a Japan-specific occupational safety and health management system (OSHMS). In 2000, the Ministry launched a project to promote OSHMS implementation in companies and in 2001, the Japanese guidelines were modified to include all elements of the OSHMS guidelines adopted by the International Labour Organization (ILO). International trends in using the ILO's OSHMS, the ageing working population, the prevention of health hazards caused by new chemicals, and fears concerning the inadequate communication of information about health and safety to the younger generation were cited as reasons for adopting the OSHMS. Rather than specifying particular measures, the guidelines encourage employers to engage in sustained, voluntary activities. Although no reference is made to OH service providers in the Japanese OSHMS, OH professionals are expected to play a key role in the development and implementation of the system.

Interest in corporate social responsibility (CSR) has been increasing in Japanese companies in recent years.[9] Although CSR is often mentioned and discussed in terms of environmental protection and compliance with laws and regulations, it should also be discussed in the field of occupational safety and health. The maintenance and promotion of employees' health through the prevention of occupational injuries and diseases should be an important company responsibility. However, very few Japanese companies so far have documented CSR that incorporates occupational safety and health.[10,11] CSR and the OSHMS share a common idea in that both activities are voluntary and do not depend on laws and regulation. Both ideas are based on ethics, which need to play a greater part in discussions about occupational safety and health.[12]

Financing structures

Employers exclusively pay the costs of occupational safety and health services in Japan. The proportion of health and safety costs in companies' total payroll expenses ranges from 4.4 to 6.4 per cent, with a mean of 5.5 per cent.[13] Health insurance premiums are the main component of health and safety costs, constituting 68 per cent of the total. The remaining 32 per cent is accounted for by occupational safety and health activities. The proportion of Workers' Accident Compensation Insurance (WACI) premiums in total occupational safety and health costs is 47 per cent.

The primary legislation concerning the compensation of workers for occupational injuries and diseases in Japan is contained in the Workers' Accident Compensation Insurance Act (WACI Act).[14-17] WACI is a compulsory state-run insurance programme. The government collects insurance premiums from employers, and provides insurance benefits to injured workers or their dependants. Contributions are based on the total pay of insured workers, and are paid exclusively by employers. Contribution rates are determined for each specific industry on the basis of accident rates and other performance data for the preceding three years; they range from a minimum of 0.6 per cent to a maximum of 1.44 per cent. The WACI Act covers employees in all workplaces in industry and commerce, with the exception of public employees and seamen, for whom separate schemes are provided. It also applies on a voluntary basis to owners of small businesses, agricultural, forestry and fishery establishments with fewer than five employees, self-employed people and farmers.

The Ministry initiated the policy of subsidising occupational safety and health activities conducted in small-scale enterprises (SSEs) in the early 1960s. Activities to be subsidised include the primary and secondary prevention of occupational injuries and diseases, and also health promotion activities. The amount of subsidy is restricted to one-third to two-thirds of the total cost of preventive activities. The long history of financial assistance for SSEs and the increasing levels of subsidy suggest that the Ministry recognises the importance of financial assistance in promoting OH activities in SSEs.[18] As it is usually difficult for SSEs to develop and implement preventive programmes by themselves, external OH service providers are expected to play a key role.

Future challenges for Japanese OH services

Measures to increase coverage

Small-scale workplaces are exempted from some requirements of the ISH Act, such as the assignment of occupational physicians and the establishment of a health committee. Considering the key roles of occupational physicians and health committees in OH activities, it is difficult for these workplaces to be covered by appropriate OH services. It has been proposed that the cut-off number of employees should be 30 instead of 50, and there has also been a recommendation that a study be conducted of a revised appointment system in which an occupational physician would work for the number of hours required to provide sufficient occupational healthcare for workers.[19,20] Another proposal is that a health committee should be established in workplaces in which 30 or more workers are employed.

ROHCs are highly valued as representing the first systematic approach to OH service provision in small companies, but many problems remain to be resolved, such as the low take-up rate, staff shortages, the relationship between existing OH service providers and ROHCs, and the lack of coverage for self-employed people.[21] Among other difficulties, the low take-up rate is a big problem, and the possibility of collaboration between ROHCs and community health centres is being examined and discussed.[22] While external OH services provide their services at market price, the services supplied by ROHCs are free.

Japanese OH services do not cover self-employed workers, including farmers and fishermen. The Ministry of Agriculture, Forestry and Fisheries is in charge of the prevention of occupational injuries and diseases in these industries. Considering that approximately 400 farmers, mostly elderly, have been killed annually in occupational accidents in recent years,[23] appropriate OH measures need to be taken.

An effective structure of OH service providers to reflect the changing working world

The socioeconomic environment of Japanese OH service providers has recently undergone drastic change.[24] Severe competition due to globalisation of the economy, the development of information technology, the ageing of the workforce amid low birth rates, and changes in people's attitudes towards working life, such as a growing tendency to prioritise family and other interests over work, have in combination led to significant change in all aspects of business operations and working patterns.[25,26] The changes have encompassed organisational structure and management style and the diversification of working patterns, such as temporary, flexible and part-time work, teleworking and 'small office, home office' models.

Current OH services, which are based mainly on essentially stable and classic socioeconomic conditions, must reflect these changes to form an effective structure of providers. Firstly, in-house OH service units should make an effort to demonstrate their effectiveness in maintaining and promoting workers' health. Reflecting severe financial restraints in companies, restructuring or streamlining of company organisation takes place frequently, and outsourcing sections with poor outcomes has become a common phenomenon. In-house OH units are no longer sacred. If they cannot show that they can contribute to the company in terms of promoting employees' health, they will be outsourced and OH professionals will lose their jobs. Secondly, present external OH service providers should make an effort to expand their business activities for the provision of comprehensive OH services, meeting the needs of their companies, and without confining themselves solely to health examination facilities. Thirdly, there is now another type of OH service provider called an 'OH consultant firm', which comprises a group of OH consultants who have come together.[20]

In any case, in order to show the effectiveness of OH service activities, they need to be evaluated.[27] In the past, this has rarely taken place in Japan. In light of the situation described above, the need for evaluation seems to be increasing. In previous years, Japanese OH professionals have contributed relatively few papers to the annual International Congress on the Evaluation of Occupational Health Services, but in 2005, at the 13th Congress, which was held in Japan, they presented more than 50 papers.[28] Although the venue of the Congress may have been a significant factor in this increase, it must also reflect the current increase in interest in evaluation of OH services in Japan.

Staffing and competence

There is a certification system for occupational physicians, and their responsibilities are stipulated in the ISH Act. On the other hand, there is no certification system with regard to OH nurses, and – in the ISH Act – their functions are defined as being limited solely to health guidance to employees following health examinations. But, in practice, many nurses engage in diverse jobs, from planning to implementation of OH activities.[29] It is difficult for occupational physicians to do their job efficiently without the help of nurses. However, it is very important to establish a certification system for OH nurses. Clinical or organisational psychologists may be necessary in order to solve employees' mental health problems, and health promoters to offer health education and the promotion of workers' health. Ergonomists and industrial hygienists are also needed to improve the quality of OH services. It is a future task for OH service providers to make best use of these kinds of OH professional.

Other challenging areas

The most recent Annual Report on health, labour and welfare has as its subtitle 'Health risks surrounding modern life – attaining safety and peace of mind with information and collaboration'.[30] Among the many health risks in modern life, there are infectious diseases, mental illnesses and biochemical terrorism. These issues must also be treated as part of a company's crisis management, which OH service providers should include in their future services.[31] Newly emerging infectious diseases, such as Severe Acute Respiratory Syndrome (SARS) and avian influenza, are threats to companies in which many people gather. Countermeasures against terrorism in the form of chemical or biological weapons are an increasingly important aspect of OH services where workers are at risk.[20] As countermeasures to biochemical threats, guidelines for equipment, manuals, information systems and human resource development should be prepared by companies or by OH service providers in local areas.

References

1. Hatakenaka N. *The occupational safety and health law of Japan*. Tokyo: The Japan Institute of Labour, 2003.
2. Muto T, Mizoue T, Araki Y, Miyazaki S & Marui E. How is 'coverage' defined for occupational health services? *International Journal of Occupational Medicine and Environmental Health* 2002; 15 (2): 147–154.
3. Statistics Bureau, Management and Coordination Agency. *Statistics survey of workplaces*. Tokyo: Management and Coordination Agency, 1996.
4. Ministry of Health, Labour and Welfare. *Survey of state of employees' health*. Tokyo: Romu Gyosei, 2004.
5. Okubo T. Specialist qualification program for physicians prepared by the Japan Society for Occupational Health. *Journal of Occupational Health* 2001; 43: 295–300.
6. Okubo T. Recent state and future scope of occupational health in Japan. *Journal of Occupational Health* 1998; 40: 161–167.
7. Ministry of Health, Labour and Welfare. *Guidelines for workers' mental health promotion in the workplace*, 2003.
8. Japan Industrial Safety and Health Association. *Present status of Japanese industrial safety and health*. Tokyo: JISHA, 2004.
9. Okamoto K. *ABC of CSR: what is corporate social responsibility?* Tokyo: Nihon Keizai Shimbunsha, 2004.
10. Kawashita F, Taniyama Y, Fujisaki J & Mori K. Industrial safety and health aspects in CSR (corporate social responsibility): publication of CSR-related reports and their contents by Tokyo Stock Exchange first section listed companies. *Journal of Occupational Health* 2005; 47: 561 (in Japanese).
11. Taniyama Y, Kawashita F, So Y & Mori K. Industrial safety and health in corporate social responsibility: a description of industrial safety and health in corporate social responsibility-related reports about mental health in particular. *Journal of Occupational Health* 2005; 47: 562 (in Japanese).
12. Westerholm P, Nilstun T & Ovretveit J. *Practical ethics in occupational health*. Oxford: Radcliffe Medical Press, 2004.

13. Muto T, Itoh I, Taira M, Harabuchi I & Sumiyoshi Y. Costs of occupational health and safety in Japanese companies. In: Mossink J & Licher F (eds). *Costs and benefits of occupational safety and health*. Amsterdam: NIA TNO BV, 1998, pages 254–258.

14. Miyatake G. *Social security in Japan*. Tokyo: The Foreign Press Center, 2000.

15. Araki T. *Labor and employment law in Japan*. Tokyo: The Japan Institute of Labour, 2002.

16. Nakane F. *Workmen's accident compensation insurance law*. Tokyo: Eibun-Horei-Sha Inc., 2003.

17. Muto T, Sakurai Y, Hsieh S D & Shimada N. Evaluation of financing methods for occupational injuries and diseases in Japan. In: Caillard J F & Westerholm P (eds). *Social security systems and health insurance: financing and implication in occupational health*. Toulouse: Octares, 1999: 221–229.

18. Muto T & Takata T. Financial assistance in promoting occupational health services for small-scale enterprises in Japan. *International Journal of Occupational Medicine and Environmental Health* 2001; 14: 143–150.

19. Muto T. International comparison highlights the standards of OHS: the Japanese case. In: Menckel E & Westerholm P (eds). *Evaluation in occupational health practice*. Oxford: Butterworth-Heinemann, 1999: 100–111.

20. Higashi T. Future challenges of occupational health services in a changing working world. In: Muto T, Higashi T & Verbeek J (eds). *Evidence-based occupational health: proceedings of the International Congress on Occupational Health Services held in Utsunomiya City, Japan, between 1 and 3 December 2005*. Amsterdam: Elsevier, 2006.

21. Muto T, Mizoue T, Terada H & Harabuchi I. Current problems and future tasks of occupational health centers for small-scale enterprises in Japan. In: Lehtinen S, Vartio A & Rantanen J (eds). *From protection to promotion: occupational health and safety in small-scale enterprises*. Helsinki: Työterveyslaitos (Finnish Institute of Occupational Health), 1998: 36–39.

22. Muto T. Collaboration between occupational health and community health for promoting workers' health in small-scale enterprises. Paper given at the International Symposium on Occupational Health in Small-scale Enterprises and the Informal Sector, 13–15 November 2004, Nagoya, Japan: page 86.

23. Muto T & Haruyama Y. Characteristics of farmer death due to farm works in Tochigi Prefecture. Paper given at the 10th Asian Congress of Agriculture Medicine and Rural Health, 2005, Kinugawa, Japan: pages 59–60.

24. Nariai O. *The modern Japanese economy*. Tokyo: The Foreign Press Center, 2002.

25. Seike A. *New trends in Japan's labor market: changes in employment practices*. Tokyo: The Foreign Press Center, 1997.

26. Sasajima Y. *Labor in Japan*. Tokyo: The Foreign Press Center, 2003.

27. Menckel E & Westerholm P (eds). *Evaluation in occupational health practice*. Oxford: Butterworth-Heinemann, 1999.

28. Muto T, Higashi T & Verbeek J (eds). *Evidence-based occupational health: proceedings of the International Congress on Occupational Health Services held in Utsunomiya City, Japan, between 1 and 3 December 2005*. Amsterdam: Elsevier, 2006.

29. Muto T, Itoh I, Horie S, Taira M, Sumiyoshi Y, Aramaki N & Tamura S. Roles of occupational physicians and occupational health nurses in Japan. *Journal of the University of Occupational and Environmental Health* 1998; 20: S68–S73.

30. Ministry of Health, Labour and Welfare. *Annual report on health, labour and welfare 2003-2004*. Tokyo: Gyosei Corporation, 2005.

31. Higashi T. Study on a model for future occupational health: proposals for an occupational health service model in Japan. *Industrial Health* 2006; 44: 541–555.

Conclusions

Peter Westerholm, University of Uppsala, Sweden

Introduction

This book, containing descriptions of professional occupational health (OH) services in 11 countries, came into being during a process of sampling of convenience. Well-known OH specialists in these countries were asked to draft articles describing the professional OH service organisations in their countries, and to give their personal views on the challenges and principal issues confronting such services in their current daily work. Clearly, this set of national narratives was never intended to be representative in any other way than to provide examples of approaches described by the authors commissioned for the task, and to give an idea of the problems to be addressed in seeking cues for progress with regard to the development of multidisciplinary professional advisory services in the field of OH. An additional motive was also a perceived need to explore in greater depth some of the observations made by Hämäläinen et al.[1] in a descriptive account of OH services in the European Union (EU), Norway and Switzerland published in 2001. These 11 chapters form the substance of this supplement to *Policy and Practice in Health and Safety*.

In these concluding remarks, I shall restrict myself to issues and observations of a general nature, which emerged from reading the national contributions. The scenario is riveting. Contrary to expectations, there are striking inter-country differences. It is not possible, nor is it meaningful, to highlight the full range of questions and problems brought up by the various authors. So I shall make only brief reference to individual countries' reports. Practically all the reports contain observed developments and present specific national scenarios that bring up important, although differing, experiences. They have implications that deserve the attention of others. Taken in their entirety, we have much to learn from all the contributions.

So, by way of general observation, there is considerable variation in the approaches and practices of OH services in this sample of countries. This is thought-provoking, since the work conditions in the countries involved are subject to largely similar impact factors. These include the rapid globalisation of national economies, technical, social and economic changes, and demographic developments – all of which have profound implications. Such changes affect health, life at work and the quality of life of millions of people. The approaches and solutions regarding roles and tasks of OH professionals in these change processes differ significantly, although the OH challenges are similar in important ways. It may have seemed reasonable to expect greater similarities between the OH systems or – at least – converging trends, in light of the intentions underlying the EU Framework Directive[2] on health and safety in European workplaces. One important conclusion is, therefore, that these differences need close examination in comparative studies, and also in the context of seeking shared policies and concerted efforts for the future development of OH service systems.

Research database

One first and quite striking observation when looking at the scientific database of occupational safety and health is the scarcity of published research that specifically addresses OH service matters. There are active centres in a few countries, such as Finland and the Netherlands, but generally OH services do not seem to occupy a prominent place in the international scientific OH literature. Factors contributing to this may be a lack of interest, low priority-setting among health professionals and researchers, and a lack of competences. All of this implies the absence of an OH research infrastructure that offers support to collaborative research undertakings. Other explanatory factors may be poorly developed or absent funding systems and their mechanisms, or even downright resistance within client systems and companies. Many OH professionals seem to prefer to publish reports in their national languages, rather than English or other languages commonly used in international scientific publishing. The scarcity of a solid international research database is clearly a weakness in this setting.

Legal basis

In most countries, employers are obliged by law to organise OH services for their employees. This obligation is strictly enforced in Finland, France and Germany, and still exists – albeit in a diluted form – in the Netherlands. It applies partially, implying exemptions for companies of a certain size or in specified sectors, in Austria, Japan, Norway and the Czech Republic. There is no corresponding legal requirement in the UK. In Sweden, there is no formal requirement, leaving it to the employer's discretion whether or not to provide OH services. In Denmark, a legal obligation was enforced in the industrial sector, and a plan was adopted for extending the employer's obligation to apply in other branches of industry and services. This obligation was, however, lifted in 2005 after a new government came into office.

Coverage

The countries that strictly enforce the provision of OH services can, for obvious reasons, demonstrate high rates of coverage of the workforce, approaching 100 per cent. In most countries, reliable assessments are difficult due to statistical uncertainties. Estimates are particularly imprecise in the UK, Japan, Austria, Sweden, and the Czech Republic. Indeed, in the category of small and medium-sized enterprises (SMEs), access to OH services is commonly very low. To some extent, the ambitions for coverage reflect whether OH is regarded as a public health or a market commodity. If it is a matter of public health, full coverage of the labour market is sought. Countries leaning towards market mechanisms to resolve needs of coverage put less weight on the public health aspects and give low priority to achieving high degrees of access to OH service organisations. In market-based systems, customer/client satisfaction is the first objective. In earlier discussions of OH service systems, coverage was commonly seen as an important objective in itself. Over time, the focus has shifted more towards questions of the quality of the service, its producers and performance, and its compliance with stakeholder expectations.

Financing

In most of the countries covered in the study, the funding of OH services is arranged by client companies and the market. This applies also in countries where OH services are legally mandatory (Finland, the Netherlands, the Czech Republic and Norway). In France, the main financing comes from regional social security funds, funded in the first instance by employers' levies. In Finland, the costs of OH services are basically borne by client companies, but there is a significant refund of roughly 50 per cent of company costs via a collective insurance scheme under government surveillance administered by the Ministry of Social Affairs and Health. The bottom line commonly seems to be that the funding of OH services is derived from the profits and production of industry and services. This applies equally in the public and private sectors. In these countries, citizens/taxpayers are apparently not major stakeholders where the funding of OH services is concerned.

Multidisciplinarity

In most countries, there are intentions to develop the competences of OH professionals and to increase the level of multidisciplinarity or, as may be the preferred term, multiprofessionalism. Presently, however, the medical professions are predominant in most countries. In Denmark, the primary task of the multidisciplinary OH service units has been one of preventive action without provision of curative services, and this has been consistently implemented. This component of the Danish system of OH professional support is, however, currently in the process of being dismantled.

Quality systems

The quality approaches adopted in the countries investigated display a wide range of variation. There are standard systems of quality assurance specific to OH services, which have been developed and applied on a voluntary basis (Sweden). There are also quality assurance systems for OH services, enforced by legal statutes as instruments for certification or authorisation (the Netherlands), whereas other countries rely heavily on good practice guidelines (Finland, the Netherlands and Norway). In some countries, professional guidelines are combined with the enforcement of regulations concerning the quality of OH services (Germany). In Denmark, the official quality system previously set up no longer applies. In the UK, quality guidelines for OH services are followed in the National Health Service, and guidelines for professional OH practice are issued by organisations such as the Faculty of Occupational Medicine of the Royal College of Physicians. There is a notable divergence of practices in this regard.

Special features

Austria

Austria has a structure of OH service organisations of a type to be found in many European countries. A noteworthy feature is that professional OH services are provided to SMEs (undertakings with fewer than 50 employees) in programmes under the auspices of the public social security agencies.

Czech Republic

Preventive action in all OH matters is the primary task of OH services, based on legal regulation. The government has more recently initiated health promotion as an important priority area within OH services.

Denmark

The existing system of professional OH service organisations acting in close relationship with client undertakings is being dismantled and replaced by a set of authorised work-environment advisers dependent on assessments made by the Labour Inspectorate. The previous OH service organisations have been given entirely new and different roles. This represents a major change in the Danish system.

Finland

OH services have been established as a comprehensive national system, successively developed over the last 30 years by the Ministry of Health and Social Affairs. Finland has, as explicitly and officially stated, significant public health motives, and is also opting for public health-oriented policies with regard to OH service functions and development. In other words, OH services are seen as an integral part of the public health system. Evaluations of the processes and outcomes achieved in this highly developed national system are expected to be published between 2007 and 2015.

France

OH services' work practices are being reoriented with a view to reducing resource use on routine annual health examinations. In addition, programmes have been adopted for the development of multidisciplinary competences in OH services. In France, major transformations are envisaged in the field of OH, implying a broadening of the scope of occupational medicine in OH service organisations, thus enabling the attainment of a more comprehensive OH perspective, including health promotion. In the longer term, integration of the approaches of OH, public health and environmental health is envisaged. France is about to embark on major transformations of its OH systems, which have, by and large, been left untouched for 60 years.

Germany

A prominent feature of developments in Germany is visible state commitment to the use of quality systems for OH services and for programmes to improve the competences of OH professionals. One particular characteristic of the German OH system is the involvement of insurance stakeholder interests through the accident insurance funds (Berufsgenossenschaften) that involve the social partners in the labour market.

The Netherlands

The case of the Netherlands is a truly fascinating narrative, taking the reader through OH service development over the last century, and explaining how the historical roots are linked to the present situation. It starts with the medically based and oriented OH services of the early 1920s through to roughly 1980, and goes on to a second period, which is characterised by multidisciplinarity – with physicians, occupational hygienists, specialists in ergonomics, psychologists and sociologists coming into and expanding OH services (1980–c.1993). This is followed by a period referred to as 'commercial' between 1994 and 2000, and the progression culminates in an ongoing stage now referred to as the 'monopolies lost' period, implying the market orientation of OH services and the present-day emphases on return to work, sickness absence management in programme form, and managed care.

Norway

In Norway, employers are legally obliged to affiliate to OH service organisations. These organisations are, however, funded by the undertakings/clients, and there is significant competition with other service providers in the health market. In seeking strategies for quality improvement, the approach chosen has been to develop and implement a good OH practice guideline, just as has been the case in Finland.

Sweden

OH services in Sweden are entirely market-based, and are subject to competitive forces. There is no funding from public sources. Sweden is one of the countries where the state, in its many guises, has opted for non-commitment, leaving market mechanisms to develop coverage, and OH service organisations to develop quality on a voluntary basis.

UK

In the UK, a new national scheme has been established to provide OH support. The programme is called Workplace Health Connect (WHC), which provides free, practical advice on workplace health, safety and return-to-work issues, in particular to small enterprises (with 5–250 employees) in England and Wales. The WHC establishes partnerships with the National Health Service and sets up locally available services for managers and workers on health matters. These strategies are founded in two government policy documents published in 2000

– *Revitalising health and safety*[3] and *Securing health together*[4] – which provide the basis for what is referred to in the UK as the 'OH support model'. The model addresses the key issues of:

- identifying health issues for recruited workers and fitness for work
- workplace risk assessments, strategies and methods to reduce exposure
- enabling workers with ill health to stay in work or to obtain rehabilitation and return to employment after sickness absence.

UK: Scotland

In Scotland, the UK programme has been taken one step further through a decision by the Scottish Executive to adopt a strategic programme named Healthy Working Lives (HWL), aiming at:

- providing access to advice for both the employed and the unemployed
- recognising the value and benefits of being in work and facilitating access to safe employment
- harnessing and co-ordinating existing services rather than creating new ones.

The HWL programme aims to address the health needs of the whole Scottish population, whether employed or unemployed, in all settings of working life, and at all ages. Issues of workplace health prevention and return to work are addressed. In taking this step, Scotland has brought OH well into the public health domain.

European overview

Laurent Vogel of the European Trade Union Confederation sets in focus the tasks of health professionals from the perspective of workers' needs for expert advice on questions, issues and challenges related to health and workplace conditions. The OH professional is expected to serve many masters, and the task of being an impartial adviser to a multitude of stakeholders with different interests at the same time is often far from easy. Further emphasis is placed on the important requirement imposed on OH service organisations to establish sound relationships, based on trust, with client companies and their staff. The professionalism, competence, impartiality and ethical conduct of OH professionals are to be seen as indispensable core values essential to the management of the numerous practical health and life quality issues that arise from production and work. In explaining workers' expectations of OH services in a local company or workplace, Vogel draws on trade union experiences from European countries beyond those represented in this book. Of course, we have yet to see the policies, strategies and solutions chosen for OH and OH services by many eastern European countries in the course of their ongoing economic transformation.

Japan

Interesting trends are to be observed in Japan. OH service organisations are increasingly seen as becoming involved in the prevention of mental health disorders, suicides and an extreme form of work-related fatigue known as *karoshi*. SMEs are receiving special attention through the organisation of regional health centres.

The wider perspective

The first question concerns the role of OH services. Is the role of an OH service to be an agent of public health, ie an instrument or tool of the state, or to be an entrepreneur in a health market, providing commodities on demand to companies, organisations and other paying customers? Or is it to be both? In countries where OH services are available as commodities on the health market, there is, of course, usually competition with other agents providing the same kind of service.

A general observation is that OH service organisations in many countries assume roles lying somewhere between that of an agent of public health and that of a provider of expert OH services – sometimes including curative services – to companies. This very duality of roles may give rise to differing expectations among consumers of the services and other stakeholders. There are customers and clients who request only curative services. Others go for health promotion and periodic health examinations. There are also, by contrast, customers and groups of customers with a highly developed awareness of health-related aspects of work, who want OH services to make a contribution to programmatic approaches with high objectives and of considerable scope. The common feature of all OH service organisations is that the stakeholders are vitally important in terms of service output and performance. This applies regardless of whether the setting is a public health domain or a health market. The concept of 'stakeholder' includes the owners, the management, the clients to be identified on the market, and also the employees and staff of undertakings. So, it needs to be recognised that OH services have no self-evident automatic right to exist. They can survive and develop as organisations only if they satisfy stakeholders' needs and interests. Laurent Vogel gives a reminder of the need of all workers to have access to professional expertise on matters of health and life quality arising from the nature of their work, from work conditions and from the organisation of work.

This multiplicity of stakeholders leads to widely differing expectations of the performance of OH service organisations. It also has implications for assessments of quality, for the choice of evaluation strategy, and for improvements in service quality. Clearly, health service organisations with primarily public health agendas need to set up a profile of professional competences which differs from that of commercial health organisations operating under competitive market conditions.

A key question concerns the commitment of the state. If OH services are understood to contribute to public health in an important way, as may be inferred from policies adopted by governments in, for instance, Finland, France, Germany and the Czech Republic, the logical next step is to extend the availability of services to the country's labour force in its entirety. This is commonly achieved through legislative action or public regulation, in other words by requiring companies to organise OH services. By contrast, in countries where OH services are seen as a supplier of market commodities, such as in Sweden, they are entirely dependent for their existence on customer demand, which implies the absence of an incentive to assume the role of a public health agent.

So, to sum up, some hard questions pertinent to the development of OH services in Europe, as well as globally, concern:

- the commitment of the state and its structures to the organisation, tasks, professional competences and funding of OH services
- the roles of OH service organisations, either as agents of public health or as commercially based organisations providing services to clients in a health market
- the required competences of OH service organisations in meeting both the expectations of the state on one hand and those of client companies and the market on the other
- the conception of service quality and its development in the field of OH services. Whose 'quality' is it to be? Quality of services as judged by assessment of their contribution to

public health? Quality of services as perceived by customers/clients and their employees to satisfy their needs? Quality as understood by health professionals? Quality implying cost-effectiveness or cost-efficiency of services? Furthermore, is there a risk of service quality being downgraded in a market where there is price competition?

- competing or conflicting objectives in national OH service systems, such as workforce coverage *v* competence/quality of service performance, and quality *v* costs, possibly carrying implications for the competitiveness of OH service organisations in the marketplace
- strategies for evaluating the effectiveness and health impact of OH services.

The essential question that remains to be tackled is this: how should the competences of OH professionals be developed, and how should use of their expertise be best organised to provide an effective contribution to the sustainable development of healthy societies? It is, as commented above, mind-boggling that highly developed countries exhibit such fundamental differences in how they organise the deployment of their OH professionals. It is all the more amazing that this remains the case despite their having most of the major features of workplace health hazards in common, and having access to OH expertise with, in broad terms, similar profiles of professional competences. It is a sobering observation that the EU Framework Directive clearly accommodates countries exhibiting widely differing policies and ensuing practices. It is reasonable to suppose that a large part of the difference may be explained by variations in structures of healthcare systems and by differences in pertinent sets of legislation or national cultures. The possibility of important inter-country differences in policies and assessments of needs of OH expertise should not be disregarded. For an overview of the scope of inter-country differences in health systems and policies in European countries see McKee *et al.*[5]

One striking aspect that emerges from discussing the roles and tasks of OH service organisations is a conspicuous lack of published evaluations of service performance and effects. This is definitely a handicap for countries considering various options that might lead to favourable development. Nevertheless, there are a few examples, although primarily in countries with public health-oriented policies for OH services. By contrast, in countries more inclined towards the demands of stakeholders in the marketplace, there are likely to be evaluations by consumers. These are only exceptionally published or otherwise made publicly available. Why is this? As mentioned earlier, part of the explanation is likely to lie in a lack of research and development with regard to professional performance in and the effectiveness of OH interventions. Contributing factors may be lack of funding, of professional competence, or simply of interest. This is, however, probably not sufficient by way of explanation. Stakeholder commitment is arguably a key factor. In countries where the state – accountable as it is for the performance of public service agencies and organisations – is a major stakeholder in the affairs of OH services, obligations to taxpayers make evaluation a logical step. Indeed, there are many objects and objectives for evaluations initiated by the state. A starting point might be to ask the following questions:

- how are we doing with respect to the task we have been given and the expectations placed on us?
- are there visible effects on OH service performance?
- are there better ways of doing it?

Since this is done in the best interests of the public, publishing and disseminating the results would be a natural step to take.

But it must be remembered that the assertion of the role of the state as an accountable public stakeholder is exceptional at the present time. The most common role assumed by an OH service organisation is one of market dependence. So, one might expect to find stakeholders in the market who would be interested in having OH service organisations evaluated as providers of specialised services. The point is, however, that most customer enterprises do not care much about vested public health interests. A market-based stakeholder is more likely to ask: what is in this evaluation for me? The evaluation would then be designed as a customer – or second-party – evaluation. Most such customer evaluations are not published, for reasons that are easily understood.

In discussing the needs for OH expertise in the labour market of modern societies, some hard questions are unavoidable. What is implied by 'needs'? Whose needs are concerned, and are there issues of priorities? The distinction between needs and demands has to be kept constantly in mind in the context of health services. These questions of need have obvious implications for competence requirements and the professional profiles of the specialists who are expected to provide the services needed. These, in turn, are determined either through norms and regulations issued by public agencies, to the extent that public health aspects are involved, or by market mechanisms and related factors, to the extent that they concern adaptation of undertakings' products and their conduct in relation to market realities. All this concerns the classical preventive tasks of OH organisations and professionals and, increasingly, discussion and adoption of programmes for workplace health promotion in OH practice. Development is expected to lead to a need to revisit the competence profiles of OH professionals and their training programmes.

In considering the concept of professionalism in the field of OH practice, the ongoing developments in training curricula of universities in health disciplines need to be reappraised. In many countries, health professions are currently renegotiating their positions and rights *vis-à-vis* the state and public agencies, and also *vis-à-vis* their markets. Even in the short term, it is not to be taken for granted that the OH professions of today will be recognised as best equipped – in terms of competence, prior training and experience – to enjoy the privileges of monopoly in handling workplace matters of health and working ability.

The question of whether a convergence of organisations and OH practices – including roles to be assumed by OH professionals – is feasible or even desirable is complex by nature. It is quite possible that such convergence would be useful and bring benefits to companies, to labour markets, and indeed to whole societies. It seems, however, important that efforts aiming at such convergence are based on international discourse and, where appropriate, the examination of factors underlying inter-country differences. In the field of occupational safety and health, just as in most other important societal fields, our first assumption must be that all governments do good things for their citizens. Indeed, it is *prima facie* reasonable to regard this principle as applying in the field of OH. When, however, we find inter-country differences in the priorities, functions and performances of OH services, which we hold to be important, it must be regarded as an elementary step to achieve a shared understanding of the factors causing the differences before taking steps to move further towards the vision and state of affairs that in common parlance we refer to as convergence. To make such a move uncritically may, in fact, and with a bit of bad luck, be mistaken and perhaps costly.

So, we have much to learn from each other. A strengthening of the international discourse on OH services, highlighting differences in strategies and approaches and in experiences gained, is what we should be looking for. It seems natural to see organisations such as the Institution of

Occupational Safety and Health and the International Commission on Occupational Health as providers of venues and meeting points for public discourse on the global level for communicative processes that carry rewards for everyone who accepts the effort to seek them. And we must see to it that we develop the requisite set of competences to take on tasks of prevention and health promotion at the workplace and social inequities in society at large. A sobering observation was made in 2007 by the World Economic Forum in its Working Towards Wellness initiative at Davos, that in 2004 only 3 per cent of all health expenditure was directed at prevention and public health in the member countries of the Organisation for Economic Co-operation and Development and that many business leaders and policy analysts acknowledge that prevention is not adequately financed. Another key finding of the forum was the expressed acknowledgement of:

> ...a potential to increase productivity – a conservative estimate of the benefits from improving the general wellness of workforce indicates a likely return of three to one or more.[6]

There are many of us who harbour a firm belief and trust in OH professionalism as an important actor in the prevention of disease and injury, in the improvement of workplace life quality and in counteracting and offsetting social inequalities in societies. The OH professions have important tasks and responsibilities in all these domains. Prevention of ill health, promotion of rehabilitation and getting people back to work are core tasks to be carried out jointly with management and trade unions. The availability of professional competence and safeguarding of professional conduct in OH matters is of fundamental importance to undertakings, to working populations and to all citizens in ensuring sustainable development of work and labour markets, and thus, both in the short and long term, in promoting health for all. In finding strategies and methods to do this with success, the commitment of the state and its determined and skilful governance is a key determinant. To leave such important matters to be determined by market forces may prove to be seriously mistaken. Do market mechanisms and commercialised OH services bring benefits, obstacles or other problems in targeting the goals mentioned above? These tough questions deserve our close attention.

References

1. Hämäläinen R M, Husman K, Räsänen K, Westerholm P & Rantanen J. *Survey of the quality and effectiveness of occupational health services in the European Union, Norway and Switzerland*. Research Report 45. Helsinki: Työterveyslaitos (Finnish Institute of Occupational Health), 2001. Preface available online at www.occuphealth.fi/Internet/partner/tthosicoh/Publications/Book_People+and+work+Research+Reports+45.htm (viewed 19 April 2007).
2. Council Directive 89/391/EEC of 12 June 1989 on the introduction of measures to encourage improvements in the safety and health of workers at work (the Framework Directive). *Official Journal* L183; 29 June 1989: 1–8.
3. Health and Safety Commission. *Revitalising health and safety: strategy statement*. Sudbury: HSE Books, 2000. Available online at www.hse.gov.uk/revitalising/strategy.pdf (viewed 23 April 2007).
4. Health and Safety Executive. *Securing health together*. Sudbury: HSE Books, 2000. Strategy document and supporting materials available online at www.hse.gov.uk/sh2/index.htm (viewed 23 April 2007).
5. McKee M, MacLechose L & Nolte E. *Health policy and European enlargement*. European Observatory on Health Systems and Policies Series. Milton Keynes: Open University Press, 2004.

6.   World Economic Forum. *Working towards wellness – executive summary*. Davos: WEF, 2007. Available online at www.weforum.org/pdf/wellness/summary.pdf (viewed 24 April 2007).